The Folklore Text

The Folklore Text
From Performance to Print

Elizabeth C. Fine

Indiana University Press
Bloomington

I gratefully acknowledge the following publishers for permission to reprint copyrighted material:

Ezra Pound. Excerpt from "Canto LXXXI," *The Cantos of Ezra Pound*. Copyright 1948 by Ezra Pound. New Directions Publishing Company.

Ray L. Birdwhistell. "Chart 3A. Linguistic and Kinesic Transcriptions," from *Kinesics and Context: Essays on Body Motion Communication*. Copyright 1970 by the Trustees of the University of Pennsylvania. University of Pennsylvania Press.

Manufactured in the United States of America

Library of Congress Cataloging in Publication Data

Fine, Elizabeth C. (Elizabeth Calvert)
    The folklore text.

    Bibliography: p.
    1. Folklore—Methodology. 2. Communication in folk-
lore. 3. Sociolinguistics. 4. Semiotics and folk
literature. I. Title.
GR40.F47 1984   390'.01'8   83-49411
ISBN 0-253-32328-2

1 2 3 4 5 88 87 86 85 84

To my parents, Sam and Mary Fine

To have gathered from the air a live tradition
or from a fine old eye the unconquered flame
This is not vanity.
Here error is all in the not done,
all in the diffidence that faltered,

Ezra Pound, "Canto LXXXI"

Contents

Preface   xi

1. INTRODUCTION   1
    The Problem   3
    Methodology and Organization   6
    Significance   11

2. THE DEVELOPMENT OF THE TEXT IN
    AMERICAN FOLKLORISTICS   16
    The Ethnolinguistic Model of the Text   18
    The Literary Model of the Text   28
    Precursors to the Performance Approach   30
    Performance-Centered Experimentation with the Text   45
    Conclusion   55

3. THE PERFORMANCE APPROACH:
    IMPLICATIONS FOR THE TEXT   57
    Key Concepts of the Performance Approach   58
    Problems of the Performance Approach:
        Making the Text Fit the Theory   66
    An Aesthetic Transaction Model of Performance   68
    Conclusion   87

4. INTERSEMIOTIC TRANSLATION FROM
    PERFORMANCE TO PRINT   89
    Objections to Translating Performance   90
    A Definition of the Text   94
    Translation Theory   97
    Conclusion   110

5. ANALYSIS OF SOURCE AND RECEPTOR MEDIA:
    PERFORMANCE AND PRINT   113
    Source Medium: Performance   114
      Aural Channel: Linguistic and
        Paralinguistic   115
      Visual Channel: Kinesic, Artifactual,
        and Proxemic   118
      Tactile and Olfactory Channels   133
    Receptor Medium: Print   133
      Digital and Iconic Projections   134
      Total Impact of Projections   145
    Conclusion   147

6. PRINCIPLES OF TRANSLATING PERFORMANCE   149
    Formal and Dynamic Equivalence   150
    Analytical and Perceptual Equivalence   153
    Making the Performance Report   158
    Making the Performance Record   161
    Conclusion   165

7. AN ILLUSTRATION OF A
    PERFORMANCE-CENTERED TEXT   166
    The Report   167
    The Record   184
    The Performance-Centered Text and the
      Literary Text: A Comparison   195
    Conclusion   202

Notes   204

Bibliography   227

Index   241

Illustrations

Figure

1. An Aesthetic Transaction Model of
   Artistic Verbal Performance   75

2. Birdwhistell's Linguistic and Kinesics Transcription   101

3. Original Performance Event   105

4. Literal Intersemiotic Translation   106

5. Adjusted Intersemiotic Translation   106

6. Hip/Hand Stance, Hip/Arm Stance   173

7. Sexy Woman Stances   174

Preface

Surely one of the great ironies for the folklorist is the making of a folklore text. Anyone who has collected folklore knows the problems of translating it to paper. The more one appreciates the telling of a tale, with all the life of a performer and audience interacting, the more frustrating this process of textmaking becomes. For those who believe that the tale lives in the telling, a text which captures only the content of the tale seems a poor and inadequate substitute for the live performance. As more and more folklorists shift their research to questions of performance, the nature and role of the folklore text becomes a subject of debate.

The issues posed by recording folklore in print are complex, and the debate over the role of the text is often heated, as the recent "text/context controversy" in *Western Folklore* attests. Some folklorists would eschew study of texts and embrace the study of live performances. Others, who work with more content-oriented research, insist that folklore texts are essential to the discipline and defend the efficacy of the traditional folklore text. This book mediates this conflict through its insistence that the folklore text can remain central to the study of folklore if we adopt a rigorous practice of treating the text as a systematic record of a performance—a record which includes nonverbal and contextual features.

I hope that my definition of the text as an intersemiotic translation from performance to the print medium will challenge more folklorists to follow in the steps of Dennis Tedlock, Dell Hymes, Barre Toelken, and others, who have endeavored to translate performance to print. I hope too that scholars of rhetoric and oral interpretation will find these concepts applicable to their study of artistic verbal performance.

It is difficult to express in a few words the debt of gratitude I feel to those who helped bring this work to fruition. To Paul Gray and Richard Bauman, I am profoundly grateful. Their probing questions and critical comments were invaluable. I profited too from the advice of Martin Todaro, Larry Coleman, and Lee Hudson. Roger Abrahams, Archie Green, Beverly Whitaker Long, and Jean Haskell Speer provided encouragement and ideas along the way. And to Thomas O. Sloane, whose interest in the relationship of text to performance first stimulated my inquiry in this area, I owe a special thanks.

I would also like to thank Jill Taft-Kaufman and Jacqueline Taylor for their comments on early drafts, as well as Daun Kendig for her research assistance. Val Alvarez provided invaluable help video recording the performance. A special thanks to Margaret Orban and Pamela Hills for their typing of early drafts, Sue Gellerman-Nilsen for her meticulous typing of the final manuscript, and Carol Nickerson and Linda Johnson-Wells for copyediting. I greatly appreciate Joan Catapano, Natalie Wrubel, and Tarry Curry of Indiana University Press, and Harry Damant, Mary Taylor, and Howard Hill of the Printing Department at Virginia Polytechnic Institute and State University for their help in bringing out this book.

I am especially grateful to James Hutchinson for allowing his performance to be taped. Without his cooperation, this work would be greatly impoverished. To Mary Jones Fine and Melissa Walker, who helped translate the video tape, and to Marilyn Carreño, who helped test the completed text by performing it, I offer sincere thanks. I am grateful to the Center for Programs in the Humanities and the Department of Communication Studies at Virginia Polytechnic Institute and State University for their support of my research. Finally, I want to thank my husband, Robert Walker, and my parents, Sam and Mary Fine, for their constant support and encouragement.

1

Introduction

Aperformance of verbal art is something more than words. Each of us has, at one time or another, sat under the spell of a performer, conscious of the artistry of voice and body. Yet this art of performance seems to elude our critical grasp. Most critical commentary on artistic verbal performances focuses on the linguistic level. We can read about themes, formulae, images, or narrative structure, but most critics invariably ignore or shortchange the elements which make artistic verbal performance different from written literature.

Certainly a major reason why we know so little about the poetics of verbal art performances is that they are ephemeral. Even when we have audio and video or film recordings to preserve them, the sounds and images are fluid—they will not hold still for analysis. If only we could make folklore texts which could combine the stability of print with the recording capabilities of film or video, then we could better understand the aesthetic patterning and social impact of verbal art.

This book is predicated on the assumption that we can indeed translate more of the performance style of folklore to print. It has grown out of my involvement with two complementary disciplines centrally concerned with the study of verbal art—oral interpretation and folklore. Both disciplines share a concern for the relationship between a verbal text and performance. Until recently, however, each discipline has approached the text with a different *telos*, or end, in mind. Oral interpreters commonly work with literary texts, critically apprehending them through performance. Hence, for interpreters, the *telos* of a text is a performance that serves as as valid interpretation. Historically, the field of interpretation[1] has focused little of its energy on making texts from performances. Yet from the British elocutionists up to contemporary linguistically oriented interpreters, interpretation scholars have experimented with notational devices to record performative behaviors

1

implicit in a literary text, or in some instances, to record the performance of a literary text.[2]

Starting at the other end, with live performances of "verbal art,"[3] folklorists record artistic verbal performances into texts which they later publish and analyze. If they specialize in documentation, their *telos* is a text that records aspects of the performed folklore, and if they seek to interpret that text, their *telos* is a written interpretation of the verbal performance they have witnessed and recorded. Thus, while folklorists commonly work from performances to texts, interpreters commonly work from texts to performances.

Not only have interpreters and folklorists approached the text with different ends in mind, they have worked with fundamentally different kinds of texts. Interpreters have confined most of their attention to texts from literary traditions, while folklorists have focused, for the most part, on texts from oral traditions. Although folklorists work with nonliterary texts, they have tended to impose a literary or ethnolinguistic model of the text on orally composed and transmitted discourse (see Chapter 2). While folklorists abstracted verbatim transcripts from performances, they often ignored recording or commenting on the contextual and nonverbal features of a performance. As MacEdward Leach says of folklore collected in the past, it was collected more as written literature than oral literature: ". . . you discover that almost without exception it was collected with little reference to how it was originally presented. It is invariably collected as if it came from written sources, as if it were eye literature, rather than ear literature. Since it was collected as eye literature, it is edited and judged as written literature."[4]

During the 1970s and 1980s, however, new orientations in both disciplines have resulted in a fusion of interests. A new "performance approach" in folkloristics, which views folklore as a dynamic communicative process rather than as an artifact from the past, has attuned folklorists to the significance of studying performance. Believing that the nature of verbal art lies in the process of performance, the performance approach seeks to study the aesthetic patterning of performances within specific cultural contexts. Consequently, many contemporary folklorists have become critical of texts that ignore or mask performative elements. In the forefront, Dennis Tedlock and Dell Hymes have experimented with new text styles which seek, when performed by the reader, to "embody the presentational form of the original."[5] As oral interpretation has turned its attention to its historical roots in folklore, it has expanded its interests from interpretation of literary texts to include folklore. Additionally, interpretation has developed a new theoretical interest in studying performance. With a dual interest in folklore and performance, interpretation has come to share the materials and *telos* of the folklorist.

THE PROBLEM

While interpreters and folklorists share a common interest in studying performance, they also share a major methodological problem obstructing that study—the folklore text. Next to the verbal art of the folk itself, the folklore text, or record of verbal art, lies at the heart of the study of folklore. Folklorists, in the peculiar position of studying an ephemeral phenomenon that exists in its living form only as it is performed, have had as their first task the recording and preservation of relevant data. Since the quality of folklore studies depends, to a large extent, on the accuracy of the texts collected and published, the folklore text is a *sine qua non*. As the medium through which the folklore performance is transmitted from collector to reader, the text plays an important role in the preservation and presentation of the folklore performance. The text not only stores the performance for future studies, it re-presents the performance in another medium. Since the reader's perception of the original performance springs from the presentation contained in the text, the study of the relationship between performance and text is critical.

Unfortunately, little attention has been focused on the folklore text as a communicative medium that reflects the analytical perspective of its maker, and in turn, influences the perspectives of its readers. Instead, taking the text for granted as an *a priori* given, and not questioning its validity and accuracy as a recording of a performance, many scholars in the past have conflated the text with the original performance. Thus, when a particular text seemed stylistically barren and flat, some scholars have concluded that the folklore itself was stylistically undeveloped and uninteresting. Indeed, as Tedlock points out, the reader of American Indian narratives who has only bowdlerized popularizations for children, or dry, scholarly texts may underrate the artistic quality of Indian narratives:

> But he will soon wonder whether the original style of these narratives was as choppy and clumsy as that of most English translations. If he takes these translations to represent, as Boas claimed, "faithful rendering of the native tales," and if he remains disappointed with popularizations, he may end by agreeing with La Farge, who said, "The literary value of a great deal of primitive literature, whether myths or tales, is nil. That of much of the rest is apparent, in the raw form, only to connoisseurs, while those who undertake to retell some of it often achieve only emasculation."[6]

As a major analytical approach becomes passé, however, and a new approach arises, the text's adequacy or inadequacy as a communicator becomes suddenly apparent. Throughout the history of American folkloristics, as Chapter 2 of this work shows, criticisms and calls for better texts emerge when followers of one approach discover that the texts collected by folklorists of another approach do not contain information necessary for their research. When the performance approach (also called the contextual approach) challenged earlier schools of folklore, the inadequacy of previous texts became apparent. For the most part, the earlier collections of texts failed to record information about the performance situation. Frequently, few, if any, descriptions of the performers, audience, or context accompany the text. Stylistic features such as opening and closing formulae, ideophones, and archaic phrases are omitted. Rarely are any paralinguistic or kinesic features notated in the text, or described in the commentary. Yet all of these features are clues to the understanding of performance as "situated behavior, situated within and rendered meaningful with reference to relevant contexts."[7]

Contemporary folklorists working from a performance perspective have commented on the inadequacy of existing texts. J. Barre Toelken, for example, says that he avoided using transcribed texts in his study because "they pose uncountable critical problems," and adds that "close literary use of published texts" is "critically hazardous for anything beyond synopses."[8] Indeed, his own fieldwork with a Navajo storyteller uncovered many important stylistic features which previous collectors had not recorded in their texts.

Noting "that the text is nothing more than the skeleton of the performed folktale," Linda Dégh argues that the skeleton must be filled out "by recording the inflection, cadence, and tempo—the rhythm of the narrator. Gestures, facial expressions, and dramatic interplay must be retained."[9] While Dégh offers no suggestions as to how to present such data within a text, Dennis Tedlock has undertaken extensive work in designing a text style which will record more performance features.[10] Working on Zuni texts, he evaluates past translations, discussing the reasons for the failure to record or transcribe stylistic features. He develops a new mode of presentation using typography and layout to record, in readable format, the style of Zuni narrative. In addition, Tedlock, along with Jerome Rothenberg, has started a new journal, *Alcheringa: Ethnopoetics*, whose goal is to stimulate new experiments with textual presentations of verbal art.[11]

In his 1974 Presidential Address to the American Folklore Society, Dell Hymes argues for a new conception of folklore as performance and a fresh examination of the role of the text in presenting a performance. To demonstrate his argument, he offers a new presentational form of a previously collected Chinookan text. Retranslating the text and performing it himself, Hymes tries "to embody the presentational form of the original." Calling attention to the problem of presentation, Hymes writes: "Short of preservation in the form of boxed storage in locked vaults, our efforts to preserve tradition through record, description, interpretation, find their natural end in presentation, that is, communication."[12]

Elsewhere, in "Breakthrough Into Performance," Hymes argues for the "systematic study of variation in performance." He notes a "virtual absence of serious stylistic analysis of native American Indian traditions and of individual performers. . . ."[13] In a footnote, Hymes adds that "there has been little or no fruitful integration of work concerned with the methodology of observational description, and work concerned with the methodology of cultural description. . . ."[14]

The current concern with the quality of the folklore text echoes earlier criticisms which resurface from the 1930s to the present. Despite continued articulations of the problem, American folkloristics has not developed any systematic approach to making performance-centered texts. As we will see in the next chapter, the content and quality of texts varies according to the analytical perspectives of the collectors.

While recent experimentation with text styles includes various paralinguistic and kinesic notations, photography, typography, and layout, the experimentation proceeds without an articulated theory of the folklore text. Performance-centered folklorists undertaking fieldwork today face a confusing problem in determining how to present the folklore on paper. Although they have at their disposal various notational devices, few theoretical principles for recording folklore performances exist to guide them.

Indeed, the new conceptualization of folklore as artistic verbal performance places much greater demands on the text than other analytical perspectives. For example, the influential Finnish historical-geographical school of folklore (see Chapter 2) treats variations in performance of tales as corruptions leading to the decay of traditional artifacts. Two leading American proponents of this method, Stith Thompson and Archer Taylor, illustrate in their writings a devaluation of performance. Thompson finds the traditional nature of folklore more important than the creative performances of storytellers: "It is handed down from one person to another, and there is no virtue in originality."[15] Similarly, Taylor labels changes in folktales as "subversive," and advocates that "as soon as a change is perceived to be intentional, it can be disposed of."[16] For adherents to this narrow view of performance as simply the annoying "devolution"[17] and corruption of a once pure artifact, making a folklore text is unproblematical. A simple text of the words alone is sufficient.

Such a simple text is sufficient too for structuralists such as Lévi-Strauss, who finds value in a tale's content rather than its style: "The mythical value of the myth remains preserved, even through the worst translation. . . . Its substance does not lie in its style, its original music, or its syntax, but in the story it tells."[18]

In contrast, contemporary performance-centered folklorists recognize
the insufficiency of a text containing only a verbal transcript. Dan Ben-
Amos and Kenneth Goldstein argue that such a text "is necessary but not
sufficient documentation." Rather, they argue that folklore texts "require
proxemic, kinesic, paralinguistic, interactional descriptions, all of which
might provide clues to the principles underlying the communicative
processes of folklore and its performing attributes."[19]

Yet the new recognition of the need to record kinesic, paralinguistic,
proxemic, and other communicative codes creates theoretical and
practical problems. The burgeoning research on such nonverbal codes,
spread among several disciplines, is often contradictory. No synthesis of
this nonverbal communication literature from a performance-centered
perspective exists to guide the textmaker. How the nonverbal features of a
performance should be recorded remains an issue. Indeed, current
experimentation with recording performance suggests two radically
different formats for presenting these nonverbal performance features.
One text style, based on structural linguistic methodology, segments the
performance into discrete codes and records them with a variety of new
symbols arranged in layers above the verbal transcript. The other text
style, borrowing the techniques of naturalistic observation and
inferential description, records the performance in natural language and
more immediately understood typographic conventions.

Underlying the oppositions between these two text styles is a
fundamental epistemological difference between positivist and
intuitionist approaches to description and meaning. Since the
performance approach has roots in both positivist and intuitionist
philosophies, both styles have an intrinsic appeal. Yet which style, or
combination of styles, best represents artistic verbal performance as an
aesthetic communicative process has not been resolved. Indeed, since the
performance approach is relatively new, its implications for the text have
not been developed. Clearly, these problems must be resolved if the
practice of making folklore texts is to grow beyond its current
experimental stages to a true *praxis,* or union of theory and practice.

METHODOLOGY AND ORGANIZATION

Essentially then, this work attacks the complex theoretical and
methodological problem of making texts which will more accurately and
completely record artistic verbal performances. Our focus on verbal
performances does not include musical forms, such as ballads. We are
concerned rather with the common ground between interpretation and
folkloristics, that large domain of performances which is variously called

oral literature, spoken art, or verbal art. The complexities of recording the artistic use of voice and body are immense; the added difficulties of recording musical tones are beyond the scope and interest of this work.

Yet it is not always easy to make a clear distinction between the boundaries of music and speech.[20] Singers and narrators employ similar vocal devices, such as rasp, falsetto, crescendo, and emphasis. Moreover, singers sometimes break into speech for emphasis while narrators sometimes intersperse their narratives with musical refrains or chants. Speech itself, with its prosodic features, can be said to possess musical qualities.

Where then does this leave us? For those cases in which intermittent melody accompanies a verbal performance, textmakers should consult ethnomusicological sources for appropriate notations. While quit-claiming the recording of musical tones, we are concerned with the musical qualities of speech so vital to aesthetic form.

In addition to folklorists and interpretation scholars, researchers in such fields as communication, sociolinguistics, sociology, philosophy, anthropology, and literary criticism may find this work on the folklore text relevant. As the social sciences and humanities have come to share paradigms based on analogies drawn from cultural performances, interest in verbal performance spans several disciplines.[21] In an effort to make this work as accessible as possible to an interdisciplinary audience, I have tried to define all specialized terms. For example, the historiographic discussion of textmaking practices in Chapter 2 takes pains to clarify theories and movements no doubt already familiar to professional folklorists.

A first and necessary step in laying the theoretical groundwork for making performance-centered texts is to understand the historical development of the text. Chapter 2 examines the development of the folklore text in American folkloristics from the inception of the American Folklore Society in 1888 to the present. For the greater part of this period, we find that folklore texts reflect the differing analytical perspectives of the two major branches of American folklorists, the anthropological and literary.

The textmaking practices follow two prevailing models: 1) the ethnolinguistic model of the text used by anthropologists; and 2) the literary model, with its scholarly and popularized formats, used by literary folklorists. Neither of these models treats verbal art performance as an integral art form. As the boundaries between the anthropological and literary folklorists begin to break down in the early fifties, we find a new concern for publishing folklore texts which will provide contextual, as well as stylistic information. The calls for better texts during the fifties and sixties laid the foundation for increasing experimentation with recording more performance features during the last two decades. This chapter ends by reviewing contemporary experimentation with making performance-centered texts.

Since the performance approach is so new, its full implications for the text have not yet been inferred. Chapter 3 examines the theoretical principles of the performance approach on which a performance-centered model of the text should be based. The three key concepts forming the nucleus of the performance approach include performance as 1) an aesthetic mode of communication, 2) integrally related to a particular event, and 3) culture-specific, cross-culturally variable. The most problematic of these principles for the textmaker, however, is to record the performance as an aesthetic mode of communication. If the text represents a performance only as a communicative process, it fails to capture the essence of the transaction that distinguishes artistic verbal performance from other modes of communication. Unless textmakers are aware of the qualitative features separating performance from other modes of communication, they may neglect to record these features.

To clarify these qualitative characteristics, Chapter 3 constructs an aesthetic transaction model of verbal art based on Arnold Berleant's work, *The Aesthetic Field.*[22] This model illustrates the components of an ideal performance-centered text which would record the aesthetic transaction (manifested through observable behaviors) between the performer and audience, and be accompanied by commentary that grounds the text in its particular aesthetic field. Such an ideal text would enable readers to reconstitute the aesthetic qualities of the original performance, perceiving its unique, integral form as an immediate, sensuous, dynamic, aesthetic communicative process. Although this ideal, like all ideals, may only be approximated, never fully reached, it provides goals and suggests solutions. The idea that the textmaker must represent a performance in another medium implies that the textmaker's essential task is a hermeneutic act of translation. Thus, the next step is to turn to translation theory for guidance in solving the problems of translating performance to print.

The next three chapters develop theoretical principles for translating performance to print. Since the central problem in recording performance is to record more of the paralinguistic, kinesic, and other nonverbal performance features in the print medium, these chapters focus on the "intersemiotic" translation of performance to print. Following precedents set by Roman Jakobson and Eugene Nida, I define intersemiotic translation as "transmutation," that is, "the transference of a message from one kind of symbolic system to another."[23] This study is limited, then, to performances in the English language and centers on the translation of the oral-physical symbols of artistic verbal performance to the two-dimensional, visual symbols of the printed page.

To approach the problems of translating performance to print, I draw primarily on the translation theories of Eugene Nida and George Steiner.[24] Although Nida's framework for analyzing the factors influencing the translation process is designed for interlingual translation, it can be adapted to the problems of intersemiotic translation. These chapters suggest principles for translating performance based on analysis of: 1) the nature of the discourse to be translated, 2) audience problems, and 3) the differences in the two media of translation, performance and print. The resulting principles for translating performance grow directly out of the analysis of these three influential factors. Let us briefly look at some of the major issues covered in these chapters.

As a prelude to this translation approach, Chapter 4 first confronts two objections to the view of the text as a translation of performance. The first objection derives from an alternative semiotic definition of "text." The second objection, rooted in a bias against the imperfection inherent in all translation, argues that since texts cannot perfectly represent performances, they should not be made.

After answering these objections, Chapter 4 defines the folklore text. This definition distinguishes between a performance record and a performance report, and argues that the text is a record of the aesthetic transaction in the print medium. This record necessarily involves intersemiotic translation. Not all performance signals, however, can be recorded. In addition, readers must have information about the participants, the event, and the performance tradition if they are to respond to the aesthetic transaction. Consequently, the record must be accompanied by a report of the performance's aesthetic field and any untranslatable features.

Three important audience relationships influence how a text is translated: 1) the various types of audiences reading the text, 2) the textmaker as an audience of the text, and 3) the textmaker as an audience to the live performance. The problem of adapting the text to different audiences is partially resolved through considering the characteristics of an adequate translation. Concepts from information theory prove useful in identifying the need to adjust the text to the audience's capacity to decode it. These concepts also help identify the dangers of overloading or underloading the text with too much or too little aesthetic information. Finally, these ideas suggest how oral interpretation can be used to evaluate the information of a text.

Just as the interlingual translator must know the characteristics of both languages, the textmaker must know the characteristics of the source and receptor media. Chapter 5 describes the signals and channel capacities of performance and print. The analysis of the performance medium covers the types of signals transmitted through the primary communication channels: aural, visual, tactile, and olfactory. Readers familiar with the better known characteristics of the linguistic and paralinguistic dimensions of the aural channel may want to bypass this part of the chapter. The analysis of research approaches to kinesics considers the key issue of description and meaning, and thus, covers important ground for the textmaker. A comparison of Ray Birdwhistell's structural linguistic model of kinesic research to the naturalistic observation model of Roger G. Barker and Herbert F. Wright provides valuable concepts for the subsequent text theory.[25] Birdwhistell's contributions to the knowledge of the communicative structure of body movements, and Barker and Wright's concepts of inferential description and molar and molecular behavior are particularly important. The concluding discussion of kinesics contrasts the heavily iconic coding of body movements with the predominantly digital coding of verbal language to clarify some of the difficulties in using verbal language to record body movements. In addition to the kinesics discussion, the chapter discusses the proxemic and artifactual signals in the visual channel, and the tactile and olfactory channels.

In comparison to the multichanneled medium of performance, the channel capacity of print is limited. Yet a number of means exist which augment the print medium's capacity to record performance. To provide a theoretical basis for choosing devices to record a performance, the analysis of the print medium examines the underlying types of signs composing existing notational and descriptive systems. This discussion concentrates on the merits and drawbacks of various printed signs for recording performance features. First, I treat the digital category of printed signs, discussing the characteristics of 1) natural language description, 2) alphabetic notations, and 3) analphabetic notations. Then, I examine the iconic category of printed signs, considering devices ranging from alphabetic icons to photographs. In addition, the discussion considers the metacommunicative impact of the entire printed page, with its configuration of printed signs.

Chapter 6 proposes general theoretical principles for translating performance to print. Four different approaches to creating equivalences in form and content are examined: formal vs. dynamic equivalence and analytical vs. perceptual equivalence. Tensions exist between these four orientations. Indeed, all folklore texts can be placed on a continuum between these polar orientations toward equivalence. Yet the performance-centered text should strive toward formal and perceptual equivalency. Inherent in the tensions between the analytical and perceptual orientations, however, is a clash between positivist and intuitionist approaches to meaning. This clash can be mediated through E. D. Hirsch's concept of "corrigible schemata."[26] Hirsch's concept provides a way to incorporate analytical procedures into the process of making a perceptual-equivalent text.

After identifying the orientations toward equivalency necessary for a performance-centered text, the chapter suggests a methodology for making the performance report of the aesthetic field and the performance record of the aesthetic transaction. The suggested methodology for making the performance report is based on Hymes' ethnography of speaking model.[27] The framework for the textual record draws on Steiner's four hermeneutic steps of translation: trust, penetration, embodiment, and restitution.[28] These steps, combined with the concept of corrigible schema and the previously discussed theoretical principles, provide general principles for making a performance-centered text.

To illustrate the theoretical principles proposed in the preceding chapters, the final chapter includes a new performance-centered text, discusses how it was made, and compares it to a literary text of the same tale. The text records a performance of "Stagolee," a well-known Afro-American "toast," or narrative monologue. Since the performance tradition of Afro-American toasts is often noted for the importance of performance style, this genre is particularly challenging to record in print. In addition, the origin of this performance in a literary version published in Julius Lester's *Black Folktales*[29] makes it possible to examine the changes made when a literary text enters oral tradition. After presenting a performance report and a performance record, the chapter compares the performance-centered text of "Stagolee" to Lester's literary text. The comparison of the two texts illustrates the value of the performance-centered text in illuminating the aesthetic patterning of performance.

SIGNIFICANCE

The development of a feasible method for making valid texts of artistic verbal performances is a necessary step in the empirical study of performance. For the fields of interpretation and folklore, performance-centered texts can help propel the new theoretical interest in performance beyond the level of generalizations.

Interpretation's theoretical interest in performance started in the late sixties, and was heralded as a new emphasis by Wallace Bacon in 1975. In "The Dangerous Shores a Decade Later," Bacon points to an increased emphasis upon performance, attributing part of this new interest to the contributions of research in other fields: "Linguists, psychologists, philosophers have been drawn upon to enhance our notions of what enters into the act of performance. Paralanguage, kinesics, phenomenology, communication theory, metalanguage—these and other fields of knowledge are helping us to understand the elements of which our art is composed."[30] Calls for research into folklore and oral tradition articulated by Thomas Sloan, Beverly Whitaker, Leland Roloff, and David Thompson;[31] articles relating oral interpretation and folklore;[32] several completed dissertations related to oral tradition and folklore;[33] an interpretation doctoral seminar on the phenomenon of performance;[34] and a national Speech Communication Association program dealing with research implications of performance[35] indicate a growing desire to understand more about performance.

For the greater part of the academic history of oral interpretation, performance has been acknowledged as one of the most effective ways to understand literature and treated as a means to that end, but it has seldom been examined in its own right. Some experimental studies tried to measure the effectiveness of certain delivery features, but the total gestalt of the performance was often characterized in metaphorical terms, thought to be an ineluctable "mystery" or "paradox," and left unexplored. As Janet Bolton points out in her response to J. T. Marshman's articles on the mystery and paradox of oral interpretation, contemporary scholars have begun to explore the phenomenon of performance.[36] She cites Thomas Sloan's application of hermeneutics and Gary Cronkhite's paradigm of oral interpretation as "the study of the interface between a written symbol system and an oral-physical symbol system" to support her contention that "the thrust today is inquiry rather than celebration, operational definition instead of metaphor."[37]

Surely a major reason for the treatment of performance as a mystery, and perhaps the greatest obstacle in the way of studying performance, is its ephemeral quality. While instructors often evaluate class performances using the fixed literary text as the referent, many of the specific features of a performance quickly fade from memory, making it difficult to analyze what Whitaker terms the "performed text," or the convergence of the text and the performer expressing.[38] Yet a study of performance-centered texts could tell teachers in interpretation a great deal about the phenomenon of performance. With the increasing availability of video recorders, performances both in and out of the classroom can be preserved and translated to paper. Such performance-centered texts can aid in the pursuit of at least five major areas of research.[39]

The first area involves the discovery and analysis of the ground rules of performance, that is, the "set of cultural themes and social-interactional organizing principles that govern the conduct of performance."[40] Knowledge of these ground rules is important for the oral interpretation of folklore from non-Western and ethnic traditions, as Jean Haskell Speer shows in her dissertation on performing folklore.[41] Ethnographic research on the performance ground rules in a variety of cultures and settings might help lay to rest that perennial debate over performance canons. It could well be that the differences in opinion on the amount of movement and gesture appropriate to the performance of literature stem from different cultural heritages as much, if not more than, allegiance to a particular school of thought. Identifying the ground rules governing the performance of literature and folklore can help expand our knowledge of the social and cultural roots of interpretation activity. But only through accurate records which make note of the interacting variables of setting, participants, ends, act-sequence, key, instrumentalities, norms of interaction and interpretation, and genre[42] can such ground rules be discovered.

A second area, research into performer competence, explores the norms and standards by which performers are evaluated. One fundamental question which the field of interpretation must answer is what constitutes "true" performance for the interpretive performer. True performance, "when standards intrinsic to the tradition in which the performance occurs are accepted and realized,"[43] may vary according to the genre, act, event, role, or speech community involved. Study of a wide range of performance-centered texts can help uncover the intrinsic standards of competence in a variety of traditions. As a case in point, J. Barre Toelken's performance-centered text of a Navaho raconteur allows him to suggest some of the performance standards intrinsic to the Navaho performance tradition of Coyote tales.[44]

A third research area, the sociological and psychological study of the performer, can be facilitated by close records of individual performances, correlated with information about the performer's background and personality. István Sándor's tentative typology of four kinds of performers, based on the study of the performance styles of famous Hungarian narrators,[45] could be tested in other cultures. Research on individual performers and the changes in their performances over a period of time could tell a great deal about the factors influencing the development of performance style.

A fourth area, performance as social interaction, has major implications for interpretation. Here, questions of context become paramount as one considers how performances are socially situated and what sociocultural functions they serve. Performance-centered texts made from such everyday performances as anecdotes, jokes, parables, and personal narratives; from ceremonial performances such as weddings, funerals, initiations; and from performances in such institutional settings as prisons, historical sites, or in the classroom, can enlarge our conception of how performance functions in social life.

Perhaps one of the greatest contributions of performance-centered texts can be their role in the development of an aesthetics of artistic verbal performance. Such texts can provide a steady data base upon which an empirical aesthetics can build. Such an empirically-based aesthetics should begin "by being primarily descriptive rather than judicial," according to Berleant, and "develop its normative standards from an observational base."[46] Study of performance-centered texts which record the performance's contextual influences, audience and performer reactions to the performance, and nonverbal features can aid in discovering the "aesthetic facts"[47] out of which aesthetic theory emerges.

At least five kinds of aesthetic facts which Berleant distinguishes can be discovered through the making and study of performance-centered texts. "Situational Facts," which describe the *"conditions under which aesthetic experience occurs,"* can be provided by recording contextual information and audience responses. "Experiential Facts," or descriptions of *"the characteristics of aesthetic experience* itself" which "distinguish it from other modes of experience, such as the practical and the cognitive,"[48] can be made from the text's notation of audience reactions to the performance. Indeed, the text itself, as it reflects the textmaker's observations and conscious selections of what to record, stands as an "experiential fact" about the performance.

Undoubtedly, performance-centered texts can contribute to the elucidation of "Objective Facts" about performance, or statements about *"The objects which are involved in aesthetic experience* and which are the central focus of our attention."[49] Objective facts about the aesthetic patterning of performance are necessary for the critical study of verbal art as performance. Unless scholars have records of performances to substantiate critical judgments, fruitful cross-examination and verification of critical claims will be hampered.

After more performance-centered texts are published, comparisons among them can provide "Judgmental Facts," or the *"body of critical judgments about these objects and events"* expressing "normative conclusions that have emerged from considerable exposure and discussion of art objects, styles, and media."[50] Certainly teachers of interpretation who are routinely involved in making judgmental decisions about performances could profit from examination of the norms undergirding their judgments and those of the audience. Texts with specific performer behaviors and audience responses can help clarify the relationship between specific behaviors and their effect on the audience.

Finally, access to performance-centered texts can facilitate the gathering of "Interdisciplinary Facts," which result from *"studies of aesthetic events and objects from the standpoint of various related disciplines."*[51] Studies in the sociology, aesthetics, semiotics, and psychology of performance, as well as cultural and historical trends in performance, can contribute to an understanding of the significance of artistic verbal performance. Since so many texts lack performance features, our actual knowledge of these areas is slim.

Since interpretation and folkloristics share a common interest in the study of artistic verbal performance, folklorists will find most of these research implications of equal significance to their field. Indeed, contemporary folklorists have been actively pursuing investigations into ground rules, performer competency, the sociology and psychology of the performer, and folklore as social interaction.[52]

Given the historic concern of folklorists with the preservation and presentation of verbal art, however, a methodological and theoretical treatment of the text is of special importance. With the advent of the performance approach in contemporary folkloristics, the role of the text has become problematical. Some folklorists concerned with performance have voiced disparaging words about the folklorist's textmaking activity: "The vitality of expressive man is thus further deadened by folklorists, fixing the transient and transitional out of a need for the objective scholar to describe and compare through the medium of the written word and the printed page."[53] Other performance-centered folklorists, instead of disparaging the text, have experimented with new presentational styles that attempt to convey the vitality of performance. Dell Hymes', Dennis Tedlock's, and J. Barre Toelken's efforts to revitalize the text indicate that folklorists can do a better job translating performance to the page.

But unless this innovative experimentation with recording performance is backed by theory and presented as a valid and productive method of recording, the great majority of folklore collectors will undoubtedly continue making texts which ignore performance. Archives of folklore will continue to expand, but will be of little use to the study and appreciation of artistic verbal performance.

Both interpreters and folklorists have only recently recognized the importance of studying performance. Consequently, we have barely begun to explore the issues involved in the intersemiotic translation of performance to the print medium. Yet considering the importance of recording and preserving verbal art, we must confront these complex issues and develop a conceptually sound and workable approach for making texts. As Hymes has said so eloquently, "The recreative aspect is both inevitable and desirable. The issue, then, is simply the character of the recreative effort, in terms of fidelity, insight, and taste."[54]

2

The Development of the Text in American Folkloristics

Since the establishment of the American Folklore Society in 1888, a dominant activity of American folklorists has been recording, publishing, and studying texts of verbal art. The text, or printed record of verbal art, remains a basic source of data for folklorists. Emphasizing the importance of the folklore text, Richard Dorson calls it the "inviolable document of oral tradition" and adds, "What the state paper is to the historian and creative work to the literary scholar, the oral traditional text is—or should be—to the student of folklore."[1] Given the importance of the textmaking activity to the folklore discipline, it is surprising to find no critical history of textmaking practices. Yet the text plays a key role in shaping folklore theory as it is influenced by, and in turn influences, the analytical perspectives of folklorists. Beginning in the late 1800s with the formation of the American Folklore Society, and ending with the most recent conceptions of the text, this chapter lays the necessary historical groundwork on which any new theory of the folklore text must stand.

This chapter identifies the major conceptual models of the folklore text, discusses their relationship to analytical perspectives, and describes the major changes in textmaking practices. In general, developments in textmaking reflect the differing analytical perspectives of four orientations within American folkloristics: 1) anthropological, 2) literary, 3) a fusion of anthropological and literary interests, and 4) the performance approach. Before discussing each of these orientations separately, let us place them in historical perspective.

16

The first two sections discuss conceptions of the text among anthropological and literary folklorists. To understand the reasons underlying the division of folklore studies into these two branches, one must consider the state of American folkloristics in the nineteenth century. The study of folklore in America began years before the American Folklore Society was founded in 1888. Ethnologists had been collecting the myths and lore of American Indians; writers and historians had been searching for a distinctive American culture; and international literary-comparative folklorists had been tracing the diffusion of tradition from the old to the new world.[2] The gathering of these diverse interests into one society created tensions and differences of opinion which still exist today.

The split between the anthropological and literary folklorists originated in a disagreement over how broadly to define American folklore. The accepted nineteenth century European definition of folklore as the "unwritten popular traditions of civilized countries" did not seem broad enough to include the traditions of the American Indians.[3] Some folklorists wanted to restrict folklore studies to the European definition and study the oral traditions of American immigrants. Others, such as William W. Newell, the founder of the American Folklore Society, wanted to include the study of American Indians.[4]

Under Newell's influential leadership, the American Folklore Society articulated a broad definition of folklore as "oral tradition—information and belief handed down from generation to generation without the use of writing."[5] This broad definition included the traditions of the American Indians and thus incorporated anthropological methodology into American folklore study.

Although literary folklorists continued collecting the European traditions of American immigrants, the anthropological folklorists dominated the field during the years from 1888 to the mid-thirties. As anthropological interest began to shift to more abstract questions of function, anthropologists showed decreasing interest in folklore.[6] Literary folklorists gained dominance in the late thirties, but reflected a growing awareness of the contributions of anthropology to folklore methodology.

If these two branches had remained separate, the holistic, interdisciplinary performance approach might never have emerged. But during the twenties and thirties, and with accelerating pace from the 1940s on, a number of intellectual influences began to break down the boundaries between these two branches. Increasingly during this period folklorists followed William Bascom's suggestion that "the most effective way to bridge the gaps between different groups of folklorists is by a common concern with common problems."[7] In this third section, we will review the major precursors to the performance approach, such as the Prague School linguists, the oral-formulaic work of Milman Parry and Albert Lord, the refiguration of social thought brought about by the application of drama and game analogies to the social sciences, and the ethnography of speaking. Against this rich backdrop of interdisciplinary work, we can better appreciate the fusion of interests among anthropological and literary folklorists which led to a new interest in improving the text as a vehicle for recording performance.

By the late sixties, the growing interest in performance found theoretical expression in a series of articles calling for a new performance-oriented perspective in folklore research. Combining anthropological methods for analyzing culture with aesthetic and stylistic interest in the patterning of verbal art, the new performance theorists conceived of folklore as a dynamic communicative process. The new conceptions of verbal art as performance have led to experiments in translating verbal art performances to print. The final section reviews the emergence of the performance approach and the recent developments in making performance-centered texts.

THE ETHNOLINGUISTIC MODEL OF THE TEXT

In general, the texts published by American anthropological folklorists follow what might be called an ethnolinguistic model. This type of text serves as an accurate verbatim transcript of connected discourse which aids in linguistic analysis of Indian languages, and which records vanishing cultural traditions. Early texts in this vein conveyed little, if any, information about the informant, setting, or the cultural significance of the tale. Nor did they record many nonverbal performance features. Such texts were often collected through dictation and through a translator. Consequently, they represented more of a report to an outsider than a traditional cultural performance in a native context. Although the ethnolinguistic model predominated, some individual texts stand out for recording more contextual and performance features than the majority. First we will examine the development of the ethnolinguistic text and then discuss some of the more innovative textmakers working in this tradition.

The basic format for the ethnolinguistic text was established by two leaders in early American anthropology, John Wesley Powell and Franz Boas. Powell was instrumental in organizing the Bureau of American Ethnology in 1879, and Boas, the Father of American Anthropology, generated a school of anthropologists, many of whom became leaders in American folkloristics.

John Wesley Powell

Powell not only started the Bureau of American Ethnology (BAE), but he directed it for twenty-three years. Under his leadership, the Bureau became the "most important source of jobs, money, and publication outlets for American anthropologists."[8] Powell's interest in philology and his belief in cultural evolution greatly influenced the textmaking policy of the BAE.

The BAE usually published verbal art texts under three areas—philology, mythology, and habits and customs. Since Powell believed that philology was the basic science necessary to the understanding of all other aspects of tribal life, he placed most of his early interests there.[9] Powell's methods of recording folklore and his statements about the role of the text reflected his linguistic interests.

One of Powell's main reasons for collecting verbal art was to provide a sample of connected discourse to aid in learning the structure of Indian languages. To facilitate accurate, scientific methods of recording texts, Powell designed a fieldwork "circular" for use by staff members, travelers, missionaries, Army personnel, or others who might have contact with American Indians.[10] Powell's circular, *Introduction to the Study of Indian Languages, with Words, Phrases, and Sentences to be Collected,* grew out of George Gibbs' *Instructions for Research Relative to the Ethnology and Philology of America,* published by the Smithsonian Institution in 1863. Gibbs stressed accurate recording and standardized English orthography by assigning one sound to each letter and adding diacritical marks. He recommended a list of vocabulary words to collect and warned against recording the pronunciation of interpreters. To ensure the purity of the language, he suggested that informants be chiefs and noteworthy Indians, since Gibbs believed they would speak more correctly than common persons.[11]

Powell's circular, however, greatly improved on that of Gibbs. Powell expanded Gibbs' alphabet with the aid of Professor W. D. Whitney, a well-known Yale linguist. In addition, Powell asked for the collection of phrases and sentences, as well as words, in order to facilitate grammatical studies. Moreover, Powell argued for recording connected discourse, and supported his argument with extensive excerpts from an article by J. Hammond Trumbull. The following excerpt from Trumbull's work illustrates Powell's rationale for recording connected discourse: "A single chapter of the Bible or a dozen sentences of familiar conversation accurately translated into an Indian language, or a few selected words and phrases translated from it to English, will give a better insight to its structures and do more to determine its relationships to other American languages than long lists of concrete names or verb forms compiled on the usual plan."[12]

Myths and folktales not only suited Powell's desire to record connected discourse, but they also furnished insights into the culture of the Indians. Powell's formal definition of the text and his rationale for publishing texts articulates both of these reasons for recording folklore: "The early publication of grammars and dictionaries connected with which are *texts, or a body of literature obtained from Indian authorities, to illustrate the facts and principles of language, while also recording the genuine aboriginal philosophy and traditions,* has, therefore, been regarded as essential (my italics)."[13]

In the interests of attaining the first goal, "to illustrate the facts and principles of the language," Powell placed great stress on accurate recording. Indeed, his insistence on accuracy is one of his greatest contributions to textmaking practices. Powell strongly criticized the poor quality of most published Indian texts: ". . . but few of these have been free from blunder or perversion. Generally, the dubious medium of interpreters was necessary and the disposition to poetize or color with European sentiment was often apparent, even when distortion in support of favorite theories did not destroy the spirit and real significance of the original." He believed folklore could be presented more accurately "When collected with thorough understanding of the language and with collation of the several versions . . . ." In his statement on the Bureau's policy for publishing texts, Powell defines the basic format of the ethnolinguistic text: ". . . by plan of the Bureau, the myths and folklore of the several tribes are preserved and recorded in their own languages, with interlinear translation and without foreign coloring or addition, in connection with the several dictionaries of those languages."[14]

As an example of this ethnolinguistic format, the first *Annual Report* of the BAE includes an "Illustration of the Method of Recording Indian Languages" by J. O. Dorsey, A. S. Gatschet, and S. R. Riggs.[15] The identifying hallmark of the ethnolinguistic text is the use of multiple, serial translations of the same performance. For example, the sample texts in this article consist of three different versions: 1) the native language transcription, 2) an interlinear translation and 3) a free translation, in which the text is presented in standard English. Presumably the native and interlinear versions would aid linguistic research, while the free version would provide a more accessible record of cultural traditions. No descriptions of informants, context, or informant interpretations of the tale's significance are printed, nor are any nonverbal performance features. This format of the ethnolinguistic text became the standard among many anthropological folklorists.

Besides facilitating linguistic research, Powell believed folklore texts could record "the genuine aboriginal philosophy and traditions."[16] As a strong believer in the cultural evolutionism of Sir Edward Tylor, Powell avidly pursued research on the evolutionary status of the American

Indian. Powell's belief in cultural evolution conditioned his attitude toward folklore and his concept of the role of the text. According to the philosophy of cultural evolutionism, culture was thought to develop unilinearly through three stages: the savage, the barbaric, and the civilized. Each culture's evolutionary status could be diagnosed by examining its cultural institutions and art forms. Analyzing folklore was particularly important in evolutionary theory, "because it is expressive phenomena that are said to most decisively reveal the nature of man's thought processes at different stages of culture. . . ."[17] Whenever evolutionists found discrepancies between the behavior in a folktale and the behavior of the culture, they attributed the discrepancies to "survivals" or cultural residues of an earlier, more primitive state.

Powell's cultural evolutionary philosophy is reflected in his writings on American Indian mythology. His definition of the scientific method of studying mythology reveals his predilection to use folklore as a key to the earlier developmental stages of a people: "The objective or scientific method of studying a mythology is to collect and collate its phenomena simply as it is stated and understood by the people to whom it belongs. In tracing back the threads of its historical development, the student should expect to find it more simple and childlike in every stage of its progress."[18] The Indians were near the bottom of the evolutionary totem pole, according to Powell. In "Sketch of the Mythology of the North American Indians," Powell writes, "After all the years I have spent among the Indians in their mountain villages, I am not certain that I have sufficiently divorced myself from the thoughts and ways of civilization to properly appreciate their childish beliefs." Since he believed that "The opinions of a savage people are childish,"[19] it is no wonder that Powell expressed little interest in asking the Indian informants for their opinion about a myth or tale.

Clearly, Powell's view of folklore as a key to the past militated against recording folklore as a dynamic communicative process.[20] Neither information about the performance context nor data about a myth's function in the current society were needed to serve evolutionary research.

Franz Boas

Powell, however, was not the only contributor to the ethnolinguistic model. Franz Boas played an equally important role in shaping the ethnolinguistic text. Not only was he active in the BAE, but he served as editor of the *Journal of American Folklore* from 1908 to 1924, and as editor of the Columbia University *Contributions to Anthropology* from 1910 to about 1936.[21] His rejection of cultural evolutionism, his respect for American Indian culture, and his appreciation of the aesthetic value and important cultural functions of Indian folklore prompted some folklorists to supplement the ethnolinguistic text with more information about such performance features as tone, music, and gestures. Indeed, several of Boas' students, who we will discuss later, expressed great interest in more accurately recording the dynamic nonverbal and contextual elements of folklore performances.

Boas exerted strong influence on the textmaking policy of the Bureau of American Ethnology. He was appointed the Bureau's Honorary Philologist in 1902, and except for John Swanton, published more material through the Bureau than any other anthropologist.[22] Like Powell, Boas believed that accurate texts of the Indian languages and traditions constituted a basic foundation for anthropological research. In a letter written in 1905 to Powell's successor, William H. Holmes, Boas urged the Bureau to continue its high standard of published texts. This letter, which George W. Stocking captions "The Documentary Function of the Text," illustrates Boas' strong "passion for texts."[23] In the letter, Boas urged Holmes to print all of John Swanton's texts rather than only fourteen, and to print them in the native language. He argued that since one would not think of studying an ancient or foreign civilization without "a thorough knowledge of their languages and of the literary documents in these languages," the same standard should apply to studying American Indians: "In regard to our American Indians we are in the position that practically no such literary material is available for study and it appears to me as one of the essential things that we have to do, to make such material accessible. My own published work shows, that I let this kind of work take precedence over practically everything else, knowing it is the foundation of all future researches." In arguing for the benefits of these texts to future scholars, Boas wrote, "future times will require new points of view and for these the texts, and ample texts, must be made available."[24]

Boas' concern for the quality of texts led him to chair a committee of the American Anthropological Association charged with drawing up a phonetic system for transcribing Indian languages. The committee's report, published in 1915, suggested two levels of phonetic transcription (a simple and more detailed system) which would facilitate the comparison of North American Indian languages.[25]

While in general, Boas' own texts followed the standard ethnolinguistic format, a few of them recorded more than linguistic features. In "The Central Eskimo," he musically scored fragments of recitative, or what he terms poetic prose. He also used musical notation to record a poem and present the words and music to several songs.[26] In his *Chinook Texts*, Boas used musical notes to score the rhythm of chanted phrases.[27] Certainly these faint indications of nonverbal performance style reflect an appreciation for the aesthetic form of performance.

Although his own texts did not go far in recording nonverbal features and were not accompanied by information about the specific performance context, his theoretical perspectives laid the groundwork for greater attention to recording performance style.[28]

In contrast to Powell's ethnocentric view of the Indians, Boas was a cultural relativist. He rejected the cultural evolutionist philosophy and brought more empirical and open-minded research techniques to the field. Rather than collecting folklore to prove *a priori* theories about the state of the Indian's mental development, Boas used folklore both as an index to a tribe's history and its relationship to other tribes, as well as a reflection of the tribe's cultural values and institutions.[29]

In his early statements about folklore in *Tsimshian Mythology*, Boas expressed the important insight that folklore reflects cultural values, thus anticipating later functionalist theory.[30] Later in his career, he voiced more concern for the aesthetic form of myths and tales. For example, in *General Anthropology*, he argued that a myth "cannot be understood solely as a result of speculative thought about the origin and structure of the world and of human life. It is no less an outflow of artistic, or more specifically literary activity." He wrote that folktales "must be considered as analogous to modern novelistic literature . . . ." Further, he appreciated the role of the individual artist in shaping folklore and argued that the stylistic dimension of verbal art should be studied.[31] To be sure, these later insights on aesthetics did not change Boas' own ethnolinguistic texts. But they pointed the way for his students to develop interest in the aesthetics of verbal art and to record more performance features.

Supplementing the Ethnolinguistic Text

Although the chief purpose of the ethnolinguistic text is to provide an accurate linguistic record of verbal art, some anthropologists included more performance information. Certain early fieldworkers and anthropologists, such as Garrick Mallery, Edward Sapir, and Bronislaw Malinowski, stand out for supplementing their texts with contextual and nonverbal features. Indeed, Sapir's sensitive descriptions of aesthetic and social uses of speech provided a strong stimulus to the ethnography of speaking, which in turn strongly influenced the performance approach. Malinowski's emphasis on recording contextual information also stimulated ethnolinguistic textmakers to include more contextual information. Like Sapir, Malinowski too provided an impetus to later performance theorists.

Perhaps the most extraordinary contributor to the development of the ethnolinguistic text is Garrick Mallery. Long before other American folklorists, Mallery used phonographs and cameras in an attempt to record nonverbal performance features. Working for the Bureau of American Ethnology in the 1880s, Mallery developed a methodology for recording nonverbal features. If his methods had been followed by his contemporaries, the texts of American Indian folklore might have been vastly enriched. Although his innovations were not adopted by other folklorists, his work illustrates that even before the easy availability of audio and film recording, methods could be devised to record more nonverbal features in texts.

Ironically, Mallery's belief in Tylor's philosophy of cultural evolution led him to develop his textmaking methods. He was not prompted to record nonverbal features out of an aesthetic appreciation of verbal art. Rather, he wanted to extend Tylor's search for the origin of language. While Tylor had explored these origins in the sign language used by deaf and mute persons, Mallery broadened this inquiry by examining the sign language of the American Indians.[32] Thus, in "Sign Language Among North American Indians Compared with that Among Other Peoples and Deaf Mutes," Mallery confronted the problems of scientifically recording gestures. Since most of his fieldworkers did not have access to cameras, Mallery had to devise a way of uniformly describing body movements.

Mallery's desire to record gestures led him to the work of a nineteenth-century elocutionist, Gilbert Austin, thus marking an early, if not the first, relationship between folklorists and oral interpretation.[33] Austin's work, *Chironomia: Or a Treatise on Rhetorical Delivery*, provided a detailed alphabetic coding system for recording gestures of the hands, feet, legs, arms, head, as well as symbols for recording vocal delivery. Mallery's system of notation was much simpler than Austin's, and concerned only with hand and arm positions. To save the fieldworker time and to promote greater accuracy, Mallery prepared a set of illustrations of hand positions, each described succinctly and coded with a letter of the alphabet. When a fieldworker found a gesture identical or similar to an illustration, he could simply refer to the sketch by its letter, and note any deviations. For notating arm positions, Mallery provided front and side view sketches of an Indian standing with his arms down at his sides, to which the investigator could add dotted lines to trace the pattern of arm movements. Although Mallery thought that his method of diagrams would provide greater accuracy than similar attempts at explanation through writing, he requested that both modes of description be used, "each tending to supplement and correct the other." Aware of the importance of recording individual stylistic features that might deviate from the set of forms, Mallery made provisions for "the notation of such striking facial changes or emotional postures as might individualize or accentuate the gestures."[34]

While the fieldworker usually lacked access to cameras and phonographs at this time, the Bureau staff in Washington, D.C. used this equipment to record visiting Indians. During 1880, many Indian delegations visited the capital, and the Secretary of the Interior made them available to the Bureau for ethnologic research. As an Indian performed a story in sign language, he would orally paraphrase the sign's meaning to an interpreter who "translated the words used by an Indian . . . and was not relied upon to explain the signs according to his own ideas." These dictated translations were "sometimes taken down by a phonographer, that there might be no lapse of memory in any particular," and "in many cases the signs were made in successive motions before the camera, and prints secured as certain evidence of their accuracy."[35]

One set of texts included in Mallery's work distinguishes itself by recording both paralinguistic and kinesic features. In order to present so many simultaneous features clearly, the contributor, Mr. Jacker, presents four texts of the same performance, along with an unusually full description of the setting in which it occurred. First, Jacker describes the narrator's position before a campfire along a shore and adds a diagram to clarify the setting. Next, he presents the full text in both the native language and English. To read the text with understanding, one almost has to perform it. For example, the first phrase in the text reads: "(1) With the exclamation *'me-wi-ja'* (a long time ago), uttered in a slow and peculiarly emphatic manner, he elevated the arm above and toward the right at the head, accompanying the motion with an upward wave of the hand and held it thus suspended a moment— *a long time ago.* (This gesture resembles sign for *time, a long,* of which it seems to be an abbreviation, and it is not sufficiently clear without the accompanying exclamation.) Withdrawing it slowly, he placed the hand back upon his knee." Following the full text, he adds a free translation of the story followed by an interlinear version of "the oral part of the story in the language of the narrator, with a literal translation into English."[36] By indicating the gestures in this text with the phrase "gestures only," the reader can more clearly see the interplay of speech and gestures.

Unfortunately, Mallery's pioneering work in recording nonverbal features had little impact on other folklorists. Far more influential was the work of Edward Sapir, one of Boas' most eminent students and a genius in the field of linguistic anthropology. Not only was he a master of formal linguistic description, but he had a comprehensive view of linguistics which "stressed the importance of dealing with the phenomena of language in the culture context, of studying speech in its social setting."[37]

Evidence of Sapir's appreciation of performance can be seen in his earliest works. In *Wishram Texts*, published in 1909, Sapir notes whispered phrases, very high pitch, and some gestures. Occasionally, he includes descriptions of performance style within parentheses in the native language transcription. For example, in one tale, "(loud and beating his hips)" appears before a chanted phrase which is notated musically.[38] As early as 1910, in "Song Recitative in Paiute Mythology," Sapir comments on the importance of performance style in Indian narratives. He notes that one of the most common stylistic devices used by narrators to differentiate the speech of characters is the use of peculiar sounds: "Thus in Takelma we find that Coyote almost regularly begins his sentences or words with a meaningless s- or c-, while Grizzly-Bear uses in parallel fashion an L, a sound not otherwise made use of in Takelma."[39]

Sapir explored linguistic and paralinguistic means of characterization further in an influential essay, written in 1915, called "Abnormal Types of Speech in Nootka." Here, Sapir investigated how various speech devices are used to imply "something in regard to the status, sex, age, or other characteristics of the speaker, person addressed, or spoken of, without any direct statement as to such characteristics."[40] This pioneering essay anticipates the concerns of ethnographers of speaking and performance with the social uses of language. Indeed, Richard Bauman cites this essay to illustrate his discussion of Sapir as "an exemplar of the spirit in which language, culture, and folklore constitute a unitary whole . . . ."[41]

No doubt the most influential early advocate for supplementing ethnolinguistic texts with contextual information was Bronislaw Malinowski. Noting Malinowski's influence on the performance or contextual approach, Dan Ben-Amos and Kenneth Goldstein write that "The use of the notion context, in this case, takes its point of departure from and does not duplicate Malinowski's concepts of context of culture and context of situation . . . ."[42]

To understand Malinowski's contribution to the development of textmaking, one must distinguish between his theoretical statements about context and his actual practice of recording context. Looking back from our vantage point today, some of his theoretical statements about context seem almost indistinguishable from those of performance theorists. Yet his contextual commentaries, despite being more extensive than the norm, fall short of the integral view of text and context advocated by the performance approach.

Malinowski's theoretical statements about the ethnolinguistic text emerged from his efforts to translate and explicate the texts which he recorded among the Trobriand Islanders. His experience convinced him that the meaning of language in this society, and indeed, all societies, was to be found in the action it stimulated. The "main function of language," he wrote, "is not to express thought, not to duplicate mental processes, but rather to play an active pragmatic part in human behaviour." It followed from his pragmatic, functional theory of language that only by situating an ethnolinguistic text within its cultural and speaking context could the meaning of the utterance be understood.[43]

Indeed, Malinowski's theory of language led him to a critical examination of translation itself. He realized that "ambiguity and confusion appear when we project words on paper after having torn them out of their context . . . ." In order to move from an interlinear to a free translation, Malinowski recognized the need to turn to context in order to discover the relation of words and sentences. But for Malinowski, even the interlinear translation must incorporate contextual features. For example, he includes deictic gestures in some texts, noting that "Here again the gesture is an integral part of language and it had to be indicated in the interlineal [sic] rendering."[44] Whereas typical ethnolinguistic texts ended with the free translation, Malinowski's texts were accompanied with extended commentaries about a variety of contextual features.

As a theorist, Malinowski thought that the ideal study of language in context should utilize a complete sound and film recording of the speaking situation. As a realist, he recognized that the technology was not yet available for ethnographic fieldwork. If only he could use a "phonographic record" to "counterfeit the living voice of Tokulubakiki: how it trembled with emotion . . .," then he "should certainly be able better to *translate* the text in the sense of imparting to it its full cultural flavour and significance." Or if he had a "cinematographic picture" to "reproduce the facial expression, the bodily attitude, the significant gestures, this would add another contextual dimension." Although his own textmaking was limited by a lack of technology, Malinowski wrote that "There is no reason whatever why, in the future, the exact and physiological study of speech should not use the apparatus of sound films for reproducing fully contextualized utterances."[45]

Without sophisticated recording equipment, Malinowski could not hope to describe fully such nonverbal features as gesture. But he did devise a systematic procedure for providing contextual information. In *The Language of Magic and Gardening*, Malinowski includes five parts to his general commentary on texts of magical formulae. The first, "sociological context," contains a description of how the words reach and affect the community, and "how the whole utterance is related to the general economic activity and to the rite of which it is a part." The second part, "ritual context," shows "the manner in which manual procedure accompanies and directs the spell." In the third section of the commentary, "structure," Malinowski provides an introduction to the linguistic analysis of the text by describing how the text is constructed. (Malinowski obviously realized that analysis of structure was out of place in the midst of a contextual commentary; he includes a footnote stating that if he were to start again, he would place this section at the beginning of the Linguistic Commentary.) The fourth part, "dogmatic context,"

details the "belief or complex of beliefs" surrounding the text. The final
part, "mode of recitation," describes the manner in which the text is
uttered. This section contains only the briefest summary statements about
the general key or tone of the performance, such as "chanted loudly and
melodiously."[46]

Clearly then, Malinowski deserves credit for focusing attention on the
importance of situating texts within a description of their contexts. But
his dominant view of folklore as a validation of culture led many of his
followers to adopt a limited approach to contextual description. Rather
than providing a full, phenomenological account of the performance and
context, functionalists tended to record only the contextual information
necessary to show a functional relationship between a text and the
society. Despite Malinowski's pronouncements on the need to record
performance fully, "only occasionally," according to Bauman, ". . . is
attention given to the immediate circumstances of folkloric performance;
when the dominant conception of folklore is as collective representation,
the expression of society as a whole, the circumstances of performance,
while perhaps colorful, are not seen to be of much analytic
importance."[47]

Except for these few attempts to supplement the ethnolinguistic text,
the majority of anthropological folklorists treated verbal art more as a
linguistic and historical artifact than as a vibrant, aesthetic performance.
Undoubtedly, the dictation process used prior to field use of tape and film
recording made it difficult to record nonverbal stylistic features. But we
should not underestimate the role of analytical perspectives in shaping
textmaking practices. Powell's cultural evolutionism, Boas' diffusionism,
and Malinowski's functionalism precluded expending much energy on
the aesthetic dimension of folklore.

THE LITERARY MODEL OF THE TEXT

While the anthropological folklorists studied the folklore of American
Indians, the literary folklorists, trained usually in literature or history,
studied the folklore of "isolated, unsophisticated, 'tradition bound'
agrarian folk."[48] The early literary folklorists adopted the European
comparative method, known also as the Finnish historical-geographical
method. This method compares many versions of a tale in order to
reconstruct a hypothetical "ur-form," or archetype of a tale, and to plot
the historical and geographical spread or diffusion of a tale. The
dominant historical orientation of the literary folklorists led to a text
model which neglected to record many contextual or nonverbal features.
The literary model assimilates the form and qualities of performance to
the conventional form of literature. Here we will review the development
of this model, in its scholarly and popularized formats, in more detail.

Before 1888, folklore studies of the English-speaking white population of the United States were primarily limited to folk song and children's rhymes and games. Major works either in progress or completed at the time were W. W. Newell's *Games and Songs of American Children* (1883); H. C. Bolton's *The Counting Out Rhymes of Children* (1888); and F. J. Child's *The English and Scottish Popular Ballads* (1882-1898). In the years following, interest intensified in recording ballads and other imported folk songs. After J. A. Lomax's *Cowboy Songs* in 1910, work with indigenous American songs grew. The majority of these collections, according to Herbert Halpert, "did little more than give a body of material with comparative notes limited to the English-American literature." Except for Clifton Johnson's *What They Say in New England* (1896), and Charles M. Skinner's two collections of legends (1896, 1903), "little of importance (except folk songs) appears outside of the society's publications until the 1920's." Then quite suddenly, interest in folklore increased: the Paul Bunyan legend was publicized, Robert Frost's *New Hampshire* appeared, Carl Sandburg used folklore backgrounds in *Abraham Lincoln: The Prairie Years,* and the Texas Folklore Society resumed publication.[49]

In 1945-46, the American Folklore Society reviewed the state of folklore research in America. Assessing the quality of the literary text collections, Herbert Halpert found that the scholarly collections followed an "unfortunate publishing practice" influenced by "the now outmoded view that folklore consisted only of 'survivals.' " Many of the collections were arranged "in tabular form with annotation but little comment." Folk beliefs were printed in a "numerical listing in colorless terms, occasionally with a few references in footnotes to other parallels." Neither accuracy nor discussions of the meaning or function of beliefs and tales were common: "With one or two notable exceptions one does not get even the exact words of informants. Attempts to determine how thoroughly or widely these beliefs are held and what purposes they serve in society are extremely rare."[50]

It is not difficult to see why even in 1947 literary folklorists were paying little attention to context. Halpert found that most folklorists at this time admired the works of Stith Thompson and Archer Taylor.[51] Both Thompson and Taylor, who trained a great number of folklorists, were instrumental in promoting widespread adoption of the Finnish historical-geographical method. This comparative method of reconstructing the history of a folktale by assembling as many versions as possible had no real need to record information about the context, retain the performer's distinctive stylistic features, or collect informant information. Neither Thompson nor Taylor valued the creative changes made by narrators. Thompson disclaimed any virtue in originality, and Taylor called all of a narrator's changes in a tale "subversive," recommending that "as soon as a change is perceived to be intentional, it can be disposed of."[52] Although Thompson wrote that accurate recordings are preferred, he said that the historical-geographical method can work with far less accurate texts than those needed by an anthropologist: "But for a knowledge of the material of the tales and the relations of that material to neighboring or remote peoples, texts taken in broken English (or another world language) are also valuable. A large number of tales we have at present were taken down from a bilingual speaker. An interpreter is also frequently used with good results."[53]

As an alternative to the bare, dry, scholarly text, many folklorists turned to a popularized text, rewriting a tale to add more color and life. Not only literary folklorists, but anthropological folklorists as well, published texts adapted to the tastes, values, and conventions of the mass reading public.[54] These rewritten tales, however, obscured and distorted the stylistic features of the original performance. In his 1947 review, Halpert criticized these popularized collections for handicapping scholarly research: "Folk tale study in the United States is extremely handicapped because most of the large body of published material has been rewritten and is of little use in stylistic analysis. Writers, in their attempt to revitalize folk material, often distort it."[55]

While the popularized format might distort a tale, it seemed to be the only way for the folklorist to present folklore in an aesthetic way. By using the techniques of a novelist and describing tones and gestures in narrative dialogue tags, the folklorist could present a more aesthetically pleasing tale than the bare plot outlines published in the scholarly format. Indeed, in 1945, Richard Dorson wrote of the advantages of using "literary effects to simulate oral art." He put forth an "heretical" argument for the "aesthetic superiority of the literary over the verbatim transcript": "The rendition of a popular tale by a *Spirit of the Times* correspondent or a local-color writer like Rowland Robinson reproduces the tones and emphases and setting of narrative art more faithfully than the literal transcript divorced from mood and audience, so that the freer translation becomes the more realistic."[56]

Halpert's dissatisfaction with both the scholarly and popularized text formats was indicative of the search for better texts that ensued from the late forties on. During the twenty years prior to the first programmatic formulations of the performance approach, a merging of anthropological and literary interests, stimulated by a convergence of intellectual currents from several disciplines, led to new developments in textmaking.

PRECURSORS TO THE PERFORMANCE APPROACH

Intellectual history rarely breaks into neat, chronological categories, and the history of developments in folklore studies is no exception. In the preceding two sections, we noted four influential precursors to the performance approach—Boas, Mallery, Sapir, and Malinowski. Our focus in these sections on the anthropological and literary branches of folkloristics precluded examining influences from other disciplines. But during the twenties and thirties and increasingly, from the 1940s on, a number of forces from outside these two branches of folklore stimulated more concern for studying performance. These forces, which often cross-fertilized each other in the following decades, make the intellectual lineage of the performance approach rich and tangled.

Here we can but untangle and briefly delineate the major strands of thought which contributed to the emergence of 'the performance approach. To discuss this rich interdisciplinary work with the depth that it deserves would lead astray from our central concern with textmaking developments. We will consider the major influences from the Prague School linguists, comparative literature, the interdisciplinary work stemming from a refiguration of social thought, and the ethnography of speaking. Against this background we will then examine the fusion of interests among anthropological and literary folklorists which led to a new interest in improving the folklore text.

The Prague School

The study of folklore has always been strongly influenced by linguistics. The Finnish historical-geographical school, as W. O. Hendricks reminds us, is clearly similar to the comparative method in linguistics.[57] When the Prague School of linguistics began to flourish in the twenties and thirties, its ideas were felt among succeeding generations of folklorists and linguists. The chief legacy of the Prague School to the study of verbal art is fourfold: 1) a synchronic emphasis, 2) a functional perspective on language, 3) a semiotic and structural analysis, and 4) a contextual approach. All of these perspectives characterize the performance approach, as well as the ethnography of speaking, with which it is closely associated.

Out of the fifty or so scholars who formed the Prague School and their associates, we can pinpoint five whose work strongly influenced subsequent folklorists. The founder of the School, Vilém Mathesius, antedated Saussure in arguing for a synchronic approach to linguistics. Mathesius' 1911 essay, "On the Potentiality of the Phenomena of Language," urged that linguists study the co-occurrence of variants within actual language use. Such a study is applicable to verbal art since the co-occurrence of variants is a source of creative usage.[58]

Although Saussure's advocacy of synchronic study received greater recognition than that of Mathesius, Saussure's preference for studying the *langue,* or abstract language system, over the *parole,* or individual usage, was quite different from the Prague School's more dialectical approach.[59] Saussure's preference for *la langue* led many linguists, including Chomsky and his followers, to downplay the significance of individual performances in their search for general, generative rules. In contrast, the Prague School theorists tended to stress the dialectical relationship between general norms and laws and individual usages.[60]

This more holistic approach to language is reflected in the work of Karl Bühler, Jan Mukařovský, and Roman Jakobson, who developed functional models of language and verbal art. Although Bühler was not a regular member of the Prague School, he contributed an essay to the *Theses.* His *Sprachtheorie,* appearing in 1934, articulated three speech functions: reference, expression, and appeal.[61] Mukařovský enlarged on Bühler's work by adding a fourth function, the aesthetic, to explain the poetic use of language. While any utterance might function simultaneously in all four ways, Mukařovský argued that in verbal art the aesthetic function is foregrounded. That is, in verbal art, attention focuses more on the structure of signs for their own sake than on the referential, expressive, or appellative functions.[62]

This metalingual or metasemiotic property of the aesthetic function led Mukařovský and the Prague School to adopt a semiotic approach to the study of verbal art. Yet his attention to the signs of art was not narrowly focused on the art work alone, since Mukařovský recognized that language could have an aesthetic appeal and still function to express an author's emotions, refer to reality, or appeal to an audience: "Indeed, these practical functions often assert themselves rather extensively in work [sic] of art—for example, the representative function in a novel, the expressive in a lyric poem."[63]

Since for Mukařovský, art was thus linked to factors outside itself, such as an author or an audience, it follows that art should be studied in context and in relationship to other social systems.[64] Such a view of verbal art is particularly applicable to folklore, which in its primary form as performance, is intimately tied to a social context.

Not surprisingly, Mukařovský's line of reasoning about verbal art undergirds Richard Bauman's definition of verbal art as performance. Bauman credits Mukařovský as one of the influences on his thinking. In defining performance, Bauman stresses that the audience holds a performer accountable for the way in which he or she displays competence as a performer, above and beyond the referential content of the message. A performance enhances experience through calling forth special attention to the "intrinsic qualities of the act of expression itself."[65] This definition bears close resemblance to Mukařovský's argument that: "In Poetic language foregrounding achieves maximum intensity to the extent of pushing communication into the background as the objective of expression and of being used for its own sake; it is not used in the services of communication, but in order to place in the foreground the act of expression, the act of speech itself."[66]

The functional perspective of Bühler and Mukařovský was refined, extended, and brought to the fore by Roman Jakobson. In his "Closing Statement: Linguistics and Poetics" presented at the interdisciplinary Conference on Style held at Indiana University in 1958, Jakobson argues that language "must be investigated in all the variety of its functions." He accepted Bühler's three functions, but used the term conative in place of appellative. Although he changed Mukařovský's aesthetic function to the term poetic function, he retained the same definition of focus on the message for its own sake. To these four functions, Jakobson added two more: the *phatic*, focused on maintaining channels of communication, and the *metalingual*, focused on clarifying or defining the code. Like Mukařovský, Jakobson recognized that verbal art is multifunctional and that the poetic function is found outside the field of poetry. Thus, Jakobson argued that the linguistic study of poetics must go beyond the conventional literary genres of poetry.[67]

Indeed, Jakobson recommended folklore as an appropriate area for investigation since it "offers the most clear-cut and stereotyped forms of poetry, particularly suitable for structural scrutiny. . . ."[68] No doubt the examples from folklore which Jakobson used to buttress his arguments helped awaken folklorists to this type of linguistic and semiotic analysis. Certainly Jakobson's broad view of linguistics, which included study of intonation and delivery, called attention to the importance of studying verbal art as performance.

This 1958 essay, however, was not the first time that Jakobson had advocated a structural and semiotic study of folklore. In his influential 1929 essay, written with Petr Bogatyrev, he argued that folklore and linguistics are analogous and that the *langue/parole* distinction can be applied to folklore.[69] This argument provided a conceptual framework for the structural study of folklore as code, as E. Ojo Arewa and Alan Dundes point out in their essay, "Proverbs and the Ethnography of Speaking Folklore."[70] This essay, published in 1964, was one of the earliest applications of the ethnography of speaking to folklore. It reflects a direct link from the Prague School theorists to the performance approach.

One final figure in the Prague School, Petr Bogatyrev, deserves mention for his application of semiotics to folklore. In his 1938 essay, "Semiotics in the Folk Theatre," he argued that folklore approximates "the phenomenon of drama." This dramatic view led him to a performance-centered concept of the folklore text. Since the hearer of folklore, in contrast to the reader of literature, cannot isolate "the artistic phenomenon, as such, from the author or reciter," Bogatyrev concludes that "it is incorrect to define the text of a tale without regard to how it is told."[71]

Comparative Literature: Parry and Lord

The Prague School's concern with the context and performance of verbal art has its analogues in other disciplines as well. In the field of comparative literature, for example, Milman Parry undertook fieldwork in 1935 with the oral poets of Yugoslavia to learn more about the oral form of poetry. Along with his student, Albert Lord, Parry discovered techniques of oral composition which shed new light on the composition of such classic epics as the *Iliad* and *Odyssey*. This work, brought to widespread attention in 1960 with Lord's *The Singer of Tales*, provided strong support for the critical advances to be made through studying the oral performances of folklore.[72] Testimonies to their influence are found in such early performance-oriented folklore essays as those by Roger Abrahams and Elli Köngäs Maranda.[73] Certainly Lord's evidence of the variable structure of oral epics, depending on audience and performer relationships, led to new attention to the emergent nature of verbal art. Indeed, Richard Bauman supports his arguments for the emergent quality of performance by referring to Lord's work as "one of the first works to conceptualize oral literature in terms of emergent structures. . . ."[74]

A Refiguration of Social Thought

To the movements within individual disciplines, such as comparative literature and linguistics, must be added the influence of the general interdisciplinary intellectual climate emerging from what Clifford Geertz has recently termed a "refiguration of social thought." In 1980, when Geertz's "Blurred Genres: The Refiguration of Social Thought" appeared, it was evident that a "culture shift" had taken place. Models and analogies borrowed from the humanities had radically altered the social sciences. Two of the most powerful analogies, based on game and drama, involve the notion of performance, and as Geertz argues, "the analogies are coming more and more from the contrivances of cultural performance than from those of physical manipulation—from theater, painting, grammar, literature, law, play."[75]

The performance approach, emerging in the late sixties and early seventies, falls squarely within this refiguration of social thought. And it is no surprise to find that the same interdisciplinary thinkers responsible for this culture shift, such as Kenneth Burke, Erving Goffman, and Gregory Bateson, to name but a few,[76] influenced the adoption of a performance approach within folklore studies as well.

Burke's theories of dramatism and of language as symbolic action, published in a series of works from 1941 through the 1960s, has had an enormous impact not only in his own fields of rhetoric and literary criticism, but on interpretation, anthropology, sociology, and folklore. Burke's dramatistic view of life and language demands a comprehensive analytical perspective, which considers not only the work or act, but the agent who creates or performs it, as well as the agency, scene, and purpose.

The influence of Burke's rhetorical, performance-oriented theories can be seen in several of the early essays of the performance approach. In his 1968 essay, "Introductory Remarks to a Rhetorical Theory of Folklore," Roger Abrahams writes that Burke "has shown in a number of works that words have power and that performance, therefore, is a way of persuading through the production of pleasure as well as the assertion of idea or course of action." He concludes that the importance of Burke's theory, "is that it causes us to consider the form and function of the isolated item: we look simultaneously at the performer, at the piece he performs, and at the effect which this has on the audience."[77] Other folklorists influenced by Burke include Brian Sutton-Smith, Joseph Doherty, Bruce Rosenberg, and Dell Hymes.[78] Applications of Burke's dramatistic perspective by such well-known anthropologists as Victor Turner, James Peacock, and Clifford Geertz, as well as by sociologist Erving Goffman, added further impetus to the growing interest in performance-oriented analyses of culture.[79]

A closely related analogy to that of drama, the game or play analogy, also cast its influence on folklorists. Of the many sources contributing to the game analogy, the most important, according to Geertz, are "Wittgenstein's conception of forms of life as language games, Huizinga's ludic view of culture, and the new strategies of von Neumann's and Morgenstern's *Theory of Games and Economic Behavior*."[80] The most influential applications of the game analogy in the social sciences and on folkloristics in particular, have come from Gregory Bateson and Erving Goffman.

In his seminal essay, "A Theory of Play and Fantasy," Bateson introduced the concepts of "frame" and "metacommunication" to account for how beings distinguish between different orders of messages.[81] He observed that animals, as well as humans, employ signals about signals, or metacommunication, to distinguish messages such as "this is play" from what otherwise might be interpreted as aggression. Bateson argued that such metacommunication constitutes an interpretive frame which helps us recognize different orders of messages, such as dreams, play, and fantasy. This concept of frame has provided a useful tool for distinguishing artistic verbal performance from other modes of communication. Richard Bauman bases much of his definition of

performance on Bateson's notion of frame, and Barbara Babcock uses the
frame concept to analyze metanarration in folk stories.[82]

Another strong impetus to study cultural performances has come from
the work of Erving Goffman, who employs both dramatistic and game
analogies. One of his earliest works, *The Presentation of Self in Everyday
Life*, published in 1959, illustrated the viability of viewing everyday roles
in work situations as cultural performances. Concepts from this work, as
well as two later works, *Encounters* (1961) and *Interaction Ritual* (1967)
are referred to in such performance-centered folklore essays as Dell
Hymes', "Breakthrough Into Performance," Barbara Kirshenblatt-
Gimblett's "A Parable in Context," and Richard Bauman's "Differential
Identity and the Social Base of Folklore."[83]

No doubt the strongest contribution to performance theory in
folkloristics has come from Goffman's work *Frame Analysis* (1974).
Building on Bateson's concept of frame, in this work Goffman explores
the different types and levels of reality signaled by frames. He advances
the concept of frame by explaining how frames are formed through
"keys" or metacommunicative signals.[84] In developing his definition of
verbal art as performance, Bauman draws on Goffman, as well as
Bateson. If performance is a type of interpretative frame, as Bauman
argues, then it can be recognized by such keys as special codes and
formulae, figurative language, parallelism, special paralinguistic
features, appeals to tradition, and disclaimers of performance.[85]

Growing out of this refiguration of social thought, as well as from the
contributions of Malinowski, Sapir, the Prague School, Parry and Lord,
and others, a new branch of linguistic anthropology called the
ethnography of speaking directly influenced the emergence of the
performance approach. Indeed, many of the same scholars who pioneered
this new ethnographic approach to the study of speaking wrote some of
the seminal essays of the performance approach in folkloristics.

The Ethnography of Speaking

In a real sense, the ethnography of speaking is the natural culmination
of the advances in the analysis of speech we have just reviewed. Credit for
harnessing and focusing the growing interest in relating language use to
social life under an approach called the ethnography of speaking, goes to
Dell Hymes. In several essays in the early sixties, Hymes advocated the
need for an ethnographic study of speaking which would examine the
range of speaking activities and genres used in societies. In contrast to
traditional linguistics, which is limited to the level of the sentence, and
traditional ethnography, which describes cultures but often neglects to
describe their speech behaviors, the ethnography of speaking aims to

discover the patterns and functions of speaking within specific cultural contexts.[86]

Postulating that determinate "ways of speaking" can be identified within various societies, Hymes suggested a methodology for describing the organization of these ways of speaking. This method begins by identifying a "speech community," that is, a group of people who share a common language and rules for conducting and interpreting speech activities. Within a selected speech community, the analyst describes speech behavior in terms of settings, participants, ends, act sequence, key (tone), instrumentalities (communication channels), norms of interaction and interpretation, and genre.[87]

By the end of the sixties, after several books on ethnography of speaking had been published,[88] it was clear that this new field was influencing and being reciprocally influenced by folklore. In an address to the American Folklore Society in 1969, Hymes outlined the contributions folklore was making to sociolinguistic research. He focused on the new performance-oriented research of Alan Lomax, Roger Abrahams, Dan Ben-Amos, and E. Ojo Arewa and Alan Dundes.[89] These new studies supported Hymes' argument that a "convergence of approach" between the ethnography of speaking and folklore had occurred. So similar were the concerns of the two fields that Hymes claimed, "It can be maintained, indeed, that folklore is a special case of the ethnography-of-speaking approach."[90] The close ties between the two fields are further illustrated by the work of Richard Bauman, who with Joel Sherzer, edited a collection of essays, *Explorations in the Ethnography of Speaking*,[91] as well as articulated some of the key concepts of the performance approach in *Verbal Art as Performance*. Interchanges between folklorists and speech ethnographers contributed to new conceptions of verbal art performance as: 1) an aesthetic mode of communication, 2) integrally related to a particular event, and 3) culture-specific and cross-culturally variable. We will discuss these concepts in depth in the following chapter.

A Fusion of Interests: New Concern for the Text

Within this interdisciplinary climate that encouraged synchronic, contextual, and performance orientations toward verbal art, it is no surprise to see anthropological and literary folklorists begin to merge interests. Among anthropological folklorists, several of Boas' students, such as Ruth Benedict, Paul Radin, Melville Herskovits, and Melville Jacobs, began a reconciliation between anthropological and literary perspectives. As early as 1935, Ruth Benedict stated an intention to study the "literary problems of the Zuni narrator." Yet her edited texts, presented without contextual or nonverbal detail, precluded adequate discussion of performance style.[92]

By 1955, however, Paul Radin, in "The Literature of Primitive Peoples," linked mistaken assessments of oral literature to the poor quality of texts. Radin presented examples of orally composed prose and poetry to refute the claims of Lévy-Brühl and Cassirer that no literature is possible without writing. He attributed their erroneous views to the "manner in which many of the recorders of these languages presented their data and the many loose statements they made." Criticizing ethnologists for not recording contemporary native narratives, Radin explained that varying texts are just as artistic as fixed texts: "We cannot emphasize too strongly the fact that the excellence of a literature has nothing to do with the number of fixed texts found in it." Although Radin mentioned native theories of composition and ways of learning the art, he gave no explicit suggestions for supplementing texts with informant interviews, or printing texts to better represent the aesthetic form of performance. His idea that the raconteur is judged more as an actor than as a transmitter of a traditional text anticipates contemporary performance theory.[93]

Like Radin, Melville and Frances Herskovits, in *Dahomean Narrative* (1958), commented on the important role performance plays in oral narrative. Their excellent introductory chapter provides native genre categories of the narratives collected. They note the importance of recording context and performance style, but in 1931, when they collected the texts, they had no access to mechanical or electronic recording devices: "Only a hidden mechanism that would simultaneously film and record a story-telling session could fully convey the artistry of the teller of tales in this setting, and give a sense of the interplay between narrator and audience that is so important an aspect of the spoken narrative tradition."[94] Despite their appreciation of performance, the Herskovitses continued the tradition of abstracting tales from their immediate contexts and providing little information about performers or performance style.

Two influential articles by William Bascom made strong contributions toward bridging the gap between anthropological and literary folklorists. In "Folklore and Anthropology," written in 1953, Bascom noted a new trend among anthropologists of studying folklore more as a process rather than a product. He described anthropological interests in narrator creativity and stylistic features, and suggested that literary folklorists could cooperate in studying them. In addition, he advocated that literary folklorists cooperate "in recording local attitudes toward folklore and its social contexts, in analyzing the relation of folklore to culture and to conduct, and finally in seeking to define its functions." Bascom suggested that "the most effective way to bridge the gaps between the different groups of folklorists is by a common concern with common problems. . . ."[95]

In "Verbal Art," written in 1955, Bascom further promoted a fusion of interests by emphasizing the aesthetic dimension in defining folklore.[96]

An important contribution to emerge from this growing anthropological interest in aesthetics was a fresh examination of the role of translation in the textmaking process. The pioneering work of C. F. Voeglin and Melville Jacobs in retranslating ethnolinguistic texts began a tradition of scholarship which is bearing fruit today in the works of Dell Hymes, J. Barre Toelken, and others.

In 1954, C. F. Voeglin developed a method to add more performance features to ethnolinguistic texts which had already been collected. In "A Modern Method for Field Work Treatment of Previously Collected Texts," Voeglin suggests a way of augmenting existing texts by having new informants reperform them. Using an Hidatsa text collected thirty years earlier, Voeglin read the text in deprosodized, monotone Hidatsa to a new Hidatsa informant. His object was to have the Hidatsa informant repeat the text, "but in the Indian fashion of speaking." He then notated intonational contours and junctures. Voeglin's experiment with this method on a Sahaptin text of a Coyote tale allowed him to identify dialects, discover that a use of connectives and conjunctions is primarily stylistic, and find that injected junctures contribute to "translating punctuation" in Sahaptin. In addition, his new translation enabled him to evaluate Jacobs' text as a sensitive recording.[97]

In contrast to Voeglin's close linguistic focus, Melville Jacobs concentrated on translating information about the contexts of ethnolinguistic texts. Whereas Voeglin's work was aimed at a scholarly audience, Jacobs tackled the difficult problem of creating a text style that would serve both scientific and literary needs. Critical of Boas' ethnolinguistic texts for being of little use to literary critics or a literature-oriented public, Jacobs asked, "Can both scientific and literary functions be combined in publication of folktales and still adhere to rigorous standards?" He answered that they could "if interpretive comments supplement the stark translations and if the additions are written so as to include, readably and pleasurably, associations and sentiments which the native audience experienced."[98]

In *The Content and Style of an Oral Literature* (1959) and a companion book, *The People are Coming Soon* (1960), Jacobs experimented with a new presentational form for the tales and myths of the Clackamas Chinook Indians.[99] His contributions to the development of the text must be evaluated against the nature of the verbal art with which he worked. By the time Jacobs began working with the Clackamas Chinook in 1929, only three persons were left who spoke Clackamas and the culture was virtually extinct. He collected his tales from a sixty-year-old woman. The tales were told in a dictating session rather than in a natural context; no nonverbal stylistic features were recorded. Indeed, Jacobs first published

these stories in an ethnolinguistic format as *Clackamas Chinook Texts*.[100]
Recognizing how bare and obscure the tales appeared in their
ethnolinguistic format, Jacobs worked to "present the stories more
vividly and intelligibly than they would be in a bare translation."[101]

Since the tales were recorded in an artificial context, and since no
native audience participated in the story-telling sessions, Jacobs had to
reconstruct the probable context and cultural interpretations of the tales.
Consequently, rather than developing a method to record the many
contextual and nonverbal features comprising a live performance, Jacobs
tried to "reconstruct for each story as much as I could of what I deduced
was happening before, during, and after the narrator's recital." To
accomplish this reconstructive effort, Jacobs interjects explanatory
phrases, enclosed in parentheses, into the original ethnolinguistic texts.
Following the initial close translation, he includes a "freer version" in
which he suggests what "may have been the intent of the raconteur and
the response of the people." Although Jacobs hypothesizes that the
narrator's ability to act out characters' voices and gestures must have been
important,[102] he adds no nonverbal descriptions to the texts.

While Jacobs' work brings us no closer to a method for recording the
nonverbal features of a performance, his efforts clearly reveal a growing
sensitivity to aesthetics among anthropological folklorists. His work also
marks one of the first efforts to improve previously collected
ethnolinguistic texts through reconstructing the performance event.

Literary folklorists during this period also advocated cooperation with
their anthropological colleagues and expressed a new concern for
improving texts. In his 1951 Presidential Address to the American
Folklore Society, Francis Lee Utley tied the conflict between the literary
and anthropological folklorists to the poor quality of folklore texts. He
criticized the lack of theory behind textmaking: "Our archives are
elementary, our collectors collect without system, our data are published
casually and without pattern or analysis—our science is, in short, in the
embryonic stage." Utley suggested that folklorists could use more
method, as well as more poetic taste and understanding. Arguing for a
rapprochement between the two branches of folkloristics, he said, "The
arts cannot be understood without ethnology, and the arts shed light on
ethnology."[103]

In 1957, Richard Dorson again addressed the issue of presenting
folklore, but from a different perspective. While in 1945 he had praised
literary revisions of verbal art as being more aesthetic, he now wrote that
"through the processes of translation, revision, bowdlerizing, and general
editorial improvement, they wander even farther from their oral sources."
Dorson identified two polar extremes in texts: the popularized and the
scientific. He characterized the popularizer as aiming for money and
distorting the folklore to appeal to the tastes of the mass reading public:

"All the storytellers narrate in exactly the same manner, and each possesses a marvelous rhythm of speech, a rare sense of idiom, and a superb fluency that transcend reality. Also, all begin their tales with 'One time there was. . . .' "[104]

In contrast to the popularizer, the scientist, aiming for truth, "reaches a tiny scholarly audience and fails to reflect the artistry attainable in oral narration." Dorson argued that the ideal folktale collector must choose among three goals: "Money, Art, and Truth." He suggested that the primary goal should be Truth, but that the "ideal book will employ enough Art to make Truth more visible, and perhaps even a little Money will follow." By Truth, Dorson meant that the collector must "faithfully render the words of his informants," and by Art, he meant that the collector should "consider his readers." Dorson hedged on the question of editing, seeming to accept the practice of revising tangled sentences, eliminating repetitions and false starts, and rearranging jumbled information. He rejected rewriting—adding words or phrases outside the speaker's vocabulary, or elaborating bare motifs—and opposed bowdlerization.[105] Unfortunately, Dorson failed to discuss how to reflect the narrator's artistry in the text. He suggested supplying descriptive notes about the informant's personality and the context, but gave no suggestions about presenting stylistic features within the text.

During this same year, in an article entitled "Classifying Performance in the Study of Verbal Folklore," William Hugh Jansen expressed the urgent need "for notes about the conditions of the actual performance, notes that reveal the informant's attitudes toward the performer and toward his handling of the particular material."[106] Jansen's argument for the importance of classifying folklore according to the degree of performance clearly anticipated the work of contemporary performance-oriented folklorists.

Jansen's work had an immediate effect on Richard Dorson, who in 1958 presented a paper, "Oral Styles of American Folk Narrators," at the Indiana University Conference on Style.[107] In this study Dorson described the backgrounds and individual narrative styles of seven folk narrators. He then applied the same descriptive technique to Lincoln's folk narrative style. Although Dorson's essay demonstrated that the individual style of folk narrators could be critically appreciated, just as the style of a literary writer could, his work did not advance any new methods of incorporating performance features into texts.

By the 1960s, the increasing interest in performance reached a critical mass. This decade marks a turning point in the development of the text as folklorists such as MacEdward Leach, Kenneth Goldstein, Alan Dundes, and E. Ojo Arewa suggested practical solutions to improving fieldwork and the quality of texts. Research on the performance style of folk songs and dances by Alan Lomax, as well as more performance-oriented

collections by Linda Dégh, Ruth Finnegan, and Daniel Crowley, further
stimulated interest in studying verbal art as performance.

Addressing himself to the "Problems of Collecting Oral Literature," in
1962 MacEdward Leach argued that the collector's first objective is to
"collect and present his material as oral literature." Noting the effects of
literacy on the collection and presentation of folk literature, Leach
claimed that oral literature had been collected and presented "as if it were
eye literature rather than ear literature." In order to present folklore as
"ear literature," he suggested that folklorists annotate their texts: "Short
of making a sound movie, he can only describe what he heard and saw,
can only annotate his text with elaborate stage directions, so to speak."[108]
These annotations would include descriptions of voice, tone, inflection,
gestures, facial expressions, attitudes, and audience reactions. As a
teacher, Leach instilled his appreciation for the aesthetic qualities of
verbal art into many of his students and vitalized interest in the aesthetics
of folklore.[109]

Until 1964, when Kenneth Goldstein's *A Guide for Field Workers in
Folklore* appeared, no comprehensive methodology for folklore collectors
had been published.[110] As a result, collectors recorded data to serve only
their particular analytical interests. One of the major contributions of
Goldstein's work is his stress on collecting folklore in such a way that it
serves both anthropological and literary folklorists. In addition, his
emphasis on recording performance context and style reflects a more
holistic approach to folklore.

Stressing the need to increase the amount of information collected and
preserved by fieldworkers, Goldstein argues that "the methods of
collecting which are to be most encouraged are those which supply the
greatest amount of reliable information to the largest number of potential
users of such information." He suggests that collecting data that would
fulfill the needs of the anthropologist would equally satisfy the needs of
comparative and literary folklorists. He finds that anthropology's
systematic approach to fieldwork has much to offer folklore research.
Consequently, Goldstein offers an ethnographic approach to folklore
fieldwork based on the problems and needs of modern folklore theory.[111]

Goldstein lists eight factors which the fieldworker should observe: 1)
the physical setting, 2) social setting, 3) interaction between participants,
4) performance, 5) time and duration, 6) sentiments expressed, 7)
miscellaneous observation, and 8) the observer. His list of specific details
to observe about performance indicates a genuine appreciation for its
importance to folklore study: "Introductory commentary; style of
performer (intonation, voice rhythm, continuity, speaking rate, pitch,
vocal intensity, pauses, facial expressions, pantomime, voice imitation of
characteristics or objects, repetition, and interjection); closing
commentary; position and attitude of body; essential equipment (e.g.,

instruments for musicians); supplemental equipment (e.g., guitar used to accompany singer, noisemakers used by storyteller); deviations from normal performance (must be based on observer's prior experiences with performer or on comments from other observers.)"[112] Beyond suggesting that the fieldworker observe all these performance features, Goldstein gives no advice on how to present this information in a text. Yet by calling for the folklorist to record more performance features, Goldstein's work implicitly raises the question of how performance data should be recorded in texts.

The strong ethnographic thrust of Goldstein's *Guide* was echoed by another work published in 1964, which adapted an ethnography of speaking methodology to folklore research. In "Proverbs and the Ethnography of Speaking Folklore," E. Ojo Arewa and Alan Dundes argue that studying texts alone cannot reveal the uses of proverbs in societies. "In order to study the ethnography of the speaking of folklore. . . , clearly one cannot be limited to texts. One needs texts in their contexts." Taking issue with contextual descriptions which make only generalized statements about the functions of folklore, they urge that the actual speech event in which the folklore occurs be transcribed. They suggest, for example, that rather than discussing the general techniques of verbal dueling, that folklorists should present "an accurate transcription of a verbal duel."[113]

Arewa and Dundes advocate recording information from the informants' points of view. In lieu of actually observing a proverb used in its natural context, they suggest that the interviewer ask informants to supply descriptions of contexts in which the proverb might be used. In fact, Arewa and Dundes suggest that folklorists record the native comments, interpretation, and criticism of all the lore which they collect. Such native interpretations constitute "part of the ethnographic context" and "influence the decision to employ a particular [proverb] in a particular situation." Foreshadowing the interest of the performance approach in studying folklore as communication, Arewa and Dundes assert that "Folklore is used primarily as a means of communication, and it is as communication that it needs to be studied."[114]

Further testament to the growing interest in ethnographic and performance-oriented research came in 1968 with Alan Lomax's pioneering work, *Folk Song Style and Culture.* Beginning in 1961, Lomax and his associates worked to develop "ways of describing recorded folk song performances in empirical terms so that songs could be compared and clustered from culture to culture." They developed "a holistic descriptive system," later called cantometrics, for "evoking performance style from sound recordings." Later they turned to dances and developed a descriptive measuring system called choreometrics in an effort to correlate dance movements to culture.[115]

The real contribution of Lomax's work lies in its demonstration of the significance of studying performance style. His methods are not, however, designed for making texts. Neither cantometrics nor choreometrics is a system for recording the complete performance of a song or dance, with all its individual stylistic features. Rather, they are generalized rating systems which can categorize the gross features of a style, such as whether the volume, rasp, or tempo of a piece falls on a scale from one to thirteen, or whether the energy of a dance is slow or fast.[116] Lomax's system for rating body movements, based on Irmgard Bartenieff's effort-shape analysis, is discussed further in Chapter 5.

No doubt the most telling work dealing with the text during the sixties is Dundes' "Texture, Text, and Context," published in 1964. It is indicative not only of the conceptual strains apparent in a discipline on the threshold of a major conceptual shift, but also of the problems inherent in defining the term text. In an effort to improve the definitions of folklore genres, Dundes proposes that folklore can be defined in terms of three analytical levels: texture, text, and context. By texture, he means "the language, the specific phonemes and morphemes employed." He also includes stress, pitch, juncture, tone, onomatopoeia, rhyme, and alliteration under texture. For the most part, he argues, these textural features cannot be translated from one language to another. In contrast to the untranslatable texture, the text, which "for purposes of analysis. . . may be considered independent of its texture," may be translated. Dundes defines the text as ". . . essentially a version or a single telling of a tale, a recitation of a proverb, a singing of a folksong." By context, he means "the specific social situation in which that particular item is actually employed."[117]

The best definitions of folklore will be based on all three analytical levels, according to Dundes. Thus, he criticizes the practice of leaving analysis of texture to linguists and analysis of context to anthropologists and concludes that "The well-rounded folklorist should hopefully attempt to analyze all three levels." This argument for examining texture, text, and context seems to point toward a more holistic, integrated approach. Yet at the same time that Dundes makes this argument, certain of his statements seem to reflect the older, fragmented disciplinary approach. For example, he argues that subjecting texture to a structural analysis will reveal linguistic structure, whereas subjecting text to a structural analysis will reveal folkloristic structure. Similarly, immediately before he concludes that folklorists should adopt all three levels of analysis, he points out that "With regard to the perplexing problem raised initially, that of the definition of folklore, it would seem that the first task of folklorists ought to be the analysis of the text."[118] Although the brunt of this essay indicates a more holistic approach, these statements suggest that the conceptual shift to an integrated performance approach had not completely taken place.

Another significant feature of this article is the definition of text, which reveals a problem of methodological import. In his definition, Dundes leaves unclear whether the text is a record of a performance or the performance itself. He seems to imply, however, that the text is the performance itself, ". . . essentially a version or a single telling of a tale. . . ."[119] Yet since he excludes the untranslatable stylistic features and context from his definition of text, then the text is not the complete performance or even a record of it, but presumably a level of analysis, such as content. Another difficulty with this definition which equates, or conflates, the text with the telling of the tale is that it encourages the mistaken notion that the written text is the tale itself, rather than a written translation of an oral event. This conflated definition of text obscures criticism and appreciation of verbal art as performance. Further, it impedes developing better quality texts. If the text is something made, then it can be improved. But if it is something given, something preexistent, then it can only be accepted. We will return to this question of definition in Chapter 4, when we deal with contemporary semiotic definitions of text which resemble the definition offered by Dundes.

During the same time that these largely methodological works were published, several new collections of folklore revealed more detailed attention to context and performance style. Daniel J. Crowley's, *I Could Talk Old-Story Good* (1966), presents Bahamian tales collected in their natural settings. His texts record the opening and closing formulae, local dialect, and audience responses. His descriptions of the narrators, their typical performance styles, and the responses of the audience enable a fuller appreciation of the art of Bahamian folklore. Ruth Finnegan's *Limba Stories and Storytelling* (1967) contains detailed descriptions of the Limba storytelling occasions. In *Folktales and Society* (1968), Linda Dégh criticizes older collections of folktales as "unauthentic" and calls for the inclusion of information about such features as the narrator's gestures, facial expressions, and dramatic interplay.[120] Although her texts do not contain these features, she provides detailed descriptions of the narrators, the tale occasions, and generalized descriptions of their style. These works demonstrate how far the field of folklore had come in its attention to textmaking. By the end of the sixties, few professional folklorists would think of publishing texts bereft of accompanying information about the performers and context.

PERFORMANCE-CENTERED
EXPERIMENTATION WITH THE TEXT

By the late sixties, the growing interest in studying folklore as a dynamic process found theoretical voice in essays articulating new conceptions about the nature of folklore. These new theoretical works had a unifying theme—that verbal art was better understood as a dynamic communicative event rather than as an item to be collected. The concepts of this new performance approach have far-reaching implications for textmaking. These concepts will be examined in depth in the following chapter. Here, we will briefly outline the emergence of this new approach and review the recent efforts to capture performance in print.

Three seminal articles by Dan Ben-Amos, Roger Abrahams, and Robert Georges expressed new conceptions about the nature of folklore. In "Folklore: The Definition Game Once Again," presented at the 1967 meeting of the American Folklore Society, Ben-Amos offered a new definition of folklore as "artistic communication in small groups."[121] He criticizes past definitions of folklore for mistaking a part of the phenomena for the whole and for defining folklore as a "thing" rather than as a process. This paper stimulated much debate in the field even before it was expanded and published in 1972 under the title "Toward a Definition of Folklore in Context," and helped crystallize awareness of a new perspective in folkloristics.[122]

Ben-Amos' redefinition of folklore as artistic communication and symbolic action found further support in Roger Abrahams' "Introductory Remarks to a Rhetorical Theory of Folklore" (1968). He argues that studies of verbal art had been hampered by the split between literary and anthropological folklorists and suggests that the best aesthetic approach to folklore would be a method which would emphasize all aspects of the aesthetic performance: "performance, item, and audience."[123] Abrahams' thesis, heavily influenced by Kenneth Burke, provided still another way of conceptualizing folklore as a communicative performance.

Adding force to this new emphasis on communication, Robert Georges' "Toward an Understanding of Storytelling Events" (1969) constructed a communication model of storytelling events. Georges attacks all previous story research on the grounds that it was based on inadequate texts: "For these texts constitute nothing more than a written representation of one aspect of the message of complex communicative events that, for convenience here, I shall refer to as 'storytelling events.' " Since storytelling events involve messages encoded through linguistic, paralinguistic, and kinesic codes, folklore texts which record only the linguistic codes are misleading, according to Georges. He suggests that these new concepts about folklore require new research directions, such as recording storytelling events in natural field situations, using "every attempt" to capture their wholeness. Georges argues that "Only by attempting to study storytelling events holistically can we begin to appreciate their true significance as communicative events, as social experiences, and as unique expressions of human behavior."[124]

Quickly following on the heels of these initial works, essays by Barbara

Kirshenblatt-Gimblett and Roger Abrahams demonstrated the wide range of application of this new perspective. In "A Parable in Context," first presented in 1969, Kirshenblatt-Gimblett skillfully shows how close attention to the social interaction of a parable's immediate context can reveal how the performance works in a corrective social ritual. Abrahams' "A Performance-Centered Approach to Gossip" (1970) demonstrates how "the function of gossip in specific groups cannot be fully understood until it is related not only to the system of ideals and the techniques of achieving power, but also to the system of performance." In "Folklore and Literature as Performance" (1972), Abrahams presents arguments "for a performance-centered approach to the study of both folklore and literature, through descriptive analysis of performance features and by a consideration of excesses fostered by the item-centered approach."[125]

The performance approach gained momentum in the seventies with the publication of three books of collected essays: *Toward New Perspectives in Folklore* (1972), edited by Américo Paredes and Richard Bauman; *Explorations in the Ethnography of Speaking* (1974), edited by Richard Bauman and Joel Sherzer; and *Folklore: Performance and Communication* (1975), edited by Dan Ben-Amos and Kenneth Goldstein. Explaining the common link among the essays in *Toward New Perspectives in Folklore*, Bauman writes that "In particular, there is an emphasis upon performance as an organizing principle that comprehends within a single conceptual framework artistic act, expressive form, and esthetic response, and that does so in terms of locally defined, culture-specific categories and contexts." The strong ethnographic focus of this work continued in *Explorations in the Ethnography of Speaking*. A number of the essays in this book specifically examine artistic verbal performances. In *Folklore: Performance and Communication*, Ben-Amos and Goldstein note the relationship of the new contextual or performance approach to work in ethnography of speaking and point out that the essays in the book concentrate upon "primary ethnographic observation."[126]

The wide range of this growing body of work seemed to demand integration and analytical development. By 1975, Bauman found the times "opportune for efforts aimed at expanding the conceptual content of folkloric performance as a communicative phenomenon. . . ." In "Verbal Art as Performance," Bauman articulates a formal definition of performance and discusses the keying, framing, patterning, and emergent quality of performance. Influenced by Hymes, Mukarovský, Goffman, and others, he defines performance "as a mode of spoken verbal communication" which "consists in the assumption of responsibility to an audience for a display of communicative competence. This competence rests on the knowledge and ability to speak in socially appropriate ways."[127] Bauman's detailed development of these concepts will be discussed further in Chapter 3. An expanded version of Bauman's article, with supplementary essays by Barbara Babcock, Gary Gossen, Roger Abrahams, and Joel Sherzer, was published in 1977 as *Verbal Art as Performance.*

All of the preceding works had sufficient strength and number to constitute a new school or approach within folkloristics. The emphasis on the primacy of performance stimulated new experimentation with ways of recording performance features in print. Our review of this experimentation begins with those who explicitly speak of the text as a translation of performance. Then we will examine the contributions of those who, in the tradition of Jacobs and Voeglin, retranslate existing texts in an effort to discover and present more performance features. Next we will look at work using kinesic notations and photography to capture nonverbal style. Finally, we will discuss efforts to record polyphonic or group performance.

Toward Translating Performance

In 1971 and 1972, Dennis Tedlock published two works calling attention to the possibility of translating performance. His article "On the Translation of Style in Oral Narrative" and his book, *Finding the Center: Narrative Poetry of the Zuni Indians,* demonstrated that much more could be done in presenting paralinguistic and nonverbal performance features in print.[128]

Tedlock's approach to recording performances reflects an ethnography of speaking perspective. Indeed, the features of performance which he describes are the components of Hymes' ethnography of speaking model: setting, participants, ends, act sequence, key, instrumentalities, norms, and genre.[129] In the introduction to *Finding the Center,* Tedlock describes the characteristic performers, situations, and native categories for two principal genres of Zuni narrative, tales and myths. In addition, he describes characteristic stylistic devices (instrumentalities and keys), norms of interaction and interpretation, and genre markings. Following each tale, he includes notes containing narrator, audience, and translator comments on the tale.

In collecting the tales, Tedlock's principal end was to study their social and psychological contexts. But in the course of translating the tapes, Tedlock searched for a mode of presentation that would communicate the poetic and dramatic features of the performances. He became convinced that written prose was inadequate to represent spoken narrative because "it rolls on for whole paragraphs without taking a breath: there is no silence in it."[130] To record performance style, Tedlock uses three techniques largely undeveloped by previous textmakers.

Following American free-verse poets who experimented with breath-pause line breaks, Tedlock uses two types of pause units. The first type, marked by the end of a line, represents a three-fourths to one-half second pause. The second type, marked by a dot between strophes, represents a two to three-second pause. Longer pauses, about six seconds, are marked by larger spaces than those between strophes. In translating line length, Tedlock tries to approximate the original contrasts in line length.

A second technique unexplored by other collectors is the use of typography to represent modes of speaking. Recognizing that the loudness of Zuni narrative "ranges from just short of a shout to just short of a whisper," and that the punctuation marks of our written tradition are ambiguous, Tedlock uses small type for soft passages or words, large type for middle-level passages, and capitals for loud passages. Occasionally, when the stressed elements in the Zuni mark off lines rather than accentuate meanings, Tedlock shifts the stress from the Zuni word on which it originally fell. For example, translating two lines, " *'Kwa' kwa'holh uhsona ho' yu'hetamME/Ma'homkwat liwan ho'no suWE,"* with the identical stress would read: "But I do NOT know about this./ Perhaps our younger broTHER there." But Joseph Peynetsa says that this type of stress means the speaker is, "saying it in a way that is not ordinary. He is trying to stress, to bring out an important idea. It shows authority, and to have a complete thought at the same time, not just trailing off [sic]." To match this function of the stress, Tedlock translates the lines, "But I do not know about THIS/ Perhaps our younger brother THERE."[131]

Tedlock also uses typography to represent chanted lines. He says that "the important lines in Zuni narrative are sometimes chanted rather than given final stress," and that in the two-pitch lines, the higher pitches tend to fall on the most important words. Unlike the case of the line-ending stress, Tedlock does not have to change the stress to preserve meaning in the English tradition. Using split lines to represent the three half-tone interval of the chant, Tedlock translates "TON^{AA}WAANA TON^{HE}SHOTAWASHNA" as "WHEN YOU HAVE ^{GONE} THERE YOU WILL BUILD HO^{U}SES."[132]

The final technique, italicized comments, describes special voice qualities and metanarrative or nonverbal elements, such as gestures, laughter, or sighs. Tedlock says that the performers made "relatively little use of gestures, mostly limiting themselves to indications (with extended arm and hand) of the position of the sun or the direction in which a story character is traveling."[133] But since Tedlock's tape recorder did not have a counter, he failed to work out a system of correlating gestures with the texts. Consequently, his texts record few gestures or body movements.

Along with Tedlock, poet Jerome Rothenberg also speaks of

translating performance and has experimented with "total translation" of American Indian verbal art. By "total translation," Rothenberg means "translation (of oral poetry in particular) that takes into account any or all elements of the original beyond the words." Rothenberg argues that the total experience of verbal art, such as Navajo song-poems, can be translated: "Everything in these song-poems is finally translatable: words, sounds, voice, melody, gesture, event, etc., in the reconstitution of a unity that would be shattered by approaching each element in isolation. A full and total experience begins it, which only a total translation can fully bring across."[134]

Although Rothenberg deserves credit for recognizing the potential of translating nonverbal dimensions of performance, his actual translations record few, if any, gestures and body movements. For the most part, they record paralinguistic features such as stress, pause, and chanted phrases, using techniques similar to Tedlock's. Further, Rothenberg provides little information about the actual context of his pieces. The absence of contextual information and translation of body movements stems partially from his practice of reworking existing texts of verbal art. Like Jacobs, much of Rothenberg's work is reconstructive; few clues about the original performance context and style exist to guide him.

Rothenberg and Tedlock spurred others to translate performance through a journal which they initiated, *Alcheringa: Ethnopoetics*. In publication throughout most of the seventies, *Alcheringa* provided "a ground for experiments in the translation of tribal/oral poetry and a forum for the discussion of the problems and possibilities of translation from widely divergent languages and cultures."[135]

Harold Scheub also conceives of the text as a translation of performance. In "Translation of African Oral Narrative-Performances to the Written Word," Scheub acknowledges that "the problems of developing literary correspondences for oral nonverbal artistic techniques are staggering." He identifies the major problem as one of "translation from the oral form into the written word. . . ." Scheub's major contribution here is simply that of recognizing the problem as one of translation. But rather than offering a concrete methodology, Scheub concludes prematurely, that "there is no useful way of transferring the nonverbal elements to paper." He suggests that the solution to translating performance might lie in developing "a hybrid art-form, neither the original narrative-performance nor a short story, yet borrowing from both art forms." Ultimately, Scheub leaves the problem "in the hands of an able translator." He ends by enjoining the translator to become an artist, but does not specify any of the tools such an artist would need: "The translator must exploit the receptor language not in any attempt to approximate the nonverbal elements of the oral performance but to give color and meaning to the transmuted work of art."[136]

Discovering Performance Through Retranslation

Following in the tradition established by Melville Jacobs and C. F. Voeglin, Dell Hymes, Richard Dauenhauer, and Barre Toelken have retranslated American Indian texts in an effort to discover and present more of the original performance style in print. Their practice of retranslation includes interlingual translation, as well as the translation of poetic form and certain paralinguistic and kinesic features.

In a series of articles published between 1975 and 1981, Hymes illustrates that much can be learned about the poetic and performance structure of tales through a retranslation based on close grammatical and rhetorical analysis of native language texts. In "Folklore's Nature and the Sun's Myth," Hymes argues for a fresh examination of the role of the text in presenting a performance.[137] Since he did not witness a live performance of the tale, he relies on close analysis of repetitions and syntactic structure to lead him to use line units, strophes, and stanzas to retranslate what he assumes must have been the rhythm in the original performance.

In much the same vein, in "Discovering Oral Performance and Measured Verse in American Indian Narrative," Hymes offers more extensive discussion of the rationale and implications of retranslation. In response to Tedlock's negative assessment of older, dictated Native American texts,[138] Hymes demonstrates that through retranslation, they may "still be grist for the ethnopoetic mill." He critiques Tedlock's reliance on breath pauses as the sole indicator for identifying poetic lines by raising a series of probing questions about the nature of pauses, such as, "Would other performances, repetitions, disclose the same placing of pause? If not, is there a pattern to which the variation is to be referred?" Even if pause "is basic to poetry," Hymes argues that "there remains the problem of differentiating pause that is motivated, that heightens the organization of lines, from pause that is inherent in the spoken medium."

Although Hymes concedes that pause demarcation is a step toward poetics, he points out that study of other features, such as repetition of grammatical features, might reveal line organization, "even not necessarily the same organization." As he astutely observes, "Perhaps pause does not so much define lines, as provide a counterpoint to them, analogous to the ways in which variation and effect are gained in European verse by caesurae within lines, enjambment and end-stopping between them, all the ways in which variations and effect may be gained by playing off sources of periodicity and rhythm against a regulated base."[139]

In both of the preceding articles, Hymes presents new translations of the texts which differ greatly in form from the original texts. For example, in "Folklore's Nature," he changes the four prose paragraphs of

103 printed lines to 298 poetic lines, "organized in seventy-three verses and thirty-three stanzas."[140] In contrast to these articles, Hymes' most recent work on retranslation does not present the retranslated features within a text. In "Reading Clackamas Texts," Hymes analyzes the rhetorical-poetic uses of noun prefixes accompanying the naming of Grizzly Woman and Waterbug. In the Clackamas language, nouns may be prefixed with *wa*, *a*, or the prefix may be omitted, Ø. Since the English language has no equivalent linguistic form, these prefixes do not appear in most translations. By carefully examining the places in the dramatic structure in which the prefixes occur, Hymes discovers that the rhetorical choice between the prefixes is based on the relative strength and activity of the character. *Wa* expresses more power and activity than *a*, and *a* in turn expresses more power than Ø. This fascinating analysis of a native language text illustrates that there is much to be discovered about ethnopoetics through retranslation. This article also illustrates, by default, the advantages of including the newly translated features within a text. Since the text included with this article does not show the prefixes, Hymes must laboriously paraphrase the text and explain each prefix occurrence. The simple expedient of substituting the Clackamas word for Grizzly Woman in the text would enable readers to see first hand where the character was named Wakitsimani or Akitsimani; or prefixing Grizzly Woman with *wa*, *a*, or Ø would accomplish the same purpose.[141]

Like Hymes, Richard Dauenhauer has retranslated early ethnolinguistic texts. Working with a Tlingit song text translated by John Swanton, and comparing it to a German translation based on Margot Astrov's translation of the same song, Dauenhauer finds that both the Astrov and German translations have deleted important aesthetic and contextual information. In a key line dealing with the death of the persona's maternal uncle, both the Astrov and the German texts substitute the phrases "loved one" and "dear one" for maternal uncle. This substitution decontextualizes the song by omitting a powerful Tlingit image. While the kinship term "my maternal uncle" is foreign to the social and aesthetic structure of English and German culture, it is "personally and poetically powerful" in Tlingit society because "of the intimate bond between uncle and nephew, and because the kinship term automatically involves a wider range of social relationships in the Gemeinschaft system."[142]

In contrast to Dauenhauer's and Hymes' efforts to examine and retranslate texts made by others, Barre Toelken has recently retranslated his own earlier translation of a Navaho coyote tale. The first version, published in 1969 as "The 'Pretty Language' of Yellowman: Genre, Mode, and Texture in Navaho Coyote Narratives," endeavored to describe the narrator's gestures and paralinguistic features in parentheses and brackets. The first version did not use lines, strophes, and stanzas to indicate pauses, but recorded the time of pause lengths in parentheses.[143] Disquieted by the prose format of this version, Toelken, with the aid of Tacheeni Scott, retranslated the story "to see what discoveries could be made about the story which *should* have been part of my original discussion."[144]

The new translation uses a poetic line-by-line format and places the descriptions of delivery style and audience responses in the right margin. It is much easier to read. Yet the second version abridges the performance descriptions "because these matters are already discussed in the earlier article." Since the first text and article are reprinted in the later article, readers can look at the first text to find the additional performance features. But their decision to omit some performance features from the second text perpetuates the notion that these nonverbal and contextual features are secondary rather than integral. Toelken and Scott's comparison of the two versions yields useful insights, such as the discovery that one intensifier, "Hááhgóóshį́," (the oral equivalent to several exclamation points) was not even translated in the first text.[145]

Using Kinesic Notations and Photography

In addition to the techniques used by the preceding textmakers, such as poetic line breaks, typography, layout, and parenthetical descriptions, special kinesic notations and photography have been used to record performance features. Beverly Brandon-Sweeney's text of a West Texas personal narrative is designed for the reader skilled in decoding Birdwhistell's kinesic symbols. She transcribes a video recording of the narrative performance, marking only kinesic features. The subsequent script was used by a trained actress to simulate the gestures of the original performance and a performance with inappropriate gestures. Although Brandon-Sweeney's text style was obviously designed for the purposes of her experiment, the text sets a precedent for the use of Birdwhistell's notations in folklore texts. Since Brandon-Sweeney gives only a short and hazy description of her method for deciding what gestures to notate, the reader cannot easily judge the validity of her transcript.[146]

With the increased interest in the nonverbal dimensions of performance, some folklorists have begun to supplement their articles with photographs of performances. Harold Scheub includes photographs of Xhosa performers in an attempt to categorize ways in which Xhosa performers use their bodies. Similarly, V. Hrdličková supplements his essay on the Japanese professional storytellers with photographs of their typical gestures.[147] Yet these essays use photography in only a supplementary role; they do not attempt to record a complete performance. In contrast, István Sándor uses photography systematically throughout a tale performance. He prints the text of a Hungarian tale in

English, divided into sections, with commentary following each section. He includes nine photos of the narrator which indicate the major shifts in narrative gestures throughout the tale. Sándor points out that, "it is a comparatively new undertaking to put narration on record in a series of photos taken at different passages of the same tale and so to make available to more thorough investigation its means of expression beyond the text."[148]

Polyphonic Texts

For the most part, the textmakers mentioned above have concentrated on recording the extended utterance of one performer, with intermittent audience response. Yet some performances are distinguished by having several persons equally sharing responsibility for performance. Recognizing that narrative can be polyphonic, Linda Dégh, Andrew Vazsonyi, and Harvey Sacks have published texts featuring many voices instead of just one.

From work recording legends in context, Dégh and Vazsonyi discovered that legend performances had been misrepresented in print. They strongly criticize legend texts as "unfit for scientific study" because they are "incomplete, mutilated by the collectors, who concentrated exclusively on the plot of the story." Experience in legend-telling sessions convinced them that legend performances are distinguished by polyphonic form. That is, listeners counterpoint, contradict, support, and otherwise interact with the initiator of a legend to such a degree that their performances are an integral part of legend-telling. Dégh and Vazsonyi argue that the co-performers' voices should be preserved in the text: "An arbitrary dissection, the elimination of the 'superfluous' voices, would be as difficult as it would be senseless to reduce the whole complex into single, homogeneous, conventional and unified stories."[149] Accordingly, they print a legend text which records the utterance of all the participants. They use a dramatic format, identifying the different speakers in the left margin.

In "An Analysis of the Course of a Joke's Telling in Conversation," Harvey Sacks uses a similar dramatic format to record the interactions of four persons having a conversation in which a joke is told.[150] The text records silences, laughs, vocalized pauses, and pauses between utterances. With all of the interruptions and interplay between participants recorded, Sacks is able to locate structural features differentiating a joke performance from a simple report of the information in the joke. His work demonstrates that more complete texts of all of the interplay surrounding and punctuating performances can aid understanding of performance structure.

CONCLUSION

From this examination of the role of the text in American folkloristics, we can see how different models of the text have been developed to serve varying analytical perspectives. The ethnolinguistic text, developed by early anthropologists and continued by modern linguistic anthropologists, serves primarily as an accurate verbatim transcript of connected discourse to aid linguistic analysis and to preserve vanishing cultural traditions. Early ethnolinguistic texts conveyed little, if any, information about the informant, setting, or cultural significance of the tale. They were often collected through dictation and through a translator, and thus constituted more of a report to an outsider than a traditional cultural performance in a native context.

The literary model of the text also ignores recording performance context and style. Developed to suit the historical, comparative interests of literary folklorists, the literary model assimilates the form of performance to the conventions of written literature. Today it remains the most widespread format for folklore publications.[151]

As we survey developments in textmaking, we can see increasing attempts to record folklore as performance. The efforts to supplement ethnolinguistic texts by Mallery, Sapir, and Malinowski, as well as the more recent attempts at retranslating older ethnolinguistic texts, reflect an appreciation of performance. Dorson's early recommendation that folklorists could improve the literary model of the text by using novelistic techniques and literary effects "to simulate oral art" shows that folklorists have long recognized the need to improve textmaking.[152] Influenced by a number of interdisciplinary forces, such as the Prague School, Parry and Lord's oral-formulaic work, the refiguration of social thought, with its game and drama analogies, and the ethnography of speaking, contemporary folklorists have expressed growing dissatisfaction with texts which ignore contextual and performance features. Indeed, the impact of the performance approach has been so strong as to prompt some folklorists to take a defensive attitude toward the text.

In 1973, D. K. Wilgus warned of a dangerous tendency to reject existing text collections in the pursuit of studying folklore as a dynamic process. In "The Text is the Thing," Wilgus asserts the value of the text as an artifact useful in historical and comparative research. His definition of the text reveals that the earlier, item-centered, static views of the text are far from dead. Wilgus defines the text as "the item, the artifact, or the record of a mentifact of folklore." He continues, "To be pseudo-Platonic, I would say that it is the manifestation of a folk idea, whether it be a song, a story, a dance, or a cooking pot."[153]

There is no need, however, to hold to static views of the text in order to defend the usefulness of texts to folkloristics. The performance approach need not mark the end of texts if folklorists recognize that performance-centered texts can be made to aid in the study of verbal art as performance. Since texts which record performance also contain the necessary information for historical, comparative studies, they can aid these research interests as well. The recent experimentation with recording performance indicates a readiness to develop a new model of the text consistent with the view of folklore as performance. In the next chapter we will examine the key concepts of the performance approach and construct a model of the performance-centered text.

3

The Performance Approach:
Implications
For the Text

We have seen how different text formats reflect the varying analytical perspectives of the folklorists who make them. When folklore is conceived of as primarily content, such as ethnolinguistic data, or themes and motifs, then recording it in print is not problematical. But when folklore is conceived of as a dynamic process encompassing speech, movement, context, and interaction, then the task of recording it in print seems quite difficult. If we are even to entertain the notion that a performance-centered model of the text can be developed, then we must begin by probing the concepts of the performance approach. Only by basing textmaking practices on a firm understanding of performance theory can we hope to develop a performance-centered praxis of textmaking.

Once the basic concepts of the performance approach have been clarified, we will examine some of the inherent tendencies within the approach which can impede such a praxis. Since the feature which most distinguishes verbal art from other modes of communication is its aesthetic nature, then one of the most important tasks will be to capture its aesthetic qualities in print. Accordingly, we will turn to aesthetic field theory in order to develop an aesthetic transaction model of performance. This model illustrates the necessary components of an ideal, performance-centered text.

KEY CONCEPTS OF THE PERFORMANCE APPROACH

While in the previous chapter we outlined the emergence of the performance approach, here we will probe the basic concepts comprising this approach. The major performance theorists share a perspective that verbal art is: 1) an aesthetic mode of communication, 2) integrally related to a particular event, and 3) culture-specific and cross-culturally variable.

An Aesthetic Mode of Communication

In observing performances of verbal art, Hymes, Bauman, Abrahams, and others recognized that they can be characterized by the *way* they are carried out. That is, while in other speech behavior, such as conversation, attention tends to focus more on the context, or *what* is said; in verbal art, attention focuses on the competence exhibited in performing, or on *how* it is said.

This attention to the stylistic and aesthetic qualities of verbal art led to the formulation of a concept of performance as a special mode of communication. Advancing a definition of verbal art as performance, Bauman writes that "performance as a mode of spoken verbal communication consists in the assumption of responsibility to an audience for a display of communicative competence."[1] On first glance, this definition of verbal art as a mode of communication might seem at odds with a common tradition in aesthetics which opposes art to communication, holding that art, like a poem, "should not mean, but be."[2] For those who define communication narrowly as "a person sending a message to another individual with the conscious intent of evoking a response,"[3] the notion that art is a species of communication seems insufficient, especially since the instrumental element in this definition seems to preclude an intrinsic focus on the art object itself.

But those who define communication broadly as an intra- and inter-active process, involving the perception and transmission of all types of signs, conceive of various modes of communication, among which is an aesthetic mode.[4] Indeed, Bauman emphasizes that the notion of performance as communicative competence is grounded firmly in the aesthetic mode of experience:

> Performance involves on the part of the performer an assumption of accountability to an audience *for the way in which communication is carried out, above and beyond its referential content. From the point of view of the audience, the act of expression on the part of the performer is thus marked as subject to evaluation for the way it is done, for the relative skill and effectiveness of the performer's display of competence. Additionally, it is marked as available for the*

enhancement of experience, through the present enjoyment of the intrinsic qualities of the act of expression itself. Performance thus calls forth special attention to and heightened awareness of the act of expression, and gives license to the audience to regard the act of expression and the performer *with special intensity* (my italics).[5]

Aware of a tradition of thought which conceives of communication solely in terms of conveying literal, or referential messages, Bauman takes pains to show how performance constitutes a different order of communication than the literal. Drawing on Gregory Bateson's idea of "frame" as an interpretive context that provides guidelines for discriminating between orders of messages, Bauman argues that performance constitutes an interpretive frame in which something in the communicative interchange says to the auditor, "interpret what I say in some special sense; do not take it to mean what the words alone, taken literally, would convey." Opposing J. L. Austin's suggestion that the literal frame is more "normal," or has greater priority over other frames, Bauman writes that aside from the notorious difficulty of defining literalness, "there is growing evidence that literal utterances are no more frequent or 'normal' in situated human communication than any of the other frames, and indeed that in spoken communication no such thing as naked literalness may actually exist."[6]

This alignment of the aesthetic with a communication perspective seems to grow out of dissatisfaction with the treatment of verbal art ensuing from formalist, object-centered aesthetic approaches. Bauman objects to formalist analyses that begin and end with the text because they fail to deal with the phenomenological reality of the live verbal art performance. Even if formalists attempt to infer performance actions from textual analysis, Bauman argues, they "proceed backwards, by approaching phenomena whose primary social reality lies in their nature as oral communication in terms of the abstracted textual products of the communication process." Indeed, Bauman suggests that although many texts may meet formalist criteria for verbal art, be recorded accurately, and even strongly resemble performances in their native contexts, they may still "not be the products of performance, but of rendition in another communicative mode."[7]

The preference for a communication-centered aesthetics rather than a formalist one also reflects the influence of rhetorical theory on folkloristics. In his "Introductory Remarks to a Rhetorical Theory of Folklore," Roger Abrahams argues that rhetorical method, and particularly, the insights of Kenneth Burke, allow a way to unify the aesthetic and functional dimensions of verbal art.[8]

The rhetorical approach Abrahams recommends, like the influence of ethnography of speaking, impelled folklorists toward a concept of folklore as a communicative process, but a distinctly aesthetic mode of communication. Abrahams' later writings on performance continue to emphasize the aesthetic dimension as he explores the relationship between pure, artistic performance and everyday life.[9]

Like Bauman and Abrahams, Hymes' writings on verbal art performance as a "way of speaking" stress that it is a particularly aesthetic mode. Hymes argues that both folklore and ethnography of speaking share an interest in speech communication and that this speech "is to be approached as having an esthetic, expressive, or stylistic dimension. The stylistic and referential are interwoven and interdependent in all of communication. Obviously there are degrees here, both of organization and of esthetic or expressive quality, and folklorists will be most concerned with the more highly organized, more expressive end of the two continua."[10]

In defining performance as a cultural behavior for which a person assumes responsiblity for presentation to an audience, Hymes cautions against using the term performance as merely a synonym for conduct and activity.[11] He argues that the assumption of responsibility for presentation distinguishes performance from *behavior*, simply anything and everything that happens, and *conduct*, behavior under the aegis of social norms, cultural rules, shared principles of interpretability. Thus for Hymes, performance is not merely behavior, nor culture, nor conduct, nor communication, but is "something creative, realized, achieved, even transcendent of the ordinary course of events."[12] In pointing to the qualitative nature of performance that distinguishes it from other forms of conduct, Hymes seems aware that we have only begun to understand performance, a "quality whose conditions and dynamics have only begun to be adequately explored."[13]

What distinguishes artistic verbal performances from other ways of speaking? Bauman, Ben-Amos, Hymes, and Abrahams all agree that certain varying and interacting features mark speech behavior as aesthetic performance. Arguing that folklore is a "social interaction via the art media" that "differs from other modes of speaking and gesturing," Ben-Amos uses Dundes' scheme of text, texture, and context, to distinguish folklore from nonfolklore. Textual markers such as opening and closing formulae set the narration apart, as when an Ashanti storyteller indicates that a story is fictional with the words, "We don't really mean to say so, we don't really mean to say so." Textural features, such as a distinct intonation or rhythm also set folklore apart. And contextual conventions such as requirements for a special time, place, and audience, also mark folklore as an aesthetic category of speech.[14] For example, among the Zuni Indians, fictional tales, by convention, may be told only "from October to March, lest the narrator be bitten by a snake, and only at night, lest the sun set early. Anyone who falls asleep during a telapnanne or who fails to stand up and stretch at the end of such a story may become a hunchback."[15] These contextual conventions, so different from the rules governing everyday speaking, set up expectations for aesthetic performance. Ben-Amos stresses that verbal art may not necessarily be cued on all three levels, text, texture, and context, but on only one or two, since different communities may vary in how verbal art is set apart from other speech.

We have already seen how Bauman's use of "frame" can distinguish between performance and other modes of communication. To explain how this interpretive frame is formed, Bauman suggests that it may be signaled by certain metacommunicative devices which, in Erving Goffman's terms, "key" performance. The most widely documented keys for performance include, according to Bauman: 1) special codes; 2) figurative language; 3) parallelism; 4) special paralinguistic features; 5) special formulae; 6) appeal to tradition; 7) disclaimer of performance. Cautioning against accepting a simple list of keys as an index to all performances, Bauman reminds the reader that the "essential task in the ethnography of performance is to determine *the culture-specific constellations of communicative means that serve to key performance in particular communities* (Bauman's italics)."[16] We will talk more about the varying patterns of performance in discussing the concept of cross-cultural variability in performance.

While Bauman uses the term "key" to refer to the metacommunicative devices signaling the performance frame, Hymes uses the same term to refer to the varying degrees of performance authenticity. He suggests that "it ought to be possible to distinguish performance according to the key in which it occurs; some performances are desultory, or perfunctory, or rote, while others are authoritative, authentic." By "authentic," "full," or "authoritative" performance, Hymes means "when the standards intrinsic to the tradition in which the performance occurs are accepted and realized."[17] As an example, Hymes cites a Navaho, "who may tell someone a tale, in the sense of knowing and telling how it goes, without embarking on a performance of the tale in the sense proper to the genre."[18] Of course, only by knowing the performance traditions for a particular group can one judge the authenticity of a particular performance. Both Hymes and Bauman suggest that many of the published folklore texts may not be records of authentic performances, but rather of reports or résumés.[19]

Abrahams also tries to define the difference between artistic performance and other ways of speaking. Like Bauman, he finds that performance calls attention to style as well as content, through self-conscious framing and marking achieved through a coordination among message channels. While in everyday behavior, a host of activities compete for our attention, performance tends to focus our attention by reducing the number of competing message channels. Thus, pure performance, according to Abrahams, involves "a high level of coordination so that prediction and participation in common may be ensured. 'Things going on' at the same time will tend to reinforce each other, a coordination achieved by the self-conscious framing and marking." Abrahams suggests the existence of "a minimal set of sociocultural preconditions for an act of pure performance":

> 1) occasions and situations in which performance is approved, indeed, expected, and which therefore carry a residuum of energies which the performance brings into focus or coordination; 2) members of the community who are given license to perform; 3) conventional patterns of expectation, stylized ideal types of expression announced by the framing of the event by which the participative energies of the performer and audience may be coordinated to some degree; and 4) a repertoire of actual items of performance which fill the formal requirements of the generic expectations are available to performers, and thus appropriate to performance events.

While each of these conditions may be found in other kinds of communication, Abrahams argues that the more they occur together, "the more we tend to categorize the event as a performance."[20]

As we have seen, proponents of the performance approach share a common definition of performance as a mode of communication that can be differentiated from other modes by its aesthetic quality. To avoid the tendency of elevating this special mode of communication into an abstract, ideal quality, a second key concept, event, reminds us that performance is grounded inextricably in a social context. While we may analytically separate the two for the purposes of definition, each performance is shaped by and, in turn, shapes a particular event.

Performance Event

A cluster of interacting variables characterizes a performance event. The physical setting, such as the season, time of day, and location (campfire circle or living room) may create expectations for the performance of certain genres, such as fictional stories or historical narratives. Within a physical setting, the psychological ambience, or "scene"[21] may further affect the performance. For example, the levity associated with a cocktail party may be conducive to the performance of jokes, whereas the formality of a wedding ceremony may make joking behavior inappropriate. The type of participants present and their particular personalities, relationships, and goals influence the potential scenes and performances that might emerge in a particular setting. As participants and scenes change within a particular setting, different expectations for verbal art performances emerge.

These implicit or explicit expectations for performance may be termed "ground rules for performance," or, "the set of cultural themes and ethical and social interactional organizing principles that govern the conduct of performance."[22] For example, a specific event may require a certain type of participant (all male), a certain physical setting (a special male-only lodge), a specific psychological scene (ceremonial), a certain cultural theme (initiation into a brotherhood), special genres (secret songs, pledges, dramatizations), and special interactional patterns (elders lead, youth follow).

Paradoxically, only by knowing the expected ground rules for a performance event can one understand the unique, creative qualities of a particular performance. For instance, a solemn, reverent recitation of the Lord's Prayer by a group of people in a church service no doubt has a different social and aesthetic impact than the same reverent rendition of the Lord's Prayer by people illegally occupying a busy intersection as an act of civil disobedience. The latter performance violates the cultural expectations for the appropriate setting and participants for the prayer and endows the prayer with political overtones. Conventional literary texts of each performance that fail to record the differing characteristics of each event will leave the reader with little understanding of the widely varying aesthetic and social significance of the two performances.

The term "emergence" is useful for referring to the new, unexpected, and unique features that often violate cultural expectations. Of course, the many interacting variables that make up a performance ensure that rules will be broken. As Bauman explains, "the emergent quality of performance resides in the interplay between communicative resources, individual competence, and the goals of the participants, within the context of particular situations."[23] Folklorists and interpretation scholars have become accustomed to thinking of texts as emergent structures, particularly after the work of Parry and Lord in uncovering the oral-compositional techniques of Yugoslav singers of epic tales. A particular Yugoslav epic may vary greatly in length, number of themes, and kinds of formulae used. Although it might be tempting to think that all oral texts display the same type of emergent structure as the Yugoslav, Bauman reminds us that much evidence also shows that "rote memorization and insistence on word for word fidelity to a fixed traditional text do play a part in the performance system of certain communities." He goes on to suggest that "completely novel and completely fixed texts represent the poles of an ideal continuum," between which lie the emergent texts found in observations of performance. Study of emergent text structures, says Bauman: "promises to bring about a major reconceptualization of the nature of the text, freeing it from the apparent fixity it assumes when abstracted from performance and placed on the written page, and placing it within an analytical context which focuses on the very source of the empirical relationship between art and society."[24]

Not only texts, but event and social structure, may be emergent in performance. The hypothetical example of demonstrators reciting the Lord's Prayer shows that while the text structure remains fixed, new aspects in event and social structure emerge during performance. The demonstrators, by performing a religious prayer rather than a political chant, can transform a pure political event into a quasi-religious one, and perhaps gain psychological leverage over police, who may feel some compunction at using force to remove "praying" citizens. Other examples come readily to mind. A performance of an apt parable in the midst of a family quarrel may point the solution to a seemingly insoluble family crisis.[25] Through the power of jokes, skillfully turned against an opponent, a person may change his social status. For instance, comedian Dick Gregory, who was bullied by other children, began to reverse the situation by gaining status as a performer. Instead of crying when he was picked on, Gregory began to make jokes: "They were going to laugh anyway, but if I made the jokes, they'd laugh *with* me instead of at me. I'd get the kids off my back, on my side." Once he had the children's attention through his power as a performer, Gregory began to turn his humor against his former victimizers. Thus, through performance, Gregory emerges in a very different social position than the one in which he started.[26] These examples point to the rhetorical power of artistic verbal performance to affect changes in attitude. Of course, the rhetorical power of verbal art has long been known in Western society, as attested by classical and medieval rhetoricians who included folklore forms such as proverbs and witty sayings in their lists of devices that could be used to praise or blame, elevate or disparage a subject.

No doubt the source of this rhetorical power to change attitudes and alter events lies in the epistemological nature of artistic verbal performance. In contrast to the types of knowledge exchanged in everyday verbal interactions, artistic verbal performance embodies knowledge in a heightened self-conscious way that binds the audience and performer together in the creation and fulfillment of aesthetic form. In addition to utilizing the power of significant form to engage the audience's attention, verbal art frequently embodies traditional values and beliefs, providing a model of appropriate cultural behavior.[27]

Influenced by Kenneth Burke's notion of poetry as "the adopting of various strategies for the encompassing of situations," Abrahams sheds light on the epistemological nature and rhetorical function of artistic verbal performance. Abrahams argues that expressive folklore, in embodying and reflecting recurrent social conflicts through a representative and traditionally recognizable symbolic form, reveals a problem situation in a controlled context. Control, Abrahams states, is "the primary tool of the rhetoric of a performance" and is ". . . 'magically' transferred from the item to the recurrent problem when the performance operates successfully, sympathetically. Because the performer projects the conflict and resolves it, the illusion is created that it can be solved in real life; and with the addition of sympathy, of 'acting with,' the audience not only derives pleasure from the activity but also knowledge." A performance exercises control, "by the use of wit, by the imposition of rules and boundaries, by the creation of an imaginary world, or by some other limiting device which proclaims artifice." With such controls, the problem seems less immediate and more universal; as in play, participants can freely expend their energies without fear of real life consequences.[28] We will return to the epistemology of performance when we consider performance's "preanalytic" qualitative characteristic. My purpose here is simply to clarify how performance, through its way of embodying knowledge, can affect event and social structure.

The concept of event, then, when added to the definition of performance as a mode of communication, results in a dynamic and systemic conception of verbal art that argues against purely formalist approaches. The many possible configurations of genre, participants, goals, settings, and scenes in which any given performance may be situated lead to the conclusion that the meaning of a particular performance can only be understood by studying it in context, integrally related to its immediate social, psychological, and physical surroundings. This conclusion leads to a third important concept of the performance approach—that performances are patterned in culturally-specific and cross-culturally variable ways.

Cultural Specificity and Variability in Performance

This third concept holds that performances are uniquely patterned within specific cultures and variable across cultures. This concept constitutes an important corrective to the prevalent tendency to generalize about the organization, style, and significance of verbal art based on the study of verbal art in one culture. As a case in point, the Parry and Lord oral formulaic theory, derived from research on Yugoslav culture, was applied to other cultures as a necessary test of oral composition. Increasingly, critics of this over-simplistic adoption of the Parry-Lord hypothesis point out that its proponents often fail to examine actual performances within various cultures. For example, Ruth Finnegan argues that "when one starts looking hard at the concept of 'oral composition,' it becomes clear that it is not a single unique process. . . but takes different forms in different cultures and circumstances."[29] Pointing to the lack of cross-cultural data behind such theorizing, Roger Abrahams notes that while the Parry-Lord theory is "really an hypothesis and a related method for collecting performances and local aesthetic observations on performance," it has been "taken as a *rule* or *law* of composition, and used as a means once again of focussing away from living performance and back onto texts. . . ."[30]

Combating these tendencies to ignore the differences in verbal art forms in various cultures, the performance approach argues that the analyst must first describe the specific ways an individual speech community organizes its verbal behavior. While many speech communities may conceptualize their traditional performances in terms of genres, others may organize their performances in terms of speech acts, social roles, or speech events.[31] According to Bauman, genres and speech acts are analytically distinct, with acts referring to speech behavior, and genres referring to the verbal products of that behavior. Oral cultures, says Bauman, may not distinguish between the speech act and the form an utterance takes. Thus, the ethnographer of performance must look for the behaviors which a community associates with performance. Likewise, specific events may or may not require performance. And certain social roles may also carry varying expectations of performance. Bauman stresses that performance genres, acts, events, and roles do not occur in isolation, "but are mutually interactive and interdependent."[32] The analytical distinction between the four provides the ethnographer with an index of possible ways in which a community may conceptualize its verbal art.

PROBLEMS OF THE PERFORMANCE APPROACH: MAKING THE TEXT FIT THE THEORY

Clearly, the performance approach resembles field and systems approaches that have been growing since the onset of quantum field theory in the disciplines of speech communication, sociology, anthropology, and psychology.[33] While these new field, contextual, ecological, systems, or performance perspectives, as they are variously termed, are more comprehensive than other approaches, their very claim to comprehensiveness creates analytical problems. Traditional scientific method has developed through abstraction and manipulation of variables and comparison and classification of such abstractions. Scientists have assumed the mask of objectivity as they have sorted, dissected, and rearranged data to test hypotheses. Unfortunately, the ground of such methods fails to hold for humanists and social scientists concerned with understanding human meaning. The interactions of persons with each other and with their environment introduce data beyond the ability of observers to explain readily.

A convenient alternative seems to solve these difficulties. One can acknowledge the importance of system and context, give a generalized report of context, proceed to isolate one or two variables in much the same way as before, and then, conveniently interpret those isolates in terms of the initial, generalized account of the context. In fact, such an alternative has already become a tendency in much communication research, as Browning and Hopper point out: "Many scholars in recent years have done lip-service to the notion that no individual sign has meaning except within contexts. But still, study of individual units continues, and study of interactive sequences (being more difficult) lags behind. In essence, we have admitted that we cannot find meaning in individual code items, then proceeded to study such items. We have consistently chosen to study what we know (conceptually) does not exist—those portions of messages which carry meanings and will 'stand still' long enough for us to record and categorize them."[34]

Another way of avoiding the complexities of contextualism is to reify contexts into containers that are thought to frame or shape meaning. The problem with the reification, as Browning and Hopper argue, is that "backgrounds are keyed . . . by items of conversation, which items themselves are part of the foreground in time and space. The items key background, and in that sense become both foreground and background, and yet not quite either." Rather than treating context as static and separable from messages, they argue that contexts should be treated as "becomings," or "interactive systems."[35]

Like other holistic strategies, the performance approach may suffer the same tendency to be pulled apart at the joints. Particularly, when one considers its interdisciplinary background (linguistics, anthropology, rhetoric, ethnography of speaking) it is easy to see how the various aims and methodologies of each discipline could subvert its holistic potential by recording only those elements of a performance useful for its particular line of research. Linguists, for example, may tape-record a performance and then make a text which systematically describes certain features such as phonemes, allophones, suprasegmentals, or paralinguistic features. Or kineticists, following the linguistic approach used by Birdwhistell, might painstakingly note the kines, kinemes, and kinemorphs of a performer. Since so many behaviors occur in any given interchange, it is tempting to separate and record only certain discrete units, which can then be referred to the general gestalt of the performance in an effort to interpret their meaning. While the resultant texts function as scientific documents of certain code uses, such texts do not record the integral form of a performance.

In constructing an ethnography of speaking, it may be convenient or necessary to arrange large groups of speaking into a taxonomy, giving representative samples of speeches to illustrate genre markings or sociological functions. Gary H. Gossen's excellent study of Chamula genres of verbal behavior, one of the most complete ethnographies of speaking, shows how a community of Maya Indians organize, name, and mark their verbal behavior, and how their system of discourse reflects their world view. Occasionally, Gossen gives specific information about the performer, situation, and audience, but usually, he presents a fragment of a text as representative of a genre, with a generalized description of the types of performers and context in which it might appear. For example, he gives a four-couplet fragment of a genre called "True Ancient Narrative" and concludes: "Not all texts are as symmetrical and redundant as this one, nor is symmetry necessarily present throughout a text. The fragment, however, illustrates a general tendency for all genres of 'Ancient Words' to utilize greater stylistic redundancy than 'Recent Words.'"[36]

Of course, such generalizations about the organization and patterning of a culture's verbal art have great value, and such comprehensive, analytical work as Gossen's has little room to include complete texts of each performance to which it makes reference. Yet, it is easy to see how the integrity of individual performances may be violated even by ethnographers of speaking, when they abstract and present only parts of a performance to illustrate general patterns of verbal art in a community. While scholarly commentary on verbal art may flourish, complete texts of verbal art performances to which other scholars can refer and to which future generations can turn for enjoyment, insight, and comparison, may become rare.

AN AESTHETIC TRANSACTION
MODEL OF PERFORMANCE

In order to fulfill the theoretical claims about the nature of verbal art as an aesthetic communicative process, the text must record and present its data in a manner consistent with the concepts of the performance approach. This means, fundamentally, that the text must represent the *aesthetic* mode of performance. Obviously, if the text represents a performance only as a communicative process, it has failed to capture the essence of the transaction that separates performance from other modes of communication. While we have pointed to a configuration of situational and formal features that tend to define a performance and separate it from other interactions, we have yet to probe the qualitative characteristics of performance as aesthetic experience. What is needed, then, is a model which will help conceptualize the nature of artistic verbal performance which the collector strives to preserve and present through the medium of the text.

An Aesthetic Field Framework

Although the key concepts, "communication" and "aesthetic" form the definition of performance, neither the well-known communication models nor aesthetic theories furnish an adequate model for verbal art performances. The common communication models, consisting of variations on the components sender, channel, message, receiver, feedback, noise, and field of experience, fail to indicate the difference between the aesthetic and other modes of communication.[37] And since most aesthetic theories fall into one of the four categories set forth by M. H. Abrams—expressive, mimetic, objective, or pragmatic—they are not sufficiently comprehensive to account for the many variables comprising the aesthetic experience of a verbal art performance.[38] Most aesthetic theories, too, have grown out of the Western high or fine arts tradition and have rarely considered performance as an important aesthetic category. Indeed, as Hilde Hein shows, when aestheticians do consider performance, they consider it as a secondary interpretation of a primary, creative work of art.[39] But Arnold Berleant's work, *The Aesthetic Field*, offers a comprehensive aesthetic theory in which the performer is a key component. Within the framework proposed by Berleant, we can find the basis for constructing a model of artistic verbal performance.

Before proceeding, I must inject a cautionary note about my use of Berleant's work. My attitude toward his work is functional; that is, I am adapting some of Berleant's ideas, without accepting all of them. Specifically, I reject Berleant's stance and arguments against communication-centered theories of art because his arguments are based on a very narrow, indeed outmoded, conception of communication. Although Berleant specifically opposes communication approaches to art, his own aesthetic transaction theory, as we will see in the following discussion, is not incompatible with the broader view of communication underlying the performance approach.

Berleant begins his phenomenological approach to aesthetics by taking issue with imitation, emotionalist, formalist, expressionist, and communicative theories of art for focusing on only parts of aesthetic experience to prove *a priori* constructs. Berleant calls these theories "surrogates" because such approaches "all seize on one aspect of the activity and thereby do an injustice to the others." In contrast to these surrogate theories, Berleant proposes an "aesthetic field" theory that defines art in terms of "the total situation in which the objects, activities, and experiences of art occur . . . ."[40]

To those familiar with contemporary "field" and transactional theories of communication, a theory of an aesthetic transaction grounded within a particular sociocultural context, or "aesthetic field," is compatible with the notion of art as an aesthetic mode of communication. But Berleant's traditional view of communication is restricted to the instrumental transference of referential meaning. For Berleant, communication theories focus only on the use of symbols and language, a focus insufficient to account for aesthetic experience: "They assume that art performs the same kind of function that language does, and by interpreting the aesthetic activity as a communicative one, the experience of art is again replaced by a surrogate."[41]

In rejecting the notion of art as analogous to language, Berleant argues that language is "rarely reflexive," but "preeminently instrumental." He finds this instrumental quality in which "language points beyond itself" incompatible with the art object as a "focal point of intrinsic perceptual awareness." Further, Berleant argues that viewing art as symbols leads into questions of meaning which lead away from art's immediacy into cognitive areas outside the "noncognitive" realm of aesthetic experience. In fact, Berleant concludes his case against communication theories with the contention that, "They commit the error of confusing the reflective analytic, symbol-using attitude and activity with the inherently noncognitive aesthetic ones."[42]

Now if communication were exclusively instrumental, if communication theory concerned itself only with language and other symbols, and if language were totally referential, one might agree with Berleant that trying to explain art through communication would neglect some important features of aesthetic experience. But the notion that language is "preeminently instrumental" or literal—a view which Berleant seems to accept unquestionably, has been called into question by many.[43] And communication theory, far from being confined to linguistics, encompasses all aspects of perception, from the biological bases of electrochemical messages to socially constructed interpretations of reality. Similarly, the idea that communication is only instrumental, as expressed by such linear stimulus-response communication models in which a source purposely transmits a message to a receiver, who responds through negative or positive feedback, has been rejected by contemporary communication theorists stressing a transactional, nonlinear model of communication. In the transactional view, meaning is not a preexistent ideal form which can be encoded, transmitted, and received, but rather is socially constructed, emergent from the interaction among participants in specific contexts.[44] Since in the subsequent discussion of the aesthetic transaction I oppose Berleant's argument that art is noncognitive, I will not repeat those arguments here, but simply point out that in refuting the contention that art is noncognitive, I refute the basic premise of Berleant's objection to communication-centered aesthetics.

Despite Berleant's narrow conception of communication, his aesthetic theory is compatible with a broad, transactional view of communication. A key element of his theory is an argument for a "reciprocal, functional relationship" between the percipient and the art object. According to Berleant, the perceiver vitalizes and activates an object's aesthetic potential in such ways as identifying the lines and figures of a painting, apprehending a play's plot, or organizing musical tones into patterns and thematic relationships. Indeed, Berleant's concept of the aesthetic transaction seems to embody the holistic concerns of the performance approach: "The work of art in its fullest dimensions is, in the final analysis, the aesthetic transaction in its entirety. It is a transaction that occurs in the context of an environment involving, in minimal terms, an art object and an individual who activates its aesthetic potential. For it is essential to remember that the aesthetic field is a unity of experience and that identifying the percipient and the art object as elements in the field, as we have been doing in order to analyze it, disrupts the real coherence and integrity of the situation."[45]

Berleant's concept of the aesthetic transaction is valuable for our inquiry not only because his theory accounts for performance, but because it reminds us of the importance of considering the reader's interaction with the text. On the basis of our adaptation of Berleant's aesthetic transaction, we will see in the next chapter that mechanical approaches to textmaking which notate various kinesic, linguistic, and other features, but neglect the reader's ability to translate the notations into the performance gestalt, will fail in the goal of recording performance as an aesthetic mode. With this caveat aside, let us, with the aid of Berleant's work, develop a model of artistic verbal performance.

Heavily influenced by John Dewey's *Art as Experience*,[46] Berleant's conception of aesthetics begins and ends in experience. He is not interested in describing art objects, or artistic creation, or perception, or the relationship between art and reality *per se*, but rather in empirically and phenomenologically describing aesthetic experience. Beginning with the premise that art is a human experience, sharing features with other human experiences, Berleant outlines the elements which identify the aesthetic mode of experience. His subsequent model of the aesthetic field and the aesthetic transaction within that field are meant to be generalized accounts of the structure of aesthetic experience. Berleant clearly states that each art form will necessitate a specific description of its aesthetic field.[47]

As the following overview of Berleant's account of the aesthetic field shows, his model reflects the dominant pattern of Western high art, in which performer, creative artist, and art object are perceptually separate entities. In most folk narrative performances, however, there is little if any perceptual difference between the performer, creative artist, and art object. Thus, verbal art performance demands its own model of the aesthetic field.

Berleant's diagram of the aesthetic field consists of four interacting elements and a set of sociocultural factors that influence the interaction. Within a large circle indicating the aesthetic field, four elements, represented by four circles connected by lines, interact in the aesthetic experience: Artist, Work of Art, Performer, and Aesthetic Perceiver (Art

Subject). Each of these elements has its own norms and traditions which influence any one aesthetic experience, and Berleant illustrates this by dividing each circle with a dotted line. The Artist, then, is influenced by Artistic Traditions and Community; the Work of Art by the Body of Art Objects; the Performer by the Community and Traditions of Performers, and the Aesthetic Perceiver by the Art Public. Further influencing each of the four elements are a set of sociocultural factors: material resources, level of technological development, biological characteristics, psychological characteristics, social forms, cultural factors, religious beliefs, moral values, ideology, aesthetic theories, historical influences, and scientific knowledge. The organizing principle of the aesthetic field is the aesthetic experience itself, when all the elements and factors come together into a dynamic relationship Berleant calls the aesthetic transaction. To help illustrate the transaction, Berleant uses a Venn diagram of four intersecting circles: Artist, Perceiver, Object, and Performer. The circle formed by the intersection of all four elements represents the aesthetic transaction.[48]

The above schematic summary of the aesthetic field cannot do justice to the dynamic process Berleant envisions. One would have to recapitulate his discussion of each element, which is beyond the interests of this work. Yet, a brief examination of his conceptualization of the Performer and the Work of Art will show how these are far from static categories. One might think that the performer would not function as an element in every aesthetic transaction, yet Berleant argues that performance is always an intrinsic element. Even when an art has no ostensible performer, Berleant holds that the role has been consolidated with that of the perceiver. The performer element, far from being superfluous, or an intruder between the artist and the perceiver, "makes us face the fact that art is an experience that is active, a process that involves knowledge and skill, and an activity that is social at heart." Likewise, Berleant conceives of the art object as a dynamic entity whose experiential limits surpass its physical limits. An individual must activate the aesthetic potential of the object through "ordering and identifying the lines and figures of the painting, following and apprehending the plot of the play, and organizing music tones into melodic and harmonic patterns and recognizable thematic relationships." Thus, the work of art "in its fullest dimensions is, in the final analysis, the aesthetic transaction in its entirety."[49]

Simply identifying the major elements and factors comprising the aesthetic field does not differentiate aesthetic experience from any other type of experience, as Berleant realizes. His real contribution, especially for the purpose of this work, lies in his phenomenological characterization of the aesthetic experience. His theory is particularly attractive to interpreters and folklorists because rather than conceiving of aesthetic experience as unique and set apart from other human experience, he sees it as: " . . . not radically different or sharply separated from other sorts of experiences. Depending upon the form, style, and period of art, aesthetic experience may verge on religious, mystical, scholarly, practical, athletic—indeed, on virtually every identifiable mode of experience. Furthermore, an aesthetic quality may be present in kinds of experiences predominantly different from it."[50] This view of aesthetic experience as a mode of experience helps explain the power of verbal art performance to transform other events into an aesthetic transaction. As we have seen, artistic verbal performance may be called into being in almost any situation, from a street corner demonstration to a family room; thus, it is not bound by any museum notion of art as separate from everyday life.

To account for the aesthetic experience, Berleant adopts a "matrix theory of definition" which delineates the set of coordinates and their relative emphasis and interrelationships "that commonly appear together and are the basis on which we recognize and distinguish this mode of experience from others."[51] Berleant's subsequent matrix for characterizing aesthetic experience makes no claim to be a final account, but is rather a hypothetical one which must be evaluated against experience with different arts. Since he does not specifically use verbal art performance to illustrate his definition of aesthetic experience, his categories must be tested against what we know of artistic verbal performance. In the following section, we will develop a model of artistic verbal performance as an aesthetic transaction and show how Berleant's coordinates of aesthetic experience help to further an understanding of the nature of verbal art performance. We will then show how this aesthetic transaction model serves as an ideal model of the performance-centered text.

The Model and Its Components

In examining the key concepts of the performance approach, we saw that one consequence of defining verbal art as performance is that when texts are evaluated against what is known about performance in the culture from which they were recorded, many turn out to be records of other modes of communication than performance. In trying to make texts that will record performance, a first step is to know the qualities and characteristics of performance that distinguish it from other communication modes.

Folklorists have made the important contribution of distinguishing between emic and etic knowledge of performance, insisting that analysis should begin with understanding the emic features deemed significant by members of the performing community.[52] Yet another distinction between types of knowledge is crucial in accounting for verbal art performance. As Berleant insightfully shows, art may be known in three distinctly different ways. First, like any other mode of experience, art may be *apprehended*, or perceived, and second, if apprehended in a specifically aesthetic way, it may be *appreciated*. Berleant finds the act of appreciation synonymous with aesthetic experience itself, and says appreciation is the source of the data with which aesthetic theory deals. The third type of knowing, to understand art, is an analytical, cognitive activity of theorizing about art, and is the business of aesthetics. Although these three distinctions are basic, they are often overlooked, creating what Berleant calls the "aesthetic error": "It is a typically aesthetic error to confuse the reflective, analytic attitude of the cognitive approach to art with the appreciative one of the experience of art." Many of the "surrogate" and incomplete aesthetic theories are the product of mistaking analytical knowledge for perceptual knowledge, argues Berleant,[53] and much the same can be said of many theories of verbal art.[54] Thus, to avoid imposing an *a priori* analytical construct on the reality of verbal art and ending up with a reductive or false conception of artistic verbal performance, we must begin with a perceptual description.

The following model (Figure 1) shows the elements, factors, and interrelationships involved in artistic verbal performance, and in addition, distinguishes verbal art performance from other speech communication. Each performance will vary, of course, according to the differences in its aesthetic field. In the following section we will examine the characteristics of the components Performer/Audience, Performance Tradition, Aesthetic Transaction, Events, and Other Modes of Speech Communication.

Performer/Audience

The distinction between performer and audience may seem obvious. Yet in some performances, audience members have more than a passive spectator role. In legend-telling sessions, as Dégh and Vazsonyi have pointed out, the audience members' participation is so active that the legend can be termed a "polyphonic form" which is collectively performed. Arguing that past texts of legends have obfuscated this characteristic by neglecting to record audience comments, Dégh and Vazsonyi insist on the importance of the counterpoint parts in legend performances, in which "the various types of participants—the proponent, the contributor, the expander, the stimulator, the critic, the challenger, and so forth—play equally important roles, and often switch them."[55]

In cases such as this, in which every participant is in some degree an

OTHER MODES OF
SPEECH
COMMUNICATION

ARTISTIC VERBAL PERFORMANCE

1. Active-Receptive   5. Preanalytic
2. Sensuous   6. Integral
3. Immediate   7. Unique
4. Intuitive   8. Intrinsic

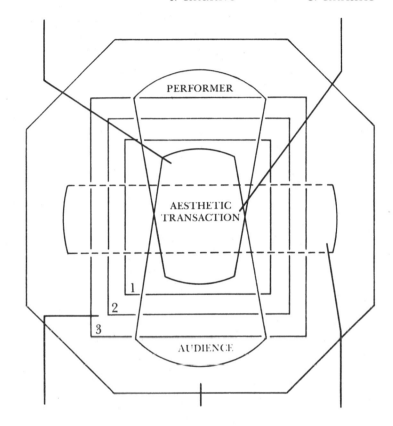

EVENTS   AESTHETIC FIELD

PERFORMANCE
TRADITION

1. Obligatory   Sociocultural Factors: Shared Knowledge of
   Performance   Technological   Genres, Acts, Roles,
2. High Expectation   Biological   Events, Themes, Norms
   of Performance   Psychological   of Interaction and
3. Optional   Historical   Interpretation
   Performance

Figure 1. An Aesthetic Transaction Model
of Artistic Verbal Performance [After Berleant]

active performer, we must recognize that each participant simultaneously plays both performer and audience roles. Likewise, we must recognize that any performer is simultaneously his or her own audience, monitoring and adapting the performance to his or her conception of how the performance should sound and look. And certainly when persons perform in solitude, they assume both performer and audience roles. Thus, the textmaker must realize that preconceived decisions about audience and performer roles may result in a recording which neglects half of a performance by including only the "performer's" words and actions. With a transactional view of performance as a process involving all participants, the textmaker will be interested in the entire transaction, not a single aspect which he or she has assumed is more significant than other parts. To illustrate the complex, reciprocal roles of audience and performer, the model shows that in the aesthetic transaction, the two spheres representing performer and audience intersect.

Performance Tradition

In contrast to Berleant's model of the aesthetic field, in which the artist, work of art, and performer are perceptually separate entities, this model contains no artist or work of art, but subsumes both in a component called performance tradition. In most experiences with artistic verbal performance, there is little sense of a creative artist separate from the performer, or a concrete fixed art object separate from the performance. In joke-telling, for example, the performer rarely knows the originator of the joke or feels compelled to cite the author of the joke, if known. The common introduction, "Have you heard the one about . . ." carries the same connotation as the expression "it is said that . . ." or "they say that . . .," implying an impersonal expression belonging to a group. And unlike a performer of literature, who feels compelled to perform with verbatim accuracy to the literary text, the performer of folklore is usually free, and often expected, to vary themes and words.

In differentiating written from oral literature, Robert Kellogg argues that even when the reader "performs" a written text, "there is still a constant authorial state of mind behind each such reading 'performance'." In contrast, says Kellogg, in oral literature, "constant behind each performance, is not the mind of an author but an ideal performance, an aspect of the tradition that is shared by performer and audience alike." According to Kellogg, the "work" of oral literature therefore has no author, since "it exists only as it is embodied in performance," and "is created anew each time it is heard."[56] A prime example of how a performance tradition, rather than a particular author, creates a story can be seen in this account of performers learning Afro-American narrative recitations: ". . . if two or three persons know the same one, one person might say part and then another person might say, 'Well, let me do the other part, I like this part,' and they do it, and another person might do it. . . . That's how they learn and find more, you know, by starting saying them around different people they don't know."[57]

The problem of authorship and fixed texts is a complicated issue, especially in literate cultures, in which folklore often enters into the written tradition, and in which written literature, such as Service's "The Cremation of Sam McGhee," circulates through oral tradition.[58] Yet even when performers learn their material from a written copy or a book, they often feel free to adapt the material to their own liking and the particular situation. For example, in the "Stagolee" tale recorded in Chapter 7, the performer said he learned his material from observing the performance of a friend who later wrote down the words for him. This manuscript version, according to the performer, came from a book called *Black Folktales* by Julius Lester. The performer had never seen Lester's book, however, and his version varies both in plot and style from Lester's. And in contrast to a performer of literature, who usually acknowledges the author of the work, this performer gave no reference to Lester in his performance. Of course, since Lester himself acknowledges that his own version is a product of oral tradition, even his rendition lacks the stamp of an authentic original.[59] Verbal art, too, frequently carries a high expectation of oral composition, as Parry and Lord's work with the Yugoslav epic singers suggests.[60] In most cases, then, the performer of oral tradition is synonymous with the creative artist; they are not separate categories.

While in literary performances, the literary text clearly exists as a fixed, concrete object which may be repeatedly activated through performance, the object status of verbal art is problematical. Certainly, the very fact that a person can say "tell me a scary story," or "tell us a joke," and a performer can comply indicates that the audience and performer share a common understanding of an entity that fits a certain genre classification. And when a person asks a performer to "tell us about the time you escaped from prison camp," or "tell the one about 'give me back my golden arm'," there is a further sense of referring to a named object which has been heard before and can be heard again. Yet the prison camp story or "give me back my golden arm" may vary greatly from one telling to the next, and no physical object can be referred to as an original work. Among aestheticians, "art object" commonly refers to a physical, concrete entity. Thus, even music, an ephemeral substance in performance, is often referred to a score to determine its authenticity and to evaluate a particular performance.[61] But since verbal art is created and circulated orally, without the mediation of a score or text, it has no object status in the usual sense of the word.

Thus, the model shows no art object, *per se*, but a circle labeled

"Performance Tradition," referring to the knowledge of genres, themes, acts, roles, events, and norms of interaction and interpretation shared between a performer and an audience. The broken line indicates the dynamic, fluid nature of a shared performance tradition. Genres and themes may change, as may performance norms of interaction and interpretation. These changes in the performance tradition, however, represent the creative choices of many performers and perceivers, not some unconscious, superorganic change of themes and motifs. When individuals assume the performer and audience roles and focus their energies in activating an item from the performance tradition, in the manner appropriate to that tradition,[62] then they are engaged in an artistic verbal performance. This performance, indicated by the intersection of performer, audience, and performance tradition, is differentiated from other modes of communication by its characteristics as an aesthetic transaction.

The Aesthetic Transaction: Qualitative Characteristics

Berleant suggests that aesthetic experience is characterized by eight qualitative characteristics—active-receptive, sensuous, immediate, intuitive, noncognitive, intrinsic, integral, and unique. To test whether these features characterize verbal art performances, we must reflect on the qualities of our own experience with such performances. A common narrative performance that most persons within our society have no doubt experienced is the scary story or ghost tale. A particular scary story that I remember telling and hearing is a tale I knew as "Give Me Back My Liver." To refresh my memory, I asked a ten-year-old girl to tell me all the scary stories she knew, and among them was a version of what I heard as a child, which she called "Johnnie I Want My Liver Back." Using this story and occasionally other genres as examples, we will examine whether Berleant's eight features characterize the aesthetic transaction in such performances, and by extension, in verbal art performance in general.

Active-Receptive. The plot of this rather ghoulish tale is simple. In the version told by the ten-year-old child, a mother tells her son to buy some liver at the store. Instead, he buys candy with the money, murders a man, and brings the man's liver to his mother. That night, when the boy goes to bed, he hears a faint voice chant "Johnnie I want my liver back. Johnnie I'm on the first step. Johnnie I want my liver back. Johnnie I'm on the fifth step." Suspense builds as the voice climbs the steps, getting louder. Finally, when the voice has climbed fifty steps, and the performer has lengthened the suspense by having the voice chant "Johnnie, Johnnie, Johnnie, Johnnie" as it opens the closet in which the boy is hiding, the performer ends the tale by startling the listener: "Johnnie,

Johnnie, Johnnie, Johnnie, BOO!" On shouting "Boo," the performer lunged at me with both hands, as if to scare me out of the mesmerization caused by the long repetitious chant.

Experience as a participant in this performance illustrates a quality present in all experiences with verbal art performance and a quality which Berleant argues is basic to the aesthetic transaction. My response could be characterized as "active-receptive"; that is, as a participant, I actively engaged my energy in the performance. As the storyteller began to build suspense through repetitions chanted in a rhythmical, quavering, mournful tone, our eyes met and we smiled. Both of us were familiar with the form of suspense being used, both anticipated the surprise ending. The storyteller continually glanced at me as she chanted the repetitions, as if trying to determine the best time to surprise me. Both of us laughed at the ending. Part of the success of the tale, as I knew from my own experience telling tales with a similar suspense-building pattern, lay in absorbing the listener in the hypnotic rhythm, building to an expected climax, and then often changing the expected climax. In this version, the storyteller expanded the action to a confrontation in the closet. Our mutual involvement in concentrating on the build-up of suspense created the sense of enjoyment we felt at the completion of the tale. Obviously, the tale's success depends on a participant willing to engage as an active listener. If the performer fails to focus the listener's attention on the performance, the story cannot work.

This active-receptive quality is similar to what Abrahams terms "receptive competence." He argues that the audience, as well as the performer, must exhibit competence: "Thus, we may distinguish between the *productive competence* of the performer and the *receptive competence* of the audience. The former recognizes that performers draw upon genres as 'an invitation to form,' utilizing conventional pattern-markers in channeling their creative energies and in terms that can be followed by the audience. The latter points to the audience's capacity to accept this invitation, their familiarity with the pattern and the markers, and their ability to bring their past experience with similarly situated performances to bear on the present experience as a means of understanding, participating in and judging what is going on."[63] In a "Knock, Knock" joke, the perceiver who fails to respond with the appropriate "Who's there?" blocks the completion of the form, and may be told by the performer, "say, 'who's there.'" In the preaching of a traditional Black sermon, audience response is crucial for the preacher to move into the chanted part of his sermon. Often, as Rosenberg points out in his book, *The Art of the American Folk Preacher*, the preacher interjects "stimulant" formulas to elicit the necessary audience response.[64]

Despite the importance of this active-receptive quality, so necessary in any face-to-face interaction, texts often record only the performer. By recording the participants' behavioral responses to the performer, our records would reflect more of the actual interchange between the performer and audience, enabling us to better comprehend how verbal art works.

Sensuous. Our active role in participating in verbal art performance, whether as performer or audience member, manifests itself in sensory features—sounds, sights, tastes, touches—giving the aesthetic transaction a sensuous quality. In arguing for the sensuous quality of aesthetic experience, Berleant objects to a long tradition in Western aesthetics of refining the aesthetic out of bodily existence into a cerebral, spiritual realm. In contrast to classical tendencies to separate the senses and keep them at a distance from art, Berleant argues that we should fully acknowledge the sensuous power of art. Further, he suggests that the sensuous experience is often perceptually integrated and nondiscrete: "Certain perceptual qualities like softness and brightness are multi-sensory, appearing to touch, taste, smell, sound, and sight. There is also the evidence of the synesthesias or intersensory effects, as when visual impressions accompany auditory stimuli."[65]

Turning to the example of the ghost tale, we can see how a performance appeals to several senses simultaneously. The auditory appeal of the chant, combined with the facial expressions of wide-eyed terror and grave seriousness conveyed the appropriate "creepiness" for a scary story. The outflung arms at the climax, coupled with the shouting and touching as the performer grabbed the listener, were especially important to the tale's success. Despite the centrality of these sensuous features, which are present in differing kinds of degrees in all verbal art performances, few texts record them.

The sensuous nature of aesthetic experience leads to a third characteristic—immediacy, which Berleant closely relates to three other characteristics—intuitive, noncognitive, and integral. All four characteristics are part of Berleant's argument that the aesthetic transaction is a direct, unmediated, precognitive or preanalytical experience. Berleant's use of the term noncognitive, however, introduces unnecessary confusion into his argument, as we will see.

Immediate. When we consider our experience with verbal art performance, we are readily aware of the immediate quality of the transaction. No intermediary interferes with our direct involvement and understanding. As Berleant says of immediacy, "art is felt with a compelling directness in which detachment, deliberation, and all other intermediate states have no place. Symbol and substitute, therefore, do not yet exist, nor does propositional truth."[66] While engaged in listening to the scary story, I felt no need or desire to search for archetypal patterns or decipher the symbolism of the liver. Rather, I directly understood the relationship between the boy's murderous act and the subsequent revenge. Yet there are times when a listener cannot comprehend a performance immediately, and these times illustrate the importance of immediacy. Sometimes, for example, after listening intently to a joke or a story, a listener will say, "I don't get it." Frequently, rather than analytically explaining the crucial relationships in the joke, the performer tries retelling it slowly, emphasizing key words. If the listener grasps the meaning of the joke in the reperformance, both performer and listener can enjoy the successful completion of the form. But when the performer must step out of the performance mode and into the role of an explicator, we feel that the transaction, now mediated by analysis and explanation, is no longer aesthetic.

Intuitive. Further explaining the immediacy of aesthetic experience, Berleant argues that intuition lies at the heart of our experience with art. Aesthetic intuition, argues Berleant, resembles what Whitehead has called *prehension*, a "seizing or grasping of something. . . ." This act is preanalytic and presynthetic: "While the activities of analysis and synthesis are largely reflective in character, aesthetic awareness takes place on a prereflective level, contextual rather than fragmented and therefore undifferentiated by any conceptual distinctions."[67]

Preanalytic. To further define intuition, Berleant introduces another characteristic, noncognitive. By cognitive, Berleant means knowledge leading to propositional truth, and art, he argues, never leads to such knowledge. Essentially, he objects to the idea that art involves reflective, analytical knowledge because such knowledge is not direct, but mediated, requiring an element of disengagement and impartiality.[68] Yet the term "cognitive" commonly applies to knowledge in general, not simply propositional knowledge, and this forces Berleant into a double bind. After claiming that art is noncognitive, he is forced to turn around and admit that there is knowledge in art, but not propositional knowledge.

Berleant's treatment of the knowledge in art, however, tends to be incomplete and definitional—a result of lumping all knowledge into one category, propositional. He fails to explain why we often feel that we have gained insights form art. Berleant admits that creating art demands a certain knowledge of craft and that a perceiver often experiences a work more fully when he understands some of the skill involved in the creation. And some arts, such as literature, he says, demand a prior knowledge of language in order to even apprehend them. But this type of knowledge, Berleant argues, "contributes to the aesthetic act and response only when it is relevant to the experience and enhances it, without deflecting attention to the cognitive rather than the appreciative."[69] If we were to reduce this statement to its tautological base, we would be left with the statement that knowledge can be in art only when it is not knowledge. The source of this confusion can be seen in the following passage in which Berleant adheres to a Platonic definition of knowledge and neglects Aristotle's definition of rhetorical knowledge:

> It is unfortunate for the development of a genuine theory of art that an intellectual model has been taken as the standard for experience since the classical age of Greek philosophy. From Plato on through the eighteenth century and into the present, all experience has been forced into a cognitive mold. Whatever did not meet the criteria of knowledge was disparaged as illusory, lowly, or otherwise inappropriate to the rational activity that is man's proper function. Aristotle, to take an influential example, began his *Metaphysics* with the famous statement, "All men by nature desire to know." Then he proceeded to account for the delight we take in our senses for their own sake by explaining that the senses, especially sight, are avenues to knowledge.[70]

But Aristotle took issue with many of Plato's ideas, and in particular, his narrow definition of dialectic. Introducing rhetoric as a counterpart of dialectic, Aristotle conceived of a type of knowledge based on probability and arrived at not through syllogistic reasoning, as in dialectic, but through enthymemes and examples.[71] This rhetorical knowledge, as opposed to dialectical, analytical knowledge, derives its proofs from ethos and pathos, as well as logos. Essentially, rhetoric deals with the "commonsense" realm of knowledge and constructs arguments based on human emotions, experiences, and assumptions.[72] In contrast to dialectic, rhetoric derives its power of persuasion from its ability to bring audiences to immediate, direct realization of knowledge.[73] This immediate type of knowledge is fully compatible with aesthetic experience and helps explain why we often feel that we have gained knowledge from art. Verbal art often seems to convey knowledge, as when a parent tells a child a fable containing a moral lesson, or someone interjects a proverb in a conversation that succinctly evaluates a situation.

Rather than using the term noncognitive to characterize aesthetic experience, we should be more specific and say that it is preanalytical. While verbal art performance imparts knowledge, the knowledge is grasped in an intuitive, immediate, and prereflective way.

Integral. The immediate, intuitive, and preanalytic qualities of artistic verbal performance lead to a concept of aesthetic form with important implications for the folklore text. Just as the aforementioned qualities describe the interaction of perceivers with a performance, Berleant's concept of "integral" form holds that artistic form encompasses a perceptual unity of perceiver and object. In contrast to object-centered aesthetics which limit artistic form to stable properties observable in objects, or what Berleant terms "analytic form," Berleant argues that we should consider the formal qualities of perceptual experience, or "perceptual form": "If art cannot be disentangled from its participation in a mode of experience without irreversibly distorting our conception of it, how then can we expect to provide an adequate treatment of form unless we expand our scope of vision to encompass the full range of aesthetic perception?"[74]

When we compare the perceptual form of various verbal art performances to the form conveyed in different folklore texts, the difference is illuminating. Although we may be quite conscious of an audience's response during a performance, not even their vocalizations appear in most texts. Even the performer's utterance may differ sharply in the text—repetitions and pauses may be removed; false starts, gestures, voice quality, and vocal dynamics eliminated. With all of these perceptual features missing from texts, analyses of verbal art are severely impoverished.[75]

Unique. Once we acknowledge the integral form of verbal art, we recognize that verbal art performances are always unique. Characterizing verbal art as unique might seem odd at first glance, since the same tale may be told by many different performers. Yet Berleant argues that "the uniqueness of art is the uniqueness of experience, not of object."[76] Certainly, the different participants and sociocultural factors in the aesthetic field of any performance guarantee that each performance is unique.

Intrinsic. A final quality by which we may distinguish artistic performance from other forms of speech communication is the intrinsic quality of our experience with performance. As participants in a performance, actively engaged in the aesthetic transaction, we focus on the performance for its own sake, not as a means to some other end. Either as performers or listeners, we surrender ourselves to the developing performance, forgetting for the time being our goals for the day and our personal concerns.

Yet to argue that performance possesses an intrinsic quality seems to be at odds with the rhetorical power of performance. It is well documented that performers often use verbal art to affect an audience or situation. The strategic use of a parable, proverb, story, or joke may affect social interaction. But if we adopt a multifunctional view of art, such as advocated by Mukařovský and Jakobson, then we can admit the instrumental potency of art while still maintaining that attention tends to focus on it for its own sake.

Paradoxically, the real power of verbal art to function instrumentally may lie in its intrinsic quality. It is precisely because the subject matter of verbal art deals with exaggerated, hypothetical, fictional, mythical, or legendary situations that it functions so powerfully as a rhetorical tool. Rather than overtly suggesting a course of action, the performer, through the apt matching of a symbolic form with a context, lets the audience infer the suggested course of action. And the aesthetic patterning that proves so pleasing to an audience, maintaining their intrinsic interest, furthers rhetorical ends by powerfully capturing their attention.

Only by engaging our attention fully on the ongoing performance can the performance be successfully realized. Performers, for example, who cannot lose their nervous self-consciousness often convey the sense that they are not really "in" the performance. And audience members who let themselves be distracted by other things show their own disengagement to the performer, who may either make a strengthened bid for their attention or terminate the performance. Prior to a performance, we can see both audience and performer begin to prepare for performance. Before the "Stagolee" performance (discussed in Chapter 7), the audience members chatted among themselves, making a good deal of noise. When the performer took the floor, putting on his microphone, the noise dimmed a little, and an audience member said loudly, "sh!" The audience members quieted down, but the performer responded, "Don't do that. Wait till I think of it first." His subsequent remarks as he prepared to perform seem to prepare both himself and the audience for performance: "Are you ready? Want to leave the door open? Can I close the door? I don't remember it. Right here's fine. If I forget it, ya'll don't laugh. You ready now?"

Sometimes when performers fail to get everyone's attention, they may break out of the performance frame and renegotiate with the audience. In a church service I recorded, the minister, shortly after beginning his sermon, was distracted by persons in the congregation. He paused, and in a solicitous tone quite different from the tone used in setting forth the scripture to be discussed, reminded the audience of the proper behavior:

> I would appreciate it if everybody would try to be as still as possible.
> That the choir member would quit paradin' and sit down that you would not attract the attention of anyone that might want to hear what the Lord's gonna speak to me this little day.
> We'll all say at the same time—
> When the Lord is gonna speak to you—you got to stop.
> God will not speak to us until he can get our attention. The Bible proved that.
> So I—I solicit your—cooperation that we might be unified to get this message.[77]

As we can see in the above samples from performances, the intrinsic quality of performance must be negotiated and maintained among participants. Far from being inherent in performance, the intrinsic quality is like the eye of a camera which must be constantly kept in focus. In a sense, the audience and performer make a tacit agreement to keep their energies focused on the performance for its own sake. But many variables influencing the performer and audience may turn this focus to other concerns.

Kenneth Pike's discussion of focus is helpful in explaining how participants can shift from attention to inattention, or from a perceptual to an analytical mode. The individual differences in focus among participants lead to an unavoidable "indeterminancy of focus" in any event. But general patterns of focus can be discerned. In a church service, for example, Pike says "there are lower limits beyond which the ordinary participant does not normally go in changing focus. If he does so, he has become an analyst, rather than a worshipper—or 'critical' rather than enjoying it."[78]

This concept of focus is complex, yet crucial to the problem of making performance-centered texts. When scholars undertake to observe and record performance, they unavoidably bring their own cultural and personal habits of focus to bear on the data. The outside observer's focus may systematically bracket out many performance features; attention may focus only on historical references or variations in plot. Although folklore texts cannot escape from reflecting the focus of their makers, we can self-consciously focus on focus, seeking to adjust our lenses to view and experience performance from the perspective of the actual participants. We will discuss this problem of focus further in the next chapter.

All of these eight qualities, then, help us to distinguish artistic verbal performance from other modes of communication. Although other modes of speech communication may have some of these qualitative features—most face-to-face communication has an active-receptive and unique quality—they are not characterized by all of these qualities: sensuous, immediate, intuitive, preanalytical, integral, and intrinsic. As George Mills, an anthropologist who also posits a qualitative definition of art says, "We may even call art communication if we remember that what is communicated is a *range* of qualities rather than a quality."[79] In delineating the qualitative features of performance, I do not mean to imply that no material or formal features distinguish performance from other modes of communication. Indeed, Jakobson, Moles, and Eco[80] offer promising approaches for investigating the semiotic structure of performance. But if we are to avoid the pitfall of murdering in order to dissect, that is, of reifying a dynamic process into a static form whose component parts somehow explain or equal the process, we must analyze performance as it is experienced. By analogy, although the skeletal remains of a human might help us distinguish it from non-humans, we would not claim that by understanding these structural features that we understand what it is to be human. Rather, to understand humanity we would need to analyze the myriad human transactions, and similarly, to understand verbal art, we would need to analyze it as an aesthetic transaction.

Other Modes of Speech Communication

Those areas of interpersonal communication in which participants do not activate a performance tradition and participate in an aesthetic transaction are represented in the model as other modes of speech communication. Many texts of verbal art, for example, may be records of other modes of communication than an aesthetic transaction. Although informants may frequently be able to gloss the content of a tale, informing the fieldworker about it, they may lack the necessary skill or context to assume responsibility for telling it in the proper manner. These cases illustrate that the performance tradition involves a knowledge of *how*, as well as a knowledge of *what*. Most Americans would not confuse the following rendition with a performance of "The Three Bears:" "There were these three bears who lived in the woods. When they went for a walk, a little girl named Goldilocks came in their house and ate some porridge. She broke one of their chairs. She went to sleep in the little one's bed. They came home and woke her up. She ran away." This text, while retaining basic plot elements, violates the norms of interaction for the performance. Any seven-year-old child would expect a performer to include the three-fold repetitions of: " 'Somebody's been eating my porridge' said the Papa Bear. 'Somebody's been eating my porridge' said the Mama Bear. 'Somebody's been eating my porridge' said the Baby Bear, 'and it's all gone'," each repetition said in a different voice quality ranging from booming bass to falsetto, to a tiny high-pitched voice.

Events

Within the aesthetic field model, the three concentric squares represent the many different events in which artistic verbal performance occurs. Some events are defined by the existence of performance—persons go to a play or a recital expecting to engage in performance. Other cultural events, as in the second square, carry a high expectation of performance. Frequently, in going to church, one expects a performance. But other interactions such as business meetings, lessons, and fellowship also occur. Going to a night club also carries a high expectation that performance might occur, but if no singer or comedian performs, the event is not a loss, as a play would be if the show did not go on. A third class of events, the great majority of day-to-day situations such as work, meals, shopping, carry little or no expectation of artistic verbal performance. Yet participants may spontaneously activate performance, as when someone during work tells a new joke, youth during recess at school tell stories and jokes, or someone during dinner tells a favorite family story. The model indicates the relative degree of expectation for performance by the size of the aesthetic transaction in relation to the size of the square. All of the elements in the aesthetic field are shaped by many sociocultural factors; thus, events, participants, and performance traditions vary from community to community.

CONCLUSION

Now that we have examined the key concepts of the performance approach in folkloristics and endeavored to distinguish performance from other modes of communication, implications for the folklore text begin to emerge. Taking as our basic premise that we value artistic verbal performance as an important cultural activity and want to record such activity in print, we assume that we want as faithful a record of that performance as possible. Accordingly, the ideal text would enable the reader to reconstitute the aesthetic qualities of the original performance, perceiving its unique, integral form as a dynamic, sensuous, aesthetic communicative process. In perceiving a performance, we are aware of its interrelationships to a particular event and specific participants; thus, in the ideal text we would want the same awareness of these situational features. Since performance is an aesthetic mode of communication, the ideal text would allow the reader to perceive the performance not simply as a communicative process, but as an aesthetic mode of communication. To satisfy these goals, the ideal folklore text must record the aesthetic transaction (manifested through observable behaviors) between the performer and audience, and be accompanied by commentary that grounds the text in its particular aesthetic field. When reading such a text, readers who have never seen the performance should be able to appreciate the performance as completely as if they were members of the performer's audience.

Naturally, many problems intercede between this ideal conceptualization of the folklore text and its realization. And this ideal, like all ideals, may only be approximated, never reached. By identifying our goals, however, we begin to see solutions. The idea, for example, that a textmaker must somehow repeat, or re-present a performance in another medium reveals the textmaker's role as a relayer, a communicator between one communication system and another. Indeed, we begin to see that the textmaker undertakes an essentially hermeneutic act of translation. The textmaker must decode an aesthetic transaction and re-encode that transaction in another medium, for another audience, so that they participate vicariously in the original performance. Once we identify the textmaking activity as that of translation, we can turn to translation theory for help in understanding the problems of translating performance to the printed page. In the next chapter, we will examine the process of translating performance, developing theoretical principles for making a performance-centered text.

4

Intersemiotic Translation From Performance To Print

Genuine translation will, therefore, seek to equalize, though the mediating steps may be lengthy and oblique. . . . The ideal, never accomplished, is one of total counterpart or re-petition—an asking again—which is not, however, a tautology. No such perfect "double" exists. But the ideal makes explicit the demand for equity in the hermeneutic process. . . . The translator, the exegetist, the reader is *faithful to* his text, makes his response responsible, only when he endeavors to restore the balance of forces, of integral presence, which his appropriative comprehension has disrupted.[1]

The preceding chapter suggests that the ideal text of artistic verbal performance would record the aesthetic transaction of the participants and be accompanied by commentary grounding the text in its particular aesthetic field. Such an ideal model of the text poses immediate theoretical and practical questions which can best be answered by approaching the textmaking process as a translation problem. The concept of "intersemiotic translation," or the translation from one kind of symbolic system to another, provides the impetus for my definition of the folklore text as an intersemiotic translation of performance to the print medium.

Before beginning this translation approach to the problems of textmaking, we must consider objections to the view of the text as a translation of performance. The first objection derives from an alternative semiotic definition of "text." The second objection, rooted in a bias against the imperfection inherent in all translating, argues that since texts cannot perfectly represent performances, they should not be made.

After answering these objections, we will formally define the folklore text. Then we will consider two important factors that determine how folklore is translated: the textmaker's conception of the nature of folklore and the audience for whom the text is intended. The problems of adapting the text to various audiences can be partially resolved by considering the characteristics of an adequate translation, three types of text styles, and the amount of information which a text can carry.

OBJECTIONS TO TRANSLATING PERFORMANCE

A Semiotic Argument for Performance as "Text"

Realizing the impossibility of perfectly translating the presentational fullness of performance to the print medium, those familiar with current semiotic literature may argue that we should define the live performance as our "text" and get on with the business of interpretation, without recording the performance into a written text. Indeed, it has become fashionable among some semioticians and anthropologists to refer to cultural events as a "text" to be "read" or interpreted by the scientist. For example, anthropologist Clifford Geertz, adopting a semiotic concept of culture, argues that culture be viewed as an "ensemble of texts,"[2] and that the anthropologist's task is to explain or interpret these texts through "thick description."[3] Similarly, philosopher Paul Ricoeur applies the term text, by analogy, to any meaningful action, and suggests that interpretation in the social sciences is analogous to text interpretation.[4]

But what appears as an innocent analogy between text and culture in Geertz and Ricoeur, takes the form of a troublesome synonym among the influential Russian Moscow-Tartu semioticians, who have expanded the common definition of text as a written message to include a wide variety of different cultural messages, from paintings, sculpture, and dance, to artistic verbal performance.

This expanded notion of text, developed in "Theses on the Semiotic Study of Cultures (As Applied to Slavic Texts)" by Lotman, Uspenskij, and others, defines text in the following way:

> 3.1.0 The concept "text" is used in a specifically semiotic sense and, on the one hand, is applied not only to messages in a natural language but also to any carrier of integral ("textual") meaning—to a ceremony, a work of the fine arts, or a piece of music. On the other hand, not every message in a natural language is a text from the point of view of culture. Out of the entire totality of messages in a natural language, culture distinguishes and takes into account only those

which may be defined as a certain speech genre, for example, "prayer," "law," "novel," and others, that is to say, those which possess a certain integral meaning and fulfill a common function.[5]

The authors further elaborate their concept of text throughout the "Theses," but in a sometimes confusing manner. As Irene Portis Winner and Thomas G. Winner aptly note in their detailed critique of the "Theses," "it is not always clear whether, in specific instances in the 'Theses,' the terms 'text' and 'message' refer only to verbal communications or whether they also refer to nonverbal communications, and whether they imply only 'cultural' texts and messages or also other texts and messages."[6]

Despite these difficulties with the expanded definition of text proposed by the Moscow-Tartu group, other scholars investigating the structure of connected discourse (or language above the level of the sentence) likewise use the term text to refer, indiscriminately, to both written and oral discourse. Such research, under a variety of names—discourse analysis, hyper-syntax, Textgrammatik, text syntax, translinguistique, semiolinguistics, and so on, has, as W. O. Hendricks says, a "common concern—the isolation of linguistic features that differentiate a coherent (connected) sequence of sentences—a text—from an agglomerate of sentences."[7] In this tradition, Hendricks uses the word "text" to refer to both oral and written compositions.[8]

Once we label a performance as a text, we will have no way of knowing whether a scholar is referring to a live performance or textual record, since both would be "texts" according to the views articulated above. A still more serious problem appears when we begin to extend the term text, whether by analogy or synonym, to apply to meaningful action or communication in general. The word text, originally from the Latin *textus,* or structure, refers in common usage to written or printed discourse: "*1 a* (1): the original written or printed words and form of a literary work. . .(2): an edited or emended copy of the wording of an original work. . . *b:* a work containing such a text. . . *2 a:* the main body of printed or written matter on a page exclusive of headings, running title, footnotes, illustrations, or margins *b:* the principal part of a book exclusive of the front and back matter. . . *c:* the printed score of a musical composition. . . ."[9] As this definition indicates, the term text bears heavy associations with printed or written discourse, and in transferring this term to oral discourse, or to nonverbal messages, we almost inevitably transfer these print-oriented, literate associations with it.

The danger is that these literate associations may fundamentally precondition our perception of performance. Before we even begin our interpretation of a performance, if we think of the performance as a "text" to be "read," we may unconsciously ignore interpreting features that fail to confine themselves to the habits of silent reading and visual literacy. For example, since the standard English orthography and typography convey little of the presentational fullness of utterance, with its paralinguistic and kinesic dimensions, we commonly conceive of the printed word as abstract, linear, disembodied, and in some cases, with greater status than the spoken word. Such preconceptions, when brought to the task of recording oral discourse, predispose textmakers to think that by recording the "words" they are recording the meaning of the utterance. Yet as current research into paralinguistcs and kinesics shows, as much as 65 percent of the social meaning of a message may be carried in nonverbal elements,[10] and often, the real import of a message lies not in "what" is said, but in "how." Although scholars, at home with print, may feel secure in assimilating all reality to a "text" to be "read," this assimilation, as Walter Ong reminds us, is a sign of our imprisonment in a literate culture:

> In his *Modes of Thought* (p. 52), Whitehead has made the point that we habitually mingle speech and writing so much that when we discuss language we hardly know whether we refer to oral performance or to written work or both. The situation is in fact much worse than Whitehead suggests. We are the most abject prisoners of the literate culture in which we have matured. Even with the greatest effort, contemporary man finds it exceedingly difficult, and in many instances quite impossible, to sense what the spoken word actually is. He feels it as a modification of something which normally is or ought to be written.[11]

My objection to expanding the term "text" to refer to performance parallels Ong's objection to using the term "oral literature" for oral performance. After showing the crippling effects of referring to oral performance as "oral literature," Ong reminds us that "our concept of oral performance has long been derived from our concept of literature despite the fact that in actuality it is literature which grows out of oral performance." In a somewhat humorous analogy, Ong argues that calling performance literature is like referring to a horse as a "four-legged automobile without wheels."[12] Surely, we can find other words than text to refer to connected discourse, meaningful actions, and messages, reserving the term text in its original sense, for anything written or printed. Rather than labeling a performance a "text" and analyzing it without the supporting evidence of a written record, we should buttress our analyses with valid written or printed texts.

The Perfectionist Argument

Others might object to making performance-centered texts on different grounds. Since no text, they might argue, can preserve or translate performance perfectly, we should work directly from the performance, without resorting to an imperfect textual intermediary. This argument against translating performance parallels arguments against translating poetry and, indeed, against the act of translation itself. George Steiner, in reviewing the history of translation in *After Babel: Aspects of Language and Translation,* notes religious and secular arguments against translation, and, in particular, against the translation of philosophy and poetry. Religious arguments center on the theme that each act of translation leads "downward" from the divine word, and secular arguments hold that there can be "no true symmetry, no adequate mirroring, between two different semantic systems." Since poetry depends so heavily on style and form, it has been particularly subject to claims of untranslatability. But as Steiner argues, "Attacks on the translation of poetry are simply the barbed edge of the general assertion that no language can be translated without fundamental loss. Formally and substantively, the same points can be urged in regard to prose."[13] When we consider that verbal art performance, like written poetry, involves subtle interplays among meaning, linguistic, and rhetorical form, but in addition, entails stylistic manipulations of nonverbal features, then it may indeed seem difficult, if not impossible, to translate performance to another medium.

Yet, the perfectionist argument that we should not translate performance because we cannot do so completely fails on several grounds. On a theoretical level, any act of communication can be considered translation, since receivers must decode the sender's message, "making sense" of it by translating it into their own frames of reference and mental sets.[14] Although cases of perfect understanding or translation between communicators may be rare or nonexistent, this does not keep us from communicating. As Steiner says, "We *do* speak of the world and to one another. We *do* translate intra- and interlingually and have done so since the beginning of human history. The defense of translation has the immense advantage of abundant, vulgar fact."[15] Even if we avoid the physical act of making a text from a performance, we still must "translate" the performance to interpret or analyze it—the only difference is that we will do so without a textual record to substantiate our claims about the performance. At least making a text gets the translation process out in the open where critics can compare claims about the performance to the textual record, and can even compare the textual record to an audio or video recording of the performance. Once we realize that translation of performance is inevitable, it makes no sense to deny it because it cannot be perfect.

Of course, it is important to recognize the limitations of translating performance to print, and we will confront the issue of untranslatability later in this work. But claims that performance cannot be translated may stem from personal biases that prevent textmakers from even experimenting with the possible. For example, Tedlock, citing Boas and Kroeber as examples, argues that some neglect of translating stylistic features "is doubtless related to a belief that style, or at least the better part of it, is simply untranslatable." Challenging this assumption, Tedlock shows cases in which linguistic style may be translated with little distortion, and adds that in the Zuni tradition, "a large part of style lies outside of what is traditionally thought of as linguistics, and I would add that even the linguistic features of Zuñi style do not create insurmountable translation problems."[16]

A DEFINITION OF THE TEXT

Once we accept the inevitability of translating performance and the value of translating performance into a text, we are faced with a host of methodological problems. First, we need a working definition of the folklore text, since, as we have seen, the dictionary definition of text spans a large area of written and printed materials. I will begin by distinguishing between a "report" and a "record" of performance and reserve the term text only for a "record" of the aesthetic transaction in written or printed media. The text must be accompanied by a "report" of the performance's aesthetic field if it is to be understood by readers unfamiliar with the live performance. In addition, I propose that the folklore text necessarily involves intersemiotic translation.

The Text as "Record" in Print or Written Media

Performance, as we saw in Chapter 3, is a mode of speech communication that involves both performer and audience in an aesthetic transaction. If we were to describe the actual behaviors observable in a performance, we would note the two-way flow of verbal and nonverbal signals exchanged between the performer and the audience. For the analyst of performance, these signals exchanged in the aesthetic transaction are the formal features comprising the performance.

There are at least two different ways that information about a performance can be recorded in print: through a "report" or a "record." In a performance report, one simply describes in one's own words, the content and/or form of the live performance. The printed report simply paraphrases the performance; it does not attempt to recreate the performance in another medium. My usage of the term report closely resembles the way Hymes uses "report" to describe a rendition in which an informant fails to assume responsibility for performance.[17]

Performance reports vary in scope and size, ranging from short synopses of a tale's plot, or a description of the performer's style and performance situation, to an extended paraphrase of the content.

In contrast, what I call a "record" attempts to preserve the formal features of the live performance in another medium. Rather than explaining, or summarizing, the record attempts to "say again" or repeat the signals constituting the live performance. In Abraham Moles' words, a record is a "transmission through time" that "preserves a message by means of printed signs, phonographic records, magnetic tapes, photography, etc."[18] Currently, two classes of performance records are available: those transmitted through film, video, and audio, and those transmitted through script or print. I will reserve the term "text" for records of performance in a written or print medium.[19] Of course, certain limitations in the channel capacity of the print medium make it impractical to record all of the signals in a performance. Yet a record, unlike a report, attempts to record systematically at least one level of signal, such as morphemes or phonemes, from the beginning to end of a performance.[20]

The advantages of limiting the term text to a record rather than a report should be apparent. Whether a report recapitulates how a narrator performed, or the content of the narrative, it is essentially a comment, not an attempt to reproduce the original message. Clearly, if our interest lies in studying artistic verbal performance, then we want as complete and close a record of it as possible. Yet texts can rarely stand alone, without some accompanying reports about the participants, the situation, and the sociocultural milieu. Indeed, in order for readers to perceive the aesthetic transaction of a performance, they must have knowledge about the aesthetic field from which it emerges. The textmaker can best present this information by framing the text with a report of the aesthetic field. Reports of performances, such as Richard Dorson's excellent descriptions of the oral styles of seven American folk narrators,[21] contain valuable information for performance studies, and I do not wish to denigrate their use. For conceptual clarity, however, it is important to maintain a distinction between a record and a report of a performance.

The Text as Intersemiotic Translation

Some contemporary textmakers, as we saw in Chapter 2, have referred to their activity as "translation." Dennis Tedlock's work, "On the Translation of Style in Oral Narrative," concerns itself with translating not only linguistic features of style, but paralinguistic and other performance features.[22] Jerome Rothenberg coins the term "total translation" for attempts at translating oral poetry which take "into account any or all elements of the original beyond the words."[23] And

Harold Scheub writes about some problems of "translation from the oral form into the written word. . . ."[24] The particular way in which Tedlock, Rothenberg, and Scheub use the term translation extends beyond the common usage of translation as referring to translating between languages. Their usage of translation complements the way oral interpreters use the term to describe their activity of performing literature. In Lee Roloff's statement that the interpreter's task is one of "translating and transforming the stimuli of written symbology into language discernible in audible and visible behavior,"[25] we can see that oral interpretation shares a complementary concern with translating performance. Interpreters seek to translate printed literature into performance, believing with Valéry, that "It is the performance of the poem which is the poem. Without this, these rows of curiously assembled words are but inexplicable fabrications."[26] Folklorists who believe that the nature of folklore lies in performance, seek to preserve this performance through translating it to print. Since this usage of the term translation may be confused with the more common meaning of interlingual translation, I will employ Jakobson's term "intersemiotic translation" to avoid ambiguity.

Jakobson suggests that translation may be divided into three classes. The first involves intralingual translation, such as defining words in the same language. The second class, interlingual translation, or "translation proper," interprets a verbal sign in one language with a verbal sign in another language. Jakobson defines the third class, "intersemiotic translation," or "transmutation" as, "an interpretation of verbal signs by means of signs of nonverbal sign systems."[27] Expanding Jakobson's definition, Eugene Nida defines intersemiotic translation as "the transference of a message from one kind of symbolic system to another": "For example, in the U.S. Navy, a verbal message may be transmuted into a flag message by hoisting up the proper flags in the right sequence. Similarly, a speech by a Kiowa chief may be transmuted into sign language without verbal accompaniment, to be understood not only by the speakers of other languages, but also by any other Kiowas who may be present.[28]

Since speech and writing employ two different kinds of symbolic systems, the former using not only acoustic signals but gestural signals as well, and the latter using only a sequence of visual signals arranged on paper, I define any movement of speech into writing, or vice versa, as an intersemiotic translation. Thus, a folklorist transcribing a performance, a linguist notating the phonemes of a speech, or an oral interpreter performing a written text are all engaged in forms of intersemiotic translation. Obviously, not all intersemiotic translations aspire to the same levels of completeness or accuracy; what is sufficient in transcribing a dictated business letter would be insufficient to transcribe artistic verbal performance—yet both texts are intersemiotic translations. Certainly one source of the difficulty in making verbal art texts is that textmakers have often taken intersemiotic translation for granted and rather mechanically applied the same procedures used in taking lecture notes or writing down a recipe to the task of recording artistic verbal performance. But by critically reflecting on the process of translating between performance and print, we should be able to improve our folklore texts.

TRANSLATION THEORY AND THE TEXT

Although Tedlock, Rothenberg, Scheub and others concern themselves with problems of translating performance, they have not developed a systematic theory of translating performance to the print medium. This is not to say that their works do not suggest individual principles which we may draw on, or that their translation efforts are not based on implicit theoretical principles. Indeed, some of their suggestions are invaluable and we will return to these later. In order to develop a performance-centered text, however, it seems best to begin by examining the processes of translating performance to print.

In turning to works on translation to see what contributions they can make toward clarifying the problems of translating performance to print, we are faced with two problems. First, most translation theory and criticism focuses on interlingual and intertextual translation. As a consequence, although some translation theory concepts may seem promising and suggestive, they must be modified to fit the special circumstances of translating performance to print. Second, although a good deal has been written about translation, much of the writing is polemical rather than analytical. In an introduction to a collection of papers given at the 1970 Conference on Literary Translation, Lewis Galantière says that translation is "not even an inexact science": "What are sometimes called rules consist in a handful of venerable clichés reiterated since the time of Cicero, Horace and the irascible St. Jerome, not one which has not been violated by one or other of the very greatest translators. What is certain is that there exists no corpus of rules on which consensus has ever prevailed. Instead, we have what I shall call *obiter dicta*—though many are not the less valid for that."[29] In a similar vein, George Steiner writes that despite the rich tradition and high caliber of translation critics, "the number of original, significant ideas in the subject remains very meager. . . . Identical theses, familiar moves and refutations in debate recur, nearly without exception, from Cicero and Quintilian to the present-day."[30]

Essentially, debate among translation critics can be reduced to two related issues: 1) emphasis on form versus concentration on content, and 2) literal versus free translating. Yet these central issues have rarely been

clearly defined and explored, according to Eugene Nida, who has
undertaken a comprehensive historical review of translation theory.
Rather, Nida finds that these issues, couched in such expressions as literal
versus free, translation versus paraphrase, are "essentially battle cries for
those who wish to defend their own work or criticize the work of
others."[31]

Obviously, rehashing arguments on the "letter" versus the "spirit" of
translation and invoking one learned translator's arguments against
another's will not help us to understand performance-to-print translation.
In recent years, however, a small but growing group of scholars have
begun to explore translation through application of insights from such
fields as linguistics, communication, anthropology, and psychology.
Although these scholars are primarily concerned with intertextual,
interlingual translation, they have advanced concepts which can be of use
in the intersemiotic translation of artistic verbal performance.

Foremost among these new translation theorists is Eugene A. Nida, a
linguist and Bible translator, whose works, *Toward a Science of
Translating*, and *The Theory and Practice of Translation* (with Charles
R. Taber), explore the problems and principles underlying the
translation of many different types of discourse, ranging from poetic,
pragmatic, religious, scientific, oral, to even translating motion pictures.
Drawing on work in structural linguistics, semantics, anthropology,
information theory, and psychology, Nida provides a descriptive analysis
of the factors influencing the translation process. Rather than providing
a set of prescriptive rules for translators, Nida analyzes the translating
activity in terms of such variables as: the different types of discourse to be
translated (e.g., poetic or scientific), the audience of the original discourse
and the varying audiences for the translation (e.g., specialists or
informally educated), and the differences between the original language
and culture and the language and culture of translation.[32] Since Nida's
methodology is dynamic, designed to specify the broad parameters and
principles governing a range of differing translation tasks, it furnishes a
framework for approaching the problems of translating folklore
performances to the print medium.

Following Nida's approach, I will suggest principles for translating
performance based on analysis of the nature of the discourse to be
translated, audience problems, and the differences in the two languages of
translation—in this case, the two media of translation, performance and
print. The analysis of these three factors greatly influences the
development of a performance-centered text style.

The Text and the Nature of Folklore

Since specific translating problems vary according to what is
translated, a first step in identifying these problems is to define the nature

of the phenomenon to be translated. After the analysis of the varying conceptions of the folklore text in Chapter 2, it should be readily apparent that how textmakers decide to present folklore is fundamentally conditioned by their view of folklore. For the greater part of the discipline's history, folklore has been treated as an artifact useful in such research as learning the linguistic structure of American Indian languages, discovering the origin and diffusion of cultural traits, and making judgments about the evolutionary status of folk groups. None of these research areas has devoted much attention to the aesthetic nature of folklore, and consequently, many of the elements constituting the integral form of performances have not been recorded. In Chapter 3, I argued that folklore's nature lies in the aesthetic transaction of performance, and accordingly, suggested that the ideal text would record this aesthetic transaction and be accompanied by commentary grounding the text in its particular aesthetic field. This performance-centered conception of folklore, then, limits our focus to a unique set of problems.

The most apparent problems stemming from this approach are the following. Since the observer cannot see inside the participants' minds, what exterior actions manifest the aesthetic transaction? What ways of recording these exterior actions most accurately portray the aesthetic transaction? Current experimentation with text styles suggests two radically different presentational forms, which I will discuss in more detail later. Not only must we determine which of these presentational forms, or mixture of these forms, provides the most valid record, we must also consider which presentational form will enable readers to experience the aesthetic transaction of the original performance. Finally, how do we furnish readers with the necessary information about the aesthetic field of the performance to enable them to participate in an aesthetic transaction with the text? I will suggest some solutions to these problems after discussing the intervening variables of audience and the characteristics of the two media, performance and print.

Although the performance approach defines our task, we must acknowledge that the study of folklore is pluralistic, and will probably always be so. Scholars will continue to approach folklore from a variety of different disciplines, not all of which are interested in the aesthetic transaction, or the situated use of verbal art. Consequently, we should consider what type of text would provide the most information for the greatest number of people. Clearly, the performance-centered folklore text would satisfy the widest audience precisely because it attempts to record the phenomenon itself, as holistically as possible. Since the performance approach values verbal art intrinsically, above and beyond its use as an index to cultural, psychological, historical, literary, or sociolinguistic research, its first task is to record and describe the performance as it emerges in a particular context. Although not all of the information recorded by the performance-centered textmaker may be needed by other scholars, that information will be available for those who want it. In addition, through attempting to record the aesthetic transaction and aesthetic field, the textmaker will enable may readers to appreciate verbal art aesthetically.

The Text and the Problems of Audience

Although the conception of folklore as artistic verbal performance defines the textmaker's goal, three different audience relationships severely constrain its realization. Beginning with the most obvious and classic problem for folklorists, we will examine the difficulties of suiting the text to the demands of different types of readers. Then, we will consider two less obvious but equally influential audience relationships—the textmaker as the reader of his or her own text, and the textmaker as an audience member to the live performance.

Adapting the Text to Readers

Adapting the text to readers is quite a knotty problem because of the widespread and diverse interest in folklore among both scholars and the public. Richard Dorson articulated this problem in 1957 when he suggested that folklorists are torn between the desire to please a public and at the same time, suit the more rigorous demands of the scientist.[33] The problem is still with us today, as Dell Hymes notes in discussing the difficulties ethnographers and anthropologists face in deciding how to present the data they collect. Often, says Hymes, ethnographers publish one book to satisfy their scientific obligations, and a second one to satisfy themselves. He goes on to argue that there is an inescapable tension between the rhetorical and literary forms considered necessary for the persuasion of colleagues, and the narrative form "natural to the experience of the work, and natural to the meaningful report of it in other than monographic contexts." Calling the alleged truthfulness and superiority of "scientific" text styles into question, Hymes suggests that: ". . . the scientific styles often imposed on ethnographic writing may produce, not objectivity, but distortion. This is an old problem—I was told of a Berkeley ethnographer in the 1930s who said, data in hand, 'Now all I have to do is take the life out of it.'"[34] Both Dorson's and Hymes' statements seem to boil down to a perceived conflict in meeting the needs of two different audiences—scientists interested in "truth" and the public interested in "art."

To a great extent, the performance approach appears to unite these two disparate audiences into one, since it insists that the "truth" of the performance is the "art." That is, the performance approach argues that to study verbal art in the most rigorous and valid manner, we must study it on its own terms, as an aesthetic transaction situated in a particular context. In terms of the performance approach, as I interpret it, a text which fails to present the aesthetic transaction, distorts performance by representing it as some other mode of speech communication. Yet even within the performance approach, a conflict between the demands of science and art can be seen in the three different text styles currently in use.

Three Types of Texts

At the present time, those who want to make a performance-centered text can choose among three text styles as precedents. The first style, building on the work of Birdwhistell, Trager, and Pittenger, Hockett, and Danehy, uses new notational symbols to record discrete elements of sound and movement in levels above the linguistic transcription.[35] The following excerpt from Birdwhistell's *Kinesics and Context* suggests a prototype for such an analytical, technical text style (see Figure 2).[36]

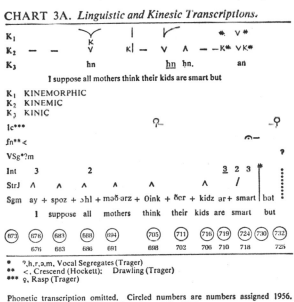

CHART 3A. *Linguistic and Kinesic Transcriptions.*

* ?,h,r,ə,m, Vocal Segregates (Trager)
** <, Crescend (Hockett); Drawling (Trager)
*** ǫ, Rasp (Trager)

Phonetic transcription omitted. Circled numbers are numbers assigned 1956. Open numbers are from edge reading of sound film 1967.

Figure 2. Birdwhistell's Linguistic
and Kinesics Transcriptions
Source: Ray L. Birdwhistell, *Kinesics and Context: Essays on Body Motion Communication.* Used by permission of University of Pennsylvania Press.

While this text is not easily accessible to those unfamiliar with
Birdwhistell's work, it is evident that Birdwhistell did not intend for it to
be understandable apart from the essay in which it is embedded. Rather
than furnishing one accompanying key to all the symbols used in the
text, Birdwhistell clarifies the meaning of symbols as he discusses various
levels of the text in the course of his essay. Indeed, before he presents this
text with both linguistic, paralinguistic, and kinesic notations, he uses
another type of text—multiple texts. That is, he presents texts of the
linguistic and paralinguistic features alone, and the kinesic features
alone.

This second style—presenting multiple texts of a performance, can be
used in several different ways. Birdwhistell uses multiple texts to clarify
various levels of performance features before presenting all of the features
in a composite text. Other users of multiple texts seem to employ them to
meet the demands of different readers. Many early ethnolinguistic
textmakers used multiple texts, including the native text, with an
interlinear and a free translation. Presumably the scholar interested in the
native language could read the interlinear text, while the general reader
could enjoy the more easily read free translation.

Still a third style of text, building on the work of Tedlock, Scheub, and
Hymes, would record a performance through a "hybrid art form."[37] As
this excerpt from a text by Toelken reveals, this presentational style is
readily understood.

> Skunk was on his way by that place to get some water.[audience:
> silent laughter, knowing looks] Ma'i was pretending he was drowned
> [audience: quiet amusement] and Skunk didn't know he was there.
> [audience: open laughter: two girls now giggling almost constantly
> throughout the rest of this scene] Skunk had a dipper, and put it into
> the water.
> "Shilna'ash." (Yellowman speaking very nasally, through side of
> mouth, lips unmoving and eyes closed, in imitation of Ma'i)
> [audience: open laughter, lasting three to four seconds].[38]

The existence of these three different ways of recording performance
again seems to place the textmaker in a dilemma. Which of these styles, or
a mixture of these styles offers the most accurate and complete record of
the aesthetic transaction? We cannot completely answer these questions
until we consider the characteristics of the two media, performance and
print. But we can begin to answer them by considering the characteristics
of an adequate translation and exploring the audience's relationship to
the text.

Characteristics of an Adequate Translation

As Nida convincingly argues, the success of any translation lies in how
well it enables its audience to understand the form and content of the

original message. He outlines four significant characteristics of an adequate translation with which "many of the most competent judges are increasingly in agreement."[39] These characteristics seem desirable for an adequate text of artistic verbal performance as well.

First, the text, like any translation, should "make sense" to the reader. Second, the text should convey the "spirit and manner" of the original message.[40] This point seems especially important for the textmaker. Since verbal art is characterized by distinctive qualitative features, any text which obscures or neglects to present these features keeps the reader from experiencing the performance as an aesthetic mode of communication.

In order to preserve the spirit and manner of the original, Nida argues that a translation should be "natural and easy" to read. This third criterion—a natural and easy form—is necessary for many reasons which we will examine in more detail later. Primarily, however, a text which is easy to read, like a good translation, carries the reader into the world of the original event with a force of immediacy. What J.B. Phillips considers the test of real translation seems to hold equally true for the folklore text: "The test of a real translation is that it should not read like translation at all."[41]

This requirement for an easy and natural style is extremely difficult to achieve, as will become clear when we examine the capacity of print to record performance. Since so many simultaneous actions occur during performance, it is hard to conceive of how they could be recorded in the two-dimensional, visual channel of print. But Nida argues that success in using an easy and natural style is essential in order to meet the fourth characteristic of a good translation: producing a "similar response." Following in the tradition of Benjamin Jowett, Alexander Souter, R.A. Knox, and Vladimir Procházka, Nida argues that the translator should aim at producing a response in his audience similar to the one produced in the audience of the original.[42] Applying this principle to the performance-centered text, I propose that a successful text should enable the audience to experience an aesthetic transaction as equivalent to the original as possible. The same qualitative features contributing to the aesthetic transaction of performance also apply to the reader's transaction with the text. If the text style is so difficult to decode that it demands laborious, analytical effort, how can the reader apprehend the performance in an immediate, intuitive, and preanalytic way?

These four characteristics of an adequate translation: 1) making sense, 2) conveying the spirit and manner of the performance, 3) having a natural and easy form of expression, and 4) producing a similar response help define how we would like readers to respond to the text. But these characteristics do not suggest any solutions to the many problems involved. Chief among the difficulties is the tension of conveying the original form of the performance without sacrificing the audience's

ability to comprehend its sense and spirit. In order to begin to solve this
and other difficulties, we must understand the forces influencing the
audience's ability to read the text with understanding. Here, Nida's
application of information theory is useful.

Information Theory and the Text

Before proceeding, it is important to stress that in using concepts from
information theory, I am, like Nida, using them as a functional analogy,
not as a basis for complex mathematical computations. Although
information theory developed out of cybernetics to explain machine
communication, its basic principles have been used to explain the
dynamics of human communication as well.[43] When information theory
is applied to human systems, it must be adapted to the nonmechanical
complexities of the human mind. Abraham Moles, who has applied
information theory to problems of aesthetic perception, argues that the
"atomistic and mechanistic" form of information theory can be made
"integrative and *Gestaltist*" when adapted to human communication.[44]

Information theory is used to measure the rate of flow of messages in a
channel. In the intersemiotic translation of performance, two types of
channels are involved: the "natural" channels of human speech and its
perception (sound, gestures, etc.) and the "artificial" channels of
"mediated" speech—print, script, film, audio and video recordings.[45]
Although I will be using information theory to examine both types of
channels and their capacities to transmit and receive artistic verbal
performance, in this chapter I will consider only the channel capacities of
the textmaker and the readers of the text.

Several concepts from information theory have direct application to
translation theory, according to Nida. First, we must understand that the
"information" communicated by any message is "a measure of the
unpredictability of the signals which are given." That is, information "is
largely equated with unpredictability." It follows that the greater the
unpredictability of a message, the greater the channel must be to transmit
and decode the message: "In ordinary language, this means that one can
readily understand a message which is commonplace, but it takes much
greater decoding effort to comprehend a message which is unusual,
unpredictable, and strange."[46]

In order to increase the efficiency of communication and minimalize
chances of distortion, languages "tend to be about 50 per cent redundant."
This redundancy seems to reflect "a kind of equilibrium between the
unexpected and the predictable," according to Nida. In addition to
linguistic redundancy, Nida argues that any communication event
contains a tremendous amount of cultural redundancy: " . . . the original

receptors were presumably acquainted with the source, knew something of his background, understood a good deal about the circumstances of the original message, and were full members of the linguistic and cultural community involved in the communication."[47]

Since the readers of a translation lack this familiarity with the cultural context, Nida argues that a literal translation "inevitably overloads" the message, so that the average receptor cannot understand it with ease or efficiency: "What may have been quite satisfactory in the source language needs to be 'drawn out' in the receptor language if the two messages are to be equivalent in terms of information theory."[48]

Adjusting the Text to the Audience. To clarify these concepts, we can adapt three of Nida's figures to show how information theory applies to the translation of performance to print.[49] In the original communication event, as Nida suggests, there would be a considerable amount of "fit" between the message and the decoder's channel, or in this case, between the performance and the audience's channel.

Figure 3. Original Performance Event [After Nida]

Participants in the live performance, familiar with the norms of the performance tradition, can readily comprehend the form and content, and even focus their attention on the fine nuances of interpretation which a skilled performer might add.

Once the textmaker abstracts a performance from its native setting and presents it to outsiders, the message can no longer be expected to fit automatically the audience's capacity to decode it. Lacking familiarity with the performance tradition, the outsider's channel capacity may be too narrow to receive the original performance easily. Either the audience must be adjusted to the culturally unfamiliar message, or the translated performance adjusted to the audience. In the literal translation, which attempts to "pack the same amount of information into substantially the same length of message," Nida argues that "it is inevitable that the linguistic awkwardness of the forms will increase the 'communication load' or 'information' in such a message."[50]

In intersemiotic translation, one type of "literal" translation would be a text style such as that of Birdwhistell's composite analytical text, which segments and layers the many performance signals so that one can read the words and accompanying gestures and other features simultaneously. To accomplish this translation, new symbols and reading habits have to be introduced into the "receptor language" of print. The average reader's unfamiliarity with these new forms creates a sort of "linguistic awkwardness," making the translated performance seem forbiddingly complicated. The translated performance text appears "wider" in the literal intersemiotic translation, while the decoder's channel capacity appears "narrower."

Figure 4. Literal Intersemiotic Translation [After Nida]

It is, of course, possible to insist that readers should invest the time and effort necessary to decode such a text style. But as Nida says of the same argument applied to literal interlingual translation, "a really satisfactory translation should not impose that sort of burden on the receptor." If the translation is too hard, he continues, the reader "is likely to give up from discouragement or to feel that the results of his efforts are not proportionate to the investment of time and trouble."[51]

In order to avoid overloading the message, Nida suggests that it is necessary to "draw out" or stretch the message by building into it "the necessary redundancy, so as to make it equivalently meaningful."[52] The translated message must be "adjusted" to the form of the receptor language. By analogy, I propose that a performance-centered text must be adjusted to the print medium, as well as to the receptor culture.

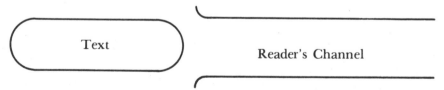

Figure 5. Adjusted Intersemiotic Translation [After Nida]

Just how to adapt a performance-centered text to the print medium, and to the readers' capacities to comprehend it, is the crux of the issue. It is not difficult to see that some verbal art texts have been so "adjusted" to readers' tastes that they misrepresent the original performance. For example, Frank Cushing's text of the Zuni Deer Boy tale seems to adjust the performance by adding stylistic devices, moralistic passages, and explanatory elements which are foreign to Zuni culture, but which make the tale more acceptable to a European-based culture.[53] These additional elements, however, make it difficult to distinguish the original narrator's discourse from the translator's. Since the performance approach values the cultural uniqueness of performance, we can see the tensions this information theory view of translation introduces. How can the text faithfully represent the original performance, and at the same time, be adjusted so as to "fit" the reading audience's capacity to comprehend both the sense and the spirit of the original?

Defining the Audience. Obviously, since audiences differ in their educational backgrounds and abilities, it is necessary to specify the types of readers for which the text is designed. For the performance-centered text which this work advocates, the audience includes both formally trained folklorists and interpretation scholars interested in artistic verbal performance, as well as educated readers, with no formal training in these fields, but who nevertheless have an interest in the verbal art forms of various cultural groups. In evaluating the merits of the three types of texts—a highly technical composite style modeled after that of Birdwhistell, multiple texts, or "a hybrid art form" modeled after texts by Tedlock or Toelken, information theory and the characteristics of an adequate translation can offer some initial guidelines.

Overloading the Text. The text, whether read by an average reader or a scholar, should not overload either's capacity to participate in the performance's aesthetic transaction. If a text tries to convey too much unsynthesized information, it will force the reader into the task of analysis and synthesis. Indeed, to decode the excerpt from Birdwhistell's composite text, one is forced to read each notation, figure out what movement or sound it refers to, and then add several of these notations into the complex action. While the scholar might have more of an interest than the average reader in going to all this trouble, the analytical focus necessary for such a reading precludes an immediate, sensory, and preanalytical perception of the performance. One might argue that such an analytical, atomistic text style provides a more scientifically sound record of the performance, but there are severe difficulties with this approach—as my discussion of current approaches to kinesics description will show. Here, it is sufficient to point out that the text, if it is to represent an aesthetic transaction, must maintain the type of perceptual "focus" employed by a participant engaged in an aesthetic transaction. One can hardly be expected to appreciate the spirit and manner of the original performance through a text which mechanically records minute particles of behavior, but fails to synthesize them into meaningful, sensuous action.

The technique of using multiple texts suggests one way of stretching the original communication so as to better fit the reader's capacity to decode it. This technique has appeal to those interested in the scientific study of specific codes. Certainly one runs less risk of overloading a text by segmenting features into several different texts, such as a text for kinesic features, a text for paralinguistic features, and a text with phonetic pronunciation. While multiple texts are well-suited for such purposes, they do not provide an answer to the central problem posed by this work—how to convey a performance as an aesthetic transaction with perceptual qualities. Two important goals for the performance-centered text are to convey the spirit and manner of the performance and to produce a similar response in the audience. Neither goals can be reached through multiple texts. It is difficult to grasp the gestalt of a performance when it is broken up into separate texts. The real challenge is to develop a way of translating several levels of information—linguistic, paralinguistic, kinesic, and so on, in such a way that readers can perceive their interaction clearly.

Let me stress that I am not arguing against using analytical methods in the textmaking process. Indeed, the textmaker will find repeated analysis of the performance into component parts useful in discovering and selecting stylistic patterns to record. But as we will see, the textmaker cannot be content to end the process by presenting only an analytical form. Instead, like the translator of a foreign language, the textmaker must move from analysis to synthesis, recognizing that the meaning of discourse is greater than the sum of its parts.

Underloading the Text. While it is possible to overload a text with too much information, it is also possible to "underload" it, and convey so little information that the readers become bored. Certainly, a text which records the frequent repetitions in a tale, but without the accompanying changes in tone and volume, leaves out the very information that makes these repetitions aesthetically interesting. As Tedlock argues, when the changes in amplitude are restored to passages with repetitions, we discover that nothing is ever said twice in the same way. In this excerpt from a tale translated by Tedlock, the phrases within parentheses are said in a softer voice:

> At that moment his mother
> embraced him, (embraced him).
> His uncle got angry, (his uncle got angry).
> he beat

    his kinswoman
    (he beat his kinswoman).[54]

Perhaps the criticisms of verbal art as banal, simple, too redundant, and of limited value stem partly from texts that fail to record enough aesthetic information. Obviously one has to find a balance between presenting so much information that the text is no longer intelligible, and so little information that it is no longer interesting.

Evaluating the Information Load. How can it be determined whether a text is overloaded or underloaded with information from the original performance? Nida suggests that one way of judging the communication load and one of the best tests of a translation is to measure the mistakes and hesitations in oral reading. He argues that "if those points at which the average reader hesitates or makes an incorrect choice of a word are carefully observed, it is very likely that these points mark an abrupt rise in communication load."[55] In the special case of translating artistic verbal performance, I propose that one way to evaluate a text's information load is through oral interpretation. The textmaker can evaluate the information load by asking several persons unfamiliar with the original performance to perform the text. These persons should have had some experience or training in performance of literature. By comparing the various performances of the text to the film or video recording, and interviewing the performers, the textmaker should be able to judge how clearly and easily the text conveys the form and content of the original performance. Just as oral interpretation can be used to reveal a person's understanding of literature, it can be used to reveal a person's understanding of a performance-centered text.

Of course, readability is only one of the demands that we make of folklore texts. Whether a textmaker overloads or underloads a text is largely influenced by two other audience relationships: the textmaker as his own audience, and the textmaker as an audience to the live performance.

The Textmaker as Audience to the Text

Like any writer, the textmaker may sometimes forget that other readers do not share his or her same field of experience. If the textmaker lacks sensitivity to those readers unfamiliar with the culture and the participants in the performance, he may put too much information in the text. Although the textmaker's prior experience with the performance may make it easy for him or her to read an elaborate scheme of notations easily, outsiders lacking this experience may find the text obscure and difficult. As long as only the textmaker reads the text, any type of private notational system may be used. But if the text is intended for readers unfamiliar with the live performance, more care must be taken in choosing a presentational style.

Paradoxically, the same familiarity with the live performance can lead to underloading the text. This tendency to furnish insufficient information is perhaps the more common. On reading a bare transcription of the words alone, the textmaker's memory of the live performance may enable him or her to fill in the missing tones and gestures. While the text may seem charged with life to the textmaker, it is likely to appear rather lifeless to those without a similar memory of the live performance.

The Textmaker as Audience to the Performance

A final cause of underloading the text stems from the textmaker's perception of the live performance. The textmaker is usually an outsider to the group being recorded and may lack familiarity with the performance tradition. If so, it may be difficult for the textmaker to even perceive significant aesthetic patterns. For example, many Afro-American performances are marked by a "call-response" pattern in which the audience is expected to punctuate the performance with audible responses. A textmaker unfamiliar with this tradition might consider such audience response as "noise," or insignificant information, and omit it from the text. Or, as Tedlock has noted, a performer might strategically interrupt a narrative by puffing on a cigarette, with each interruption designed to build suspense.[56] Yet, the textmaker, lacking sensitivity to the narrator's performance style, may not even transcribe these important gestures. Certainly, the textmaker should strive to acquire the "cultural redundancy" to perceive the event from an emic point of view. Much has been written on fieldwork techniques for acquiring familiarity with a culture, and it is beyond the scope of this work to discuss these techniques. If the initial film, video, or sound recording (from which a text is made) is to capture adequately the key participants and elements in the aesthetic transaction, the person making the recording needs to have a minimal knowledge of where to focus the recording equipment. As Jean Rouch, a noted ethnographic filmmaker says, "the decisive factor" in making a good film is that "the ethnographer must spend a long time in the field before beginning to shoot. This period of reflection, apprenticeship, and mutual awareness might be quite long. . . ."[57]

CONCLUSION

In this chapter we have laid the preliminary groundwork for a translation approach to the problems of textmaking. Defining the text as a "record" in the print medium helps avoid the confusion resulting from a semiotic definition of the performance itself as a text. Viewing the text as an intersemiotic translation clarifies the textmaker's task of translating the integral presence of performance to the print medium.

Since the textmaker's conception of the nature of folklore determines how he or she will translate a performance, we have defined the textmaker's task as one of *recording* the aesthetic transaction and *reporting* the aesthetic field. In order to enable the audience to understand the form and content of the original performance, the text should have the characteristics of an adequate translation: 1) make sense, 2) convey the spirit and manner of the performance, 3) be natural and easy to read, and 4) produce a similar response. The same qualitative features contributing to the aesthetic transaction of performance also apply to the reader's transaction with the text.

Since translating performance often demands crossing cultures as well as media, it is difficult to convey the original form of the performance without sacrificing the audience's ability to comprehend its sense and spirit. We have defined the specific audience for the performance-centered text as one including not only folklorists and interpretation scholars, but also educated readers with no formal training in these fields, who nevertheless, have an interest in artistic verbal performance. This broad definition of audience, which includes both the scientist and the educated public, seems well-suited to the performance approach. Yet choosing a text style, or styles, that will best suit the demands of both scholars and the public is difficult.

By applying concepts from information theory, we clarified the sources of this difficulty and suggested some initial solutions. In order to avoid overloading or underloading the information level of the text, it must be adjusted to the form of the receptor media, as well as the receptor culture. One way of evaluating the information load is through having other readers perform the text. This act of restitution, or second intersemiotic translation from print to performance, should enable the textmaker to judge how clearly and easily the text conveys the form and content of the original performance.

Our considerations of the information load, as well as the characteristics of an adequate translation, led us to reject the use of the analytical, composite text. While this style may suit specialized readers, it is not only difficult to decode, but it fails to synthesize minute particles of sound and movement into meaningful action with its attendant perceptual qualities. Although the technique of multiple texts lessens the information load of any one text, it fails to synthesize the gestalt of a performance.

Although a third potential text style, the "hybrid art form," is more easily read than the analytical, composite text style, we have not yet evaluated its potential as a vehicle for recording performance. Before choosing any notational symbols or presentational forms, we must examine the two media of intersemiotic translation. The next chapter discusses the signals and channel capacities of performance and print in order to provide a rational basis for selecting *what* to record and *how* to record it.

5

Analysis of Source and Receptor Media: Performance and Print

In interlingual translating, we expect a translator to have a knowledge of both languages. Indeed, Nida suggests that an important step in translating is to analyze the characteristics of the source and receptor languages. Similarly, the textmaker, as a translator from one medium to another, needs to know the characteristics of the source and receptor media. The source, artistic verbal performance, is a multichanneled medium, capable of transmitting information through all the senses. In contrast, the receptor medium, print, conveys information only through the visual channel. As the subsequent discussion illustrates, the complexity and number of signals transmitted in performance and the severely limited channel capacity of print, make it impractical and unproductive to insist that the textmaker mechanically record all the signals present in performance. Some principles of selection are needed if the text is to present performance in an aesthetic mode. If the textmaking process is to be rational rather than left completely to intuition, these selection principles should be based on a knowledge of the signals and channel capacities of performance and print.

Before proceeding, I should stress that in the following analysis, my purpose is simply to describe the signals and channels present in the two media, not to specify which signals should be recorded, or how. Since work on nonverbal communication is not widely known, and since so many divergent approaches exist, I will critically review the work in this area to abstract principles of most value in translating performance. The discussion of the structural linguistic and naturalistic observation approaches to kinesic description and the sections on digital and iconic print projections are particularly important.

SOURCE MEDIUM: PERFORMANCE

As in any other face-to-face interaction, a performer and audience transmit communication signals through any or all of the five senses—sight, sound, touch, taste, and smell. These five senses comprise the primary sensory "channels" through which individuals receive signals. (The term channel simply means any material system which conveys a message from sender to receiver). Performances vary in the number of channels used. In a Catholic Communion service, the ritualized performance involves all five senses—the sound of scripture, sight of vestments, wine, bread, and so on, the smell of wine and incense, the taste of bread and wine, and the touch of the sacraments being administered. In contrast to the full sensory appeal of Communion, a ghost story told at night between children lying in bed may use only one channel—the aural. Some riddles or stories, in addition to the aural and visual channels of the participants' voices and gestures, involve touch between the performer and audience. For example, the success of a simple "catch" riddle in which one person asks, "Did you get the letter I sent you?" the respondent says "No," and the person replies, "Must have forgot to stamp it" as he "stamps" his foot down on the respondent's toes, depends heavily (and perhaps painfully) on the tactile contact between the two participants.

As these few examples of the varying channels employed in different performances illustrate, it would be an oversimplification and misrepresentation to define verbal art as employing simply aural, or aural and visual channels of communication. Yet as we saw in Chapter 2, most folklore texts record only a limited portion of the signals conveyed through the aural channel—phonemes, morphemes, and a few terminal markers represented by question marks, periods, and exclamation points. Yet the aural channel contains signals other than words—signals that can now be recorded through progress in paralinguistics. And research on other communicative channels, particularly the visual channels of gestures and facial expressions, indicates that these signals too can be recorded and analyzed. We will examine the primary channels used in performance, discussing the characteristics of the signals transmitted through them, and the interrelationships between them. Our examination begins with the aural channel, with its linguistic and paralinguistic dimensions. Then, we look at the visual channel, subdivided into kinesic, artifactual, and proxemic dimensions, and conclude with the tactile and olfactory channels.

Aural Channel: Linguistic
and Paralinguistic

Our experience in everyday spoken interactions points to the complexity of speech. We know that as listeners, we not only listen to words and their arrangement into phrases and sentences, but to the way in which these words are uttered—the particular rhythm, intonation, stress, voice quality, and tone of voice used by the speaker. In many cases, these extralinguistic, or so-called "paralinguistic" features may have more import for us than the words themselves. For example, simple informative sentences such as "Dinner is ready" or "Time to go to bed" must often be recouched in an emphatic, perhaps threatening tone before the hearers will react to the information by coming to the table or going to bed. In order to better understand the aural channel and its signals, it is helpful to break speech into its constituent parts. To begin with, let us refer to Kenneth L. Pike's excellent diagram of the layers of structure in speech.[1]

According to Pike, the signals composing speech are not linked together linearly, but are layered like an onion, with the various layers of form accompanied by concomitant layers of meaning. Within these layers of form, Pike identifies two distinct groups—those whose organization utilizes "systematic" contrasts and those which utilize "gradient" differences. To define the difference between these two groups, Pike gives the following illustration:

> The sounds, for example, have a limited number of contrastive types—phonemes—with a limited number of sequences in which they may be found within words; there is no infinite number of significant sounds. English intonation, also, has systematic contrasts, in that it is built up of contours which in turn are based upon a limited number of contrasts, the four relative pitch levels. On the other hand, voice quality in its various characteristics seems to be largely gradient—since there is no significant limited number of degrees of harshness, or resonance, for example.[2]

Within the layers organized by systematic contrasts, Pike identifies two subgroups: the "linear structure" and "superimposed" features. Inside the "linear structure," according to Pike, we have three layers of form: phonemes, morphemes, and words. Superimposed on these layers, Pike identifies systematic contrasts of lexical stress, four contrastive pitch levels, intonation contours with internal structure, and contrasts of rhythm, pause, and sentence stress.[3] These suprasegmental phonemes are sometimes called "prosodic phonemes."

Modifying the linguistic structure are certain extralinguistic, gradient features which convey important information about the speaker's sex, age, social status, and attitudes. Among the gradient features Pike identifies are general type of utterance—song, whisper, falsetto, and so on; general modification of key—pitch gap, rate, loudness, abruptness, crescendo, decrescendo, and so on; and general quality of harshness, resonance, etc.[4]

Since Pike developed his model of the layers of structure in speech in 1945, research has refined our understanding of the suprasegmental and gradient features. Some linguists recognize twelve suprasegmental phonemes.[5] The seven intonational suprasegmental phonemes consist of four pitch levels and three terminal contours. In these terminal contours, the final segmental phonemes and pitch level are either retained slightly at the same pitch level; raised slightly, or lowered slightly. The five nonintonational suprasegmentals consist of four degrees of stress and one juncture.[6] In recent years, the so-called gradient characteristics to which Pike refers have been further described and analyzed under the rubric of "paralinguistics."

Working with Henry Lee Smith, Jr., Norman A. McQuown, and Ray L. Birdwhistell, George L. Trager defined the term paralanguage and developed a tentative notational system for describing paralinguistic features. In "Paralanguage: A First Approximation," Trager breaks the act of speech into three categories: *voice set, vocalizations,* and *voice qualities.* The latter two categories, *vocalizations* and *voice qualities,* he terms paralanguage. By voice set, Trager refers to the physical and physiological characteristics of voice from which such cultural identifications as sex, age, state of health, body build, status, and location are derived. After describing a speaker's particular voice set as a backdrop for measurement, the analyst describes the speaker's vocalizations and voice qualities that are found in systematic association with language.[7]

Vocalizations are noises or aspects of noises not having the structure of language. Vocalizations can be divided into three kinds: vocal characterizers, vocal qualifiers, vocal segregates. Vocal characterizers are noises one may "talk through," such as laughing and crying, giggling, snickering, whimpering, sobbing, yelling, whispering, moaning, groaning, whining, belching, and yawning. Modifying these vocalizations, as well as large or small stretches of language, are the vocal qualifiers of intensity, pitch height, and extent. These qualifiers vary in range, with intensity extending from overloud to oversoft; pitch height ranging from overhigh to overlow; and extent varying from drawling to clipping. A third kind of vocalization, vocal segregates, refers to such sounds as the English "uh-huh" for affirmation, "uh-uh" for negation, the "uh" of hesitation, and other sounds outside the ordinary phonological patterns of a language.[8]

In addition to vocalizations, paralanguage consists of voice qualities which modify both language and vocalizations. The voice qualities identified by Trager include pitch range, vocal lip control, glottis control, pitch control, articulation control, rhythm control, resonance, and tempo. Each quality may range in degree between polar extremes; for example, vocal lip control varies from a heavy rasp of hoarseness through a slight rasp to various degrees of openness. Trager suggests a tentative group of symbols to use in transcribing all the paralinguistic features.

In addition to Trager's work, major research on paralinguistics includes that of David Crystal, J. C. Catford, and David Abercrombie.[9] The best synthesis of this research can be found in Howard R. Martin's *The Prosodic and Paralinguistic Analysis of Dramatic Speech: A Practical System*.[10] While Martin broadly follows Trager's system, he includes clarifications and modifications based on other paralinguistic research. Moreover, Martin offers a simple taxonomy of paralinguistic variables in an effort to provide a perceptually-based description of dramatic utterance. He provides a simple notation for each paralinguistic feature. Folklorists will find Martin's work useful in alerting them to the variety of paralinguistic features available to a speaker.

Knowledge of how a performer manipulates paralinguistic variables can provide an indispensable tool for differentiating a performance of verbal art from a mere report or paraphrase. When John H. McDowell asked a Quechua informant to report the content of a story and then to perform it as he would to his friends, he noted a strikingly different paralinguistic style between the two versions. In the reported version, the informant used a "deadpan intonation," sometimes subsiding into "a virtual mutter." Weak accentuation and stress, a very thin voice quality, relaxed articulation, and a leisurely rate with little or no acceleration characterized the report. In contrast, in the performed version, the informant used thick resonance, strong accentuation, precise articulation, a wide pitch range, and an insistent tempo.[11]

Now the aural channel is quite elastic, and at the same time that it transmits purely referential information, it may be "stretched" through particular configurations of linguistic and paralinguistic features to convey information about: 1) a speaker's membership in a group, 2) his individual idiosyncracies, and 3) his changing moods and states. David Abercrombie terms such nonlinguistic information "indexical features," and labels the three aforementioned kinds of information "regional indices," "idiosyncratic indices," and "affective indices," respectively.[12] The regional index of dialect, the particular idiosyncracies that distinguish one performer's style from another's, and such features as rate, intensity, and volume, which a performer may vary to indicate changing emotions, can convey important aesthetic information. Yet too often, textmakers fail to record these indices, or worse, falsify these indices through stylistic embellishments such as "eye dialect," which they think suit some preconceived ideal of what constitutes "folksy" or "quaint" speech.

Visual Channel: Kinesic, Artifactual, and Proxemic

The aural channel rarely functions in isolation from other channels. We see a performance as well as hear one: indeed, what we hear is often conditioned by the visual signals that supplement and modify speech. Yet in contrast to the aural channel, the communicative signals of the visual channel have frequently been ignored by folklorists, or relegated to that slippery catch-all category, "context." The various gestures and movements of the participants (kinesics), the objects used in the performance (artifactual) and the participants' use of space (proxemics), rarely receive more than cursory treatment.

This lack of recording visual signals is understandable, however, when we consider the incredible complexity of sensory input transmitted through the visual channel and the still fledgling status of the modern scientific study of nonverbal communication. Currently there are several conflicting approaches to the study, and as a result, the burgeoning literature on the subject is perplexing and often full of contradictions. Unlike linguistics, no widely accepted notational system, such as the alphabet or the IPA exists to transcribe these signals to print. Indeed, as Albert Scheflen points out, the critical problem in publishing studies of nonverbal communication is to find a way to describe nonverbal behavior: "Many events and behaviors in communication are almost entirely outside the realm of language and consciousness. There are no words for them, and these infrasystems of behavior are so complex that few readers will wade through a systematic description of their integration. Thus, intricate nonlinguistic behaviors must be transformed into the system of speech and metabehavior, and the major effort of this research and others like it has been, not the detailed observation, but the search for a way to tell what the slowmotion analysis of a film has revealed."[13]

The problem of description, as the subsequent discussion illustrates, is closely connected with the problem of interpreting the meaning of nonverbal signals. The interrelated issue of description and meaning is especially important for the textmaker, who seeks to record the formal signals of a performance in such a way that they recreate in the reader an aesthetic transaction equivalent to the original.

Kinesics: Approaches to Description and Meaning

Most nonverbal communication studies center on kinesics, a term popularized by Ray L. Birdwhistell for the study of how bodily movements communicate. At the present time, body motion studies proceed under six different models: 1) choreographic, 2) acrobatic, 3) expressive behavior, 4) external variable, 5) structural linguistic, and 6) naturalistic observation. Each model has a different approach to description and meaning, not all of which are suited to the study of artistic verbal performance.

In delimiting the field of kinesics studies to those of use to the textmaker, we can dismiss those approaches based on choreographic and acrobatic models. In the choreographic model, body motion is described in terms of the skeletal musculature as it moves in space. Epitomized by Rudolph Laban's system for recording dance, Labanotation,[14] the choreographic model records the visual result of movement in space. Since this model does not concern itself with the interaction of speech and movement, it is not well-suited for the holistic performance-centered perspective. Like the choreographic model, the acrobatic model, a term coined by Norbert Freedman for Paul Bouissac's approach in *La Mesure des Gestes,* considers movement in abstraction, unrelated to its social use or interaction with speech. Bouissac, who strives for "the mathematization of body movements as construed in a volume of three-dimensional space so that behavioral sequences can be delineated as successive volumes," treats movement as an end in itself.[15]

Still another approach, called Effort-Shape Analysis, seems to be, on first glance, of potential use to the textmaker. Also developed by Rudolph Laban, this approach follows an *expressive behavior* model. Its chief proponents, Irmgard Bartenieff and Martha Ann Davis, claim that effort-shape: "1) is a replicable technique for describing, measuring, and classifying human movements; 2) describes patterns of movement which are constant for an individual and distinguish him from others; and 3) delineates a behavioral dimension related to neurophysiological and psychological processes."[16]

Effort-shape has been used by folklorist Alan Lomax as part of his choreometrics research on the relationship of dance style and culture. As used by Lomax, the system does not attempt to record the complex movements of a dance performance. Rather, it rates dance movements "in extremely general qualitative terms."[17]

Indeed, Effort-Shape is ill-suited for recording artistic verbal performance. It does not aim to record the actual body movements used, nor does it record these movements in conjunction with speech. Instead, it describes a person's movement patterns in terms of the parameters *gesture-posture, gathering-scattering* (shape flow) and *free-bound* (effort flow): "One characteristic pattern of this woman was a bilateral forearm gesture widening and narrowing without effort dynamics. Frequently her hand gestures were indirect and bound opening and widening, fully exposing the palms. . . ." Each parameter suggests correlated psychological states and neurophysiological factors. Thus, the above excerpt from an effort-shape analysis is accompanied with this interpretation: "After several weeks of seeing the hand gesture of opening and exposing the palm, the effort-shape observer felt that, quite literally, it was an exposing and offering of herself."[18] While this method might be of some use in making a *report* about a performer's movement style, it does not serve our purpose of making a textual *record*.

A fourth research model, the "external variable" tradition, is of little use in translating performance. The "external variable" method typically isolates one variable, such as facial expression, and then relates it to an external variable, such as personality.[19] Through rating scales, or check lists, observers describe behavior in terms of predetermined categories. While these procedures are efficient, they do not record and preserve the behavior itself. As Barker and Wright argue, the "one great deficiency" with such procedures is that they "do not preserve the complexities, the interdependencies, and the continuity of behavior and situation."[20]

In contrast to the aforementioned models, the last two models, the *structural linguistic* and *naturalistic observation*, offer distinct contributions to translating performance.

The Structural Linguistic Model. The structural linguistic model of kinesic research treats body motion as culturally patterned behavior and seeks to describe the structural units of this behavior. It should be no surprise that the same scholars instrumental in expanding the study of language to include paralinguistic features were also instrumental in formulating approaches to kinesics study based on the methodology of structural linguistics. Linguists Henry Lee Smith, Jr., George L. Trager, Kenneth Pike, and Charles Hockett, anthropologists Edward T. Hall, Gregory Bateson, and Margaret Mead, and psychologists R. E. Pittenger, J. J. Danehy, and Roger Barker—all heavily influenced the pioneering work of Ray L. Birdwhistell.

Using a structural linguistic approach, Birdwhistell has laid important foundations for kinesic research. As an anthropologist, Birdwhistell approaches kinesics as a culturally patterned system; he is concerned with "the learned and visually perceptible shifts in the body which contribute to the peculiar communication systems of particular societies." With the premise that nonverbal communication is an ordered and interdependent activity, Birdwhistell sees the primary task of the anthropological kineticist as that of "developing a methodology whereby units and subsystems can be abstracted and manipulated." Birdwhistell's research is based on four methodological canons: 1) establishing and maintaining a given level of analysis, 2) isolating units for manipulation, 3) establishing the independent identity of these units by contrast analysis, and 4) weighing the analytic value of these newly established units by examining the contexts in which they regularly or never appear.[21]

Through repeated viewings of slow-motion filmed interactions, Birdwhistell has delineated four hypothetical units of movement: the kine (kineme), the kinemorph, the complex kinemorph, and the kinemorphic construction. All of these units are based on emic observations of North Americans; that is, they are units that members of North American speech communities recognize as having contrastive value. For example, Birdwhistell's definition of the first and smallest unit, the kine, emphasizes its emic status: "A kine is an abstraction of that range of behavior produced by a member of a given social group, which, for another member of that *same social group*, stands in perceptual contrast to a different range of such behavior" (my italics). In the case of an eye wink, the majority of Americans do not seem to distinguish between a right or left eye wink. Thus, Birdwhistell terms these two variations of the same kine, "kine variants," and calls a class of kine variants a *kineme*.[22]

These smallest units, the kines or kinemes, are combined in the next unit, the kinemorph. The kinemorph is an assemblage of kines in a given body area, such as the head region, or the trunk region, forming a complex in which all the components are not only necessary for the production of the unit, but found within a given time frame. To establish that a group of movements is a kinemorph and not some arbitrary grouping of kines, Birdwhistell not only relies on informant reports that "'these movements fit together,'" but finds transition devices such as a pause, or a shift to a different body area, that mark its start and finish and establish its unitary function in larger contexts. The third unit, the complex kinemorph, involves kines from two or more areas that form a complex "which, under contrast analysis, behaves precisely like a kinemorph."[23]

The largest unit, the *kinemorphic construction*, is roughly analogous to the sentence and is made up of combinations of kinemorphs and or kines. Birdwhistell has abstracted three different types of construction. The simplest, the *kinemorphic combination*, is composed of two or more kinemorphs, either in parallel or in series. The *complex kinemorphic complex combinations* consist of two or more complex kinemorphs. The *kinemorphic compound* consists of complex kinemorphs plus single kinemorphs.[24]

Just as a method is needed to distinguish a sentence from a phrase, the kineticist must find a way to delimit the unitary nature of a kinemorphic construction. To do so, Birdwhistell moves to a larger field of body movements which he terms action. Since his research has not discovered any kinesic system comparable to linguistic grammar and syntax, Birdwhistell hypothesizes that the "meaningful segmentation and binding together of kinesic construction sequences is handled, in all likelihood, parakinesically . . . through the medium of stance." By stance, Birdwhistell means:

> . . . a pattern of total body behavior which is sustained through time, within which one or a series of constructions takes place, and which contrasts with a different stance. *Stance* subsumes *position* (p), (which is a statement of the relative position of all the body parts in space), *locomotion* (l), (the movement of the body through space) and *velocity* (v) (which covers sustained velocity of movements of the total body).

To discover a stance shift, Birdwhistell looks for a variation in posture, locomotion, or velocity (or any combination of these) to such an extent that there is a "marked shift in the total message." These stance shifts provide "structural frames for extended stretches of kinemorphic constructions."[25]

With these four units established—the kine (kineme), kinemorph, complex kinemorph, and kinemorphic construction, Birdwhistell enlarges his analysis to include modifiers of motion, action, and interaction, which he terms *parakinesics*. Modeling his procedure after that used in paralinguistics, he begins by identifying a base line of body type and activity analogous to Trager's term *voice set*. The *body-base*, or "the basic image of other members of the social group which must be internalized by the group member in the socialization process," consists of such socially recognized physical characteristics as position, sex, age, state of health, body build, rhythm phase, territoriality, mood, and toxic state.[26]

Against this body-base which establishes an expectancy pattern, *body qualities*, varying with different interactions, may be derived. These qualities constitute the *body-set* and consist of such characteristics as status, gender, age grade, health image, body image, rhythm image, territorial status, mood, and toxic image. To clarify the relationship between *body-base* and *body-set*, consider cases in which a man of sixty projects the image of a forty-year-old, a heavy set woman projects a slender image, or an ill person presents a healthy image. In these cases, the body-set contradicts the expectancy created by the body-base. Conversely, the body-set may confirm the body-base, as when a ten-year-old displays the age grade behavior of a ten-year-old. It is necessary to analyze the body-base first, since it "constitutes the zero-line which any communicant must have internalized in order to recognize the special cross-referencing message carried by the body-set signal-complex." Recognizing these body-set cross-referencing signals is especially important since they "may be seen as overall frames for the system of interaction occurring within their boundaries."[27]

Under parakinesics, Birdwhistell suggests tentative modifiers of motion, action, and interaction. The motion qualifiers, *intensity, duration,* and *range* (or width) occur across segments of complex kinemorphic constructions, and function to modify the kinesic meaning of the passage. For most "middle majority American movers," says Birdwhistell, these qualifiers seem to be distributed on a three-to-five degree scale. An actor with a narrow spread of intensity, duration, or range incongruent with that of the interaction, may convey a "flattened affect," a term used by psychiatrists to describe abnormally bland movements of some schizophrenics. Conversely, when the spread is too wide for the interaction, we have, in Birdwhistell's terms, a "fattened affect." Birdwhistell suggests seven ways in which *action,* or the movement of a person's whole body, may be modified. In the following list I have included abridged definitions of only the less familiar categories:

1. unilateral—bilateral (as when a mover favors both sides of the body or just one)
2. specific—generalized (as when a mover utilizes only one body area or several)
3. rhythmic—disrhythmic (as when the movement has a definite rhythm as opposed to a pattern of rhythm interruptions)
4. graceful—awkward
5. fast—slow
6. integrated—fragmented
7. intertensive—intratensive (the intertensive mover is highly responsive to the behavior of others, as opposed to the intratensive mover who looks for little feedback)[28]

Finally, on an interaction level, Birdwhistell has found three types of interaction modifiers involving two or more actors. Again, I have briefly defined only the less familiar categories:

1. mirror—parallel (in mirror behavior one or more actors *acts* in mirror image of a central actor; in parallel behavior two or more actors move in parallel)
2. rhythmic—disrhythmic.
3. open—closed (in open behavior the actors search the environment for other stimuli, while in closed behavior the actors are so interactive that they do not react appropriately to other stimuli)[29]

With the parakinesic and kinesic units established, Birdwhistell approaches the most difficult area of research—the interrelationship between speech and body motion. Birdwhistell has found that some movements, which he calls *motion markers,* seem to punctuate speech. He warns, however, that "while the punctuational behavior can be located in the speech context in certain positions, the analysis has not yet reached a point where we can posit obligatory binding between linguistic and kinesic events." He then lists five "derived functions" that these markers have in the interaction sequence. Birdwhistell has such a low confidence in the ability to attribute "meaning" to such markers that he uses the term "derived function," (an "observable set of behaviors in a given context which can be abstracted and interpreted as related"), rather than the term "meaning."[30]

The first derived function, *cue,* includes gestures such as hand, foot, and head nods, or stance shifts that mark anticipated interruptions, termination or initiation of phonation, or signal "proceed, I'm listening." The second function, *selection,* includes behaviors that emphasize a selected item in a series of items, a selected connection between items in series, or selection of certain items as related to other items. Such behaviors might include a qualifier shift, a head nod or head sweep, or a special lip protrusion or retroflection. The third function, *duration,* signals an "increase" or a "decrease" through behaviors such as a duration qualifier shift to staccato or allegro; lateral sweeps of hands or feet, and eyeball sweep. The fourth function, *area,* consists of behaviors such as pointing with head, hands, feet, torso, hand sweeps, and head sweeps that signal a nearby locale, a distant locale, or traversing distance. The fifth and final function, *pronominal reference,* includes these same types of pointing gestures to clarify who is the speaker, auditor, "we," "they," and "it."[31] In later research, Birdwhistell elevated these motion markers into a system of kinesic stresses and junctures roughly analogous to the linguistic stresses and junctures.[32]

Birdwhistell's delineation of structural units and functions of body motion ends with this last category, motion markers. Having briefly reviewed his research methodology, we are now in a position to assess his contributions to our problem of translating performance. What has his research discovered about body motion that is of use to the textmaker? Can his research methods and notational system be adapted to our purpose?

First, we should note that Birdwhistell's research does not include three areas of body motion which occur in artistic verbal performance: 1) iconic gestures illustrating a concept (such as forming the hands in a circle to illustrate the sun, which he calls *demonstratives* 2) task-oriented gestures, such as lighting a cigarette, which he calls *instrumental,* and 3) shifts in interpersonal distance, which he calls *interactional behavior* (and which we will deal with under proxemics). Although Birdwhistell recognizes the existence of these three types of behavior, he does not include them in his system of description because he thinks they have "differing structural properties than those which could be traced for the phenomena assigned to kinesics proper."[33]

Acknowledging these shortcomings, the textmaker may find some of Birdwhistell's categories useful in analyzing the body motion used in performance. Most revealing, it seems to me, are the parakinesic categories, such as stance, body base, body set, and the action, interaction, and motion markers. Looking for physical stance shifts, for example, might help reveal thematic or logical shifts in the discourse. Scheflen profitably uses stance shifts, which he calls position units, to shed light on the communication structure of psychotherapy sessions.[34] By first describing the performer's body-base, one is in a better position to assess how a performer changes his body-set to impersonate different social types. These parakinesic categories can serve as investigatory points for the textmaker to examine as he or she analyzes a video or film recording.

The four kinesic units—kine, kinemorph, complex kinemorph, and kinemorphic construction—do not seem to be as useful. After painstaking analyses, Birdwhistell admitted that these heuristic units, modeled after linguistic units, do not seem to constitute a hierarchically organized grammatical system: "While there are encouraging leads in the data, I am forced to report that so far I have been unable to discover such a grammar. Neither have I been able to isolate the simple hierarchy which I sought." With this conclusion that body motion is not a "language" with a distinct grammar and syntax, Birdwhistell argues that body motion is best understood in interrelationship with the linguistic system.[35]

An immediate consequence of Birdwhistell's two findings is that the textmaker cannot expect to find any valid dictionary of body "language" whose "words" have a discrete meaning. To believe that gestures have "real" meanings such as words is to succumb to what Birdwhistell calls the "carrier" temptation: "If the investigator succumbs to this, his attention is directed into a kind of 'lexicon' wherein he draws up a list of moves and their meanings only to discover that most human beings are kinesically illiterate and move improper English."[36] Certainly, we can confirm this conclusion that most body movements do not carry discrete meanings from simply reflecting on everyday experience. Folding the arms across the chest may convey defensiveness, or it may mean that the person is physically cold. Yet if most gestures do not have clearly definable meanings which hold across varying contexts, how can the textmaker describe a gesture in such a way that the reader knows its import in a particular context? If no grammar governs the combination of kines into kinemorphic constructions, does it make sense to describe behavior in discrete, atomistic units?

These two questions bring us to the heart of the difficulty in recording body movements. We know from experience that gestures and facial expressions convey specific meanings in specific contexts. Yet Birdwhistell's approach to description brackets out the question of meaning by denying the important role of subjective interpretation. Instead, Birdwhistell argues that the question of meaning cannot be asked until the context and social system are exhaustively analyzed: "I have tried to make it clear that the question 'What does X mean?' is nonadmissible unless the system within which X operates has been subjected to sufficient analysis so that X in its multiple of transforms can be described. . . . The final answers to 'What does X mean' *can only be arrived at when all of the other social systems interacting in any situation are equally thoroughly analyzed.*"[37]

This approach to meaning leads to an infinite regress of descriptive tasks in which the investigator assumes that sheer quantity and scope of behavioral descriptions will reveal meaning. As Roger Poole aptly notes, Birdwhistell's approach is based on the assumption that "*quantitative* increases of information will suddenly magically be transformed into a *qualitative* change in the level of explanation (possibly, one day, even 'meaning')." Yet by deliberately setting aside the question of meaning, continues Poole, practitioners of Birdwhistell's approach "have no means of ascertaining or isolating those movements and expressive gestures which have a meaning to the agent himself or herself, and segregating those which do not. Both at the level of practice, and of theory, it is thus impossible for Birdwhistell to distinguish acts which have a high *subjective* significance for his individuals from those which are *subjectively* insignificant to them."[38]

Obviously, the translator of performance is not interested in recording insignificant behavior. As our discussion of information theory shows, the textmaker cannot afford to expand description endlessly without overloading the text with so much information that it is no longer intelligible. What we need is a descriptive approach that records body motion as meaningful action. Poole suggests that "we cannot examine bodily expressivity with our eyes alone. The exact inverse of the Birdwhistell procedure is the right one: erudition, knowledge, historical grasp has to be present." Poole argues for a methodological stance in which the "intersubjective world" is acknowledged: "Meaning involves an agent, and an observer who is himself intersubjectively in communication with the agent, be it ever so distantly. There must be some mutual point of reference."[39]

At the root of Poole's critique of Birdwhistell's approach is a clash of differing epistemologies. Birdwhistell's structural linguistic approach rests on the philosophical foundations of positivism, while Poole's call for intersubjective interpretation rests on intuitionism. Here, I simply want to point out the need for coming to terms with this epistemological problem. We will confront this problem in greater detail in Chapter 6.

The Naturalistic Observation Model. A developed intersubjective approach to describing behavior can be found in Barker and Wright's work on naturalistic observation. Their philosophy of behavioral description sheds light on the problems with the structural linguistic approach and suggests concepts which clarify the textmaker's descriptive task.

In *Midwest and Its Children*, psychologists Roger G. Barker and Herbert F. Wright undertake two difficult problems of description: to make naturally occurring human action a matter of scientifically adequate record, and to analyze and to reconstruct systematically the recorded behavior and its relevant context. Behavior, they argue, can be broken down into two interdependent levels—*molar* and *molecular*. Briefly defined, molar units are *actions*, usually goal directed and generally recognized by the person performing them. Hurrying to school, tying one's shoe, or saluting the flag are examples of molar units. *Molecular* units (also called *actones*) are the subordinate parts of an action. The molecular units in the action saluting the flag, for example, are "elbow bending, extensor adjustment of the fingers, visual fixation." While persons are generally aware of their actions, they frequently lose sight of the molecular details composing them. Whether movements are molar or molecular depends on their context, not on some arbitrary definition of size:

> The size of a behavior sample, as defined by how long it lasts or how much of the physical organism it uses, cannot be made a test for this distinction. Bodily massive and long extended patterns of behavior, like the movements in walking, swimming, or dancing, can be molecular whenever they only mediate action by the person. Conversely, very small behavior samples are often molar. A footstep can be molar in the context of crossing a muddy street; and so can a wink in the context of a love affair. The determining context, as defined above, makes the difference in these and other cases.[40]

These concepts of molar and molecular behavior reveal the problem with Birdwhistell's emphasis on recording discrete, atomistic units. While molecular actones serve as "media" for a particular action, they are not interconnected with actions in any simple one-to-one way:

> First, an action is transposable from one to another manifold of actones. There are different ways to skin a cat. A child can memorize

the rule for dividing fractions by writing it, reading it or speaking it. Different letters and words might have been used for this paragraph.

Second, the same actones can be used for different actions. The same molecular manifold in walking or looking or speaking can mediate numberless different molar behavior units. Grasping with the hand can serve a thousand "purposes." So can saying *yes, no, why, I agree with you,* or almost any word or word combination.

As a result of these two observations, Barker and Wright conclude that describing molar behavior requires special procedures. A thorough scrutiny and description of actones is insufficient, they argue, since description at the molecular level alone "will not yield an adequate description of actions. Insofar as the same action can be mediated by different actones and the same actones can mediate different actions, this must be true."[41]

The point Barker and Wright make is that behavioral description must proceed at both levels, molar and molecular, through an "inferential shuttling back and forth between molecular details and the larger contexts of action." Describing only molar behavior, such as "George took a basket from the kitchen table and walked outdoors where he mounted his bicycle and went to pick berries for his mother" reveals little about the actor's motivation or attitude. Adding molecular details, however, allows one to see the qualitative characteristics of the action: "George, with his *lips quivering,* his *brows knit,* and the *corners of his mouth turned down,* took a basket from the kitchen table, and, with the *fingers of his left hand wound limply around the handle of the basket,* his *shoulders hunched,* his *chin sagging against his chest,* and his *feet dragging,* walked outdoors, where he mounted his bicycle and, with his *head still bent,* went to pick berries for his mother."[42] Conversely, recording only the actones, without the actions of which they are a part, will not give enough context to interpret the significance of these gestures.

A flaw in Birdwhistell's approach lies in the emphasis on recording molecular units. Segmenting and recording behavior into component parts does not guarantee that the parts alone will enable the reader to reconstruct the meaningful action. The whole is greater than the sum of the parts. Indeed, as Norbert Freedman argues, nonverbal behavior has a "Gestalt configuration often demanding anecdotal linguistic (stenographic) description. Gestures often have the properties of icons and emblems. They are thus not readily reducible to digital dimensions."[43] Unless the larger frames of action are recorded, the reader will not be able to tell how to interpret a gesture. In order to record the larger actions, Barker and Wright argue, the analyst must include "inferential description." To use their example, while a motion picture can clearly show John throwing a ball toward Jim, it cannot show "whether John was trying to hurt Jim or to engage him in a game of catch in the same positivistic sense that a photograph can show the position of a star":

> Only observation involving explicit or implicit inference would enable one to say what John was really doing. Trying to hurt Jim or to play catch with him and, to lift other examples from our records, saying things "proudly and with definiteness," showing "evident surprise," being "motherly," speaking in an "authoritative tone," talking "firmly and with agitation," acting as if one had a "bright idea," . . . go to make up the minimal phenomena of molar behavior; and any recording instrument which will not register them is no good for the purposes of ecological studies of molar behavior. We see no course for discouragement on this score, for every normal adult has the needed instrument built into him.[44]

Using inferential description, however, poses the problem of where description ends and theorizing begins. This problem will be addressed later. My purpose here is to illustrate the complexity of recording body movement as meaningful action. It is precisely because individual gestures can combine in so many ways and because they function interdependently with speech and larger actions, that we cannot record them as discrete parts and hope to capture the whole which they signify at a particular instant.

How then can we record the body motions used in performance in such a way that the reader perceives their meaning and qualities? Barker and Wright argue that common language provides the best and only practicable tool. In everyday social experience, persons commonly describe and interpret behavior using the idiom of common language. It offers the needed breadth and flexibility to preserve the qualitative refinements of human actions:

> Common language has much to recommend it for the purpose. It has been adapted by centuries of daily practice to the variability, the complexity, and the richness of human conduct. It should not surprise us therefore that, in the judgment of Lewin: "The most complete and concrete descriptions of [behavior and] situations are those which writers such as Dostoevski have given us. These descriptions have attained . . . a picture that shows in a definite way how the different facts in an individual's environment are related to one another and to the individual himself." In the hands of a Dostoevski, conventional speech can make us see subtleties in behavior beyond the range of our ordinary daily perceptions and far above the level of our best statistics and experiments.[45]

In the absence of such skilled writers as Dostoevski, Barker and Wright specify how observers, with no specialized education in psychology, can be trained to provide reliable, accurate descriptive records of behavior. I will return to some of their methods later. Here, I have simply tried to sort out some of the issues involved in recording body motion. As should now be clear, description necessarily involves the question of meaning. In rejecting certain models of behavioral description, I do so on the grounds that either they record movement in isolation from speech, or treat movement as an end in itself, without the accompanying detail which allows the reader to understand the movement's meaning. Birdwhistell's findings on the interdependency of gesture and language, and his parakinesic categories give us some ideas about what to observe as we analyze body motion in performance. Barker and Wright's philosophy of behavioral description points to the need for intersubjective interpretation.

Coding of Kinesics. To conclude this discussion of kinesics, let us contrast the way in which verbal and body movements are coded. Knowledge of how movements are coded helps clarify some of the difficulties in recording them. In comparing spoken language to kinesics and paralinguistics, Bateson finds that they differ in the types of signs or codes used. The code system of verbal language is almost entirely arbitrary or digital. The signs, for the most part, have no natural connection with their referents. In contrast, Bateson finds that many body movements and paralinguistic features in some way resemble what they represent through analogy or iconicity (Bateson uses these terms interchangeably): ". . . in kinesic and paralinguistic communication, the magnitude of the gesture, the loudness of the voice, the length of the pause, the tension of the muscle, and so forth—these magnitudes commonly correspond (directly or inversely) to magnitudes in the relationship that is the subject of discourse."[46]

Like Bateson, Ekman and Friesen argue that many bodily movements are iconic rather than arbitrary. Their use of the term iconic is based on Morris' definition of an iconic sign, which "is any sign which is similar in some respect to what it denotes. Iconicity is thus a matter of degree. . . the strength of the iconic sign lies in its ability to present for inspection what it signifies." One of Ekman and Friesen's five categories of body movement, *illustrators,* is almost entirely tied to speech, "serving to illustrate what is being said verbally." Illustrators which are clearly iconic include *pictographs,* which sketch pictures of their referents, *kinetographs,* movements that depict bodily actions, and *spatial movements,* depicting spatial relationships.[47]

There are, of course, arbitrarily coded movements, and as well, indexically coded gestures, or pointing movements which, according to

Sebeok, signify by contiguity.[48] Part of the power of iconic gestures seems to be the richness resulting from the union of sign and referent. For example, when a performer narrating "Stagolee" (see Chapter 7) imitates Stagolee's actions by pulling an imaginary gun (made from his pointer finger), dealing imaginary cards, or throwing a would-be guitar over his shoulder, he both refers to Stagolee and partially becomes Stagolee. No matter how carefully these iconic gestures are described in words, the digital quality of verbal language cannot match the presentational force of the icon.

Artifactual and Proxemic

In contrast to the lengthy discussion of kinesics, the treatment of artifactual and proxemic communication will seem brief. Although researchers are increasingly aware of how objects and space affect communication, the literature on their description and functioning is comparatively scant. Since the use of specific objects or spatial relations may be an integral part of a performance, the translator must consider recording them.

"Artifactual" communication refers to the communicative use of objects, including cosmetics and clothing.[49] Certainly in many performances, participants make use of various props or costumes. The norms of interaction for ceremonial performances may specify that both performers and audience wear formal attire. Performers may have special costumes or props which play an important role in keying the performance. For example, Hrdličková notes that the Japanese professional storyteller gets the audience's attention by tapping the table with a special bamboo stick. Apparently, the way in which the storyteller taps carries aesthetic significance, since "experienced listeners claim that from the first blow they can gauge the measure of the storyteller's art."[50]

Proxemics, a term coined by Edward T. Hall, refers to the way cultures use space.[51] Proxemic studies consider how the spatial designs of rooms and the distances between persons affect communication and behavior. The impact of a room's size or design and the distances maintained between persons may not be readily apparent. Often, it seems, we only notice the effect of a room or physical distance when we sense that an unspoken norm has been broken. Thus, if a relative stranger stands "too close," and intrudes into a space reserved for personal or intimate relationships, one suddenly becomes aware of the spatial ground rules governing interactions.

Different types of verbal art performances have their own norms of how space is used. The importance of space as an instrumentality of performance was illustrated to me in my classroom teaching of folklore. In one assignment, students were asked to perform examples of the verbal art performed in their families, recreating as closely as possible the appropriate setting, scene, norms of interaction, and performance style. In one instance, a student performed a scary bedtime story, but at a distance of about ten feet, a distance which Hall classifies as the far phase of social distance. After the performance, the audience members said that they felt like the performer was too far away from them for maximum impact. The student performer acknowledged that in the original performance in the family, her father used a personal distance of two to three feet, from which he would strategically touch the listening children at appropriate points in the story. Regna Darnell's article, "Correlates of Cree Narrative Performance," devotes considerable attention to describing the interpersonal arrangements and distances among the participants in the performance. Darnell notes that when her husband, unfamiliar with Cree Culture, first drew a diagram of the participants' positioning, he unconsciously changed the arrangements to accord with European habits.[52]

Several of Hall's proxemic concepts furnish useful points of investigation. In describing the relationship of the performer to the physical setting, the textmaker could consider whether it occurred in "fixed-feature" space, "semi-fixed" feature space, or "informal space." In fixed-feature space, rooms are set aside for specific functions. Sleeping does not occur in the kitchen, nor would a public speech occur in a bedroom. Some types of performances may be associated only with a well-defined, fixed-feature place: a theatre, a church, a bedroom, a playground. Semi-fixed feature space refers to the arrangement of objects within a room. The seating arrangement in a room affects the type of interaction among participants. If the seating pattern allows all participants face-to-face contact, the participants may find it easier to respond vocally to a performer. Hall describes a spatial arrangement that encourages social interaction as *sociopetal*, while an interaction that impedes social interaction he terms *sociofugal*.[53]

In contrast to fixed and semi-fixed feature space, which refer to physical features (objects, rooms), the third category, "informal space," refers to the unstated, but apparently rule-governed *distances* maintained between individuals. Hall identifies distance zones for middle-class, healthy adults, native to the Northeastern seaboard of the United States. The intimate distance of zero to eighteen inches, includes activities such as wrestling, lovemaking, comforting, and protecting. In the personal distance (1-1/2 to 4 feet), touching is possible. Subjects of personal interest and involvement may be discussed. In social distance (4 to 12 feet) common in business interactions, communication takes a more impersonal quality. In public distance (12 to 25 feet or more), interaction often assumes a formal nature. At the far phase of thirty feet or more, the "subtle shades of meaning conveyed by the normal voice are lost as are the details of facial expression and movement. Not only the voice but everything else must be exaggerated or amplified. Much of the nonverbal part of the communication shifts to gestures and body stance."[54] Hall discusses each of these distance zones in greater detail, and contrasts the variations in space use among differing cultural groups.

Tactile and Olfactory Channels

Although the senses of touch and smell are inevitably present in social interaction, we do not usually consider them major instrumentalities of artistic verbal performance. Still less is written about the communicative use of these channels, and my treatment of them will be brief. Different folklore genres vary in the kinds and amount of touch used. In children's hand clap games, touching is pronounced and, indeed, a defining characteristic of the genre. Not only do hand clap games involve touching others, they also frequently involve the participants touching parts of their own bodies as well. It is important to know who touches whom, on what part of the body, and how touch interacts with the verbal message.

Olfaction is probably the least employed channel. I mention it only as a possible instrumentality in some performances. In the European tradition of North American culture, as Hall points out, olfaction is repressed. In contrast, Hall finds that Arabs stress olfaction by enhancing body odors and using them in building human relationships.[55] The only self-conscious appeal to smell that I know of used in artistic verbal performance among European-origin North Americans is the use of incense in religious services.

In concluding this analysis of the communicative channels and signals of the source medium, performance, I want to stress that while these channels are analytically separable, they are often perceptually interdependent. Since all of the senses function simultaneously, the information received by any one sense may be modified by the information of any other. Consequently, analysis of performance may be misleading if it proceeds by dissecting the signals into separate strands or levels, without examining how these levels interact. The configuration of aural, visual, and tactile signals may form a gestalt perceptibly different from the analytical sum of dissected strands.

RECEPTOR MEDIUM: PRINT

When we compare the multichanneled medium of performance to the simple printed line, we immediately recognize the comparatively limited channel capacity of print. A performance modulates both time and three-dimensional space. Print transmits information only through the visual channel. If the print medium's channel capacity were limited solely to standard English orthography and the simple printed line, it would indeed be difficult to record much of a performance beyond the words. A number of means exist, however, which augment or stretch the channel capacity of the print medium, making it more attractive for recording performance. Poets, dramatists, linguists, and others have, over the years, developed different descriptive and notational devices to represent various performance features.

The following discussion of the print medium is based on a broad definition of print as the application of "inked types, plates, blocks, or the like, with direct pressure to paper or other material."[56] Thus, this discussion includes many aspects of the printed page, ranging from the composition of notational devices, printed drawings and photographs, to typography.

Certainly, the textmaker should understand the capabilities of the print medium as a receptor for performance and be familiar with the different codes which can be utilized to record performance. One way of providing this familiarity with print's potential would be to review, in detail, the history of individual notational and descriptive systems, evaluating their strengths and weaknesses. Such a historical approach, however, could easily fill an entire book, and is beyond the scope of this work. A more efficient, and I believe more enlightening procedure, is to examine the underlying types of signs from which existing notational and descriptive systems are composed.

Digital and Iconic Projections

Since devices for recording performance features differ so greatly— ranging from a printed photograph to natural language, or special alphabetic symbols, the terms notation, description, and transcription seem inadequate to refer to the whole class of recording devices available. I prefer to use the term *projection* for recording a performance because, in the special sense in which I use it, it calls attention both to the phenomena being recorded and the rules of transformation governing the projection. Umberto Eco uses the term projection to refer to the way in which any content is expressed: "Thus, given a content-type that is in some way cognizable, its pertinent features must be 'projected' into a given expression continuum by means of certain transformational rules."[57] This definition of projection calls attention to the codes used in expressing an idea. J.M. Lotman also uses projection in this way, defining projection as the rules of transformation by which an image represents an object.[58] Katherine Loesch applies the term projection specifically to recording a performance. In her prosodic studies of written texts, Loesch uses a "projected performance approach" in which prosodic features "not mapped out directly by the written text" are "projected in some way into a transcription."[59]

Applying these concepts to textmaking, I define projection as the codes and rules of transformation by which performance features are encoded on paper.[60] Projection, in this sense, covers all graphic means of recording a performance. I like the emphasis projection places upon the rules of transformation because a reader's ability to learn these rules marks the success or failure of a text in facilitating an equivalent aesthetic transaction. For example, in order to pronounce a word correctly, we need a minimal knowledge of the rules governing the transformation of letters into sounds. Similarly, to read the special kinesic or paralinguistic notations, we must know how the symbols translate into sound or action. As we will see later, some performance-centered textmakers use specialized devices, but either fail to let the reader know how to decode the devices, or have so many varied and complicated transformational rules as to make performing the text akin to working a jigsaw puzzle or painting-by-the-numbers.

Printed signs may be classified into two broad types: arbitrary or digital signs, which have no natural connection to their referents, and iconic signs, which in some way resemble their referents. Within the digital category, we may identify three subsets: 1) natural language description, 2) alphabetic notations, and 3) analphabetic notations. The iconic category is not so neatly divided, but in general, we can group these devices by the degree to which they resemble their referents. Some iconic notational systems are alphabetic in principle; that is, one single symbol represents one segment. While the degree to which iconic alphabetic symbols resemble their referents is often tenuous, other iconic devices, such as sketches or photographs, may bear a more immediate natural connection.

Digital: Natural Language Projections

Most published folklore texts use natural language to record the verbal utterance. The Roman alphabet used in natural language writing is, of course, composed of digital letters which represent sounds. The words formed by the alphabet are also, for the most part, arbitrary symbols. Except for some ideophones—words that imitate sounds, such as *buzz*— words symbolize their referents by convention. As anyone who has struggled with the irregularities of English orthography knows, standard spelling practices are inadequate for representing the actual sounds of an utterance. But by deviating from the rules of standard spelling, either through literary dialect or special phonetic definitions of letters, a writer can imitate speech sounds more precisely. Similarly, although natural language lacks discrete words to represent every possible gesture, tone, or movement, through combining words into descriptive phrases, natural language can become an effective tool for recording performance features. Let us consider the ways in which natural language can represent idiosyncrasies of pronunciation, paralinguistic, kinesic, artifactual, proxemic, and other characteristics of the aesthetic field.

Rather than using a special phonetic code such as the International Phonetic Alphabet (IPA), the textmaker can use the conventional alphabet to represent certain dialect features. Since few readers are fluent in reading IPA, natural language can reach a wider audience. One way of recording a performer's dialect is through the use of "literary dialect." At its worst, literary dialect has been used in paternalistic, chauvinistic ways to caricature a folk type. Rather than truly seeking to imitate the speech of the folk, some writers have employed "eye dialect" such as "*tu* (to), *ove* (of), *conversashun* (conversation), *operashuns* (operations)" and so on. Frontier humorists such as George Washington Harris, Artemus Ward, Petroleum V. Nasby, and Josh Billings used such eye dialect to develop humorous "dialect characters." One such character drawn by Harris, Sut Lovingood, speaks like this: "Well, to cum to the serius part ove this conversashun, that is how the old quilt-mersheen an coverlidloom cum to stop operashuns on this yeath." As Paul H. Bowdre says of this passage, "The many Eye Dialect spellings indicate that the writer is not making a serious effort to convey any regional or class dialect. Rather he is using an easy method of conveying to the reader the impression that Sut Lovingood is funny, an ignorant yokel to be laughed at."[61]

Yet at its best, literary dialect can be an effective indicator of certain dialect features. In "A Theory of Literary Dialect," Sumner Ives illustrates persuasively how literary dialect can be a reasonably accurate dialect indicator if readers first know the dialect which the author considers "standard." According to Ives, since "the phonetic interpretation given to the letters and combinations of letters in the conventional orthography varies in different sections of the country," an author trying to represent spellings other than his own, "will select those which 'stand for' the deviant sounds in his *own* speech type, not in that of other varieties of English." Thus, continues Ives, "in order to interpret his dialect spelling, it is necessary to know how these spellings would be pronounced in the region to which the author belongs."[62]

Illustrating this core principle in interpreting literary dialect is the controversy over Joel Chandler Harris' spelling of "brer." Although H. L. Mencken faults Harris' "er" spelling as an inaccurate representation of the Black dialect "BRUH-UH" or "BRUH," Ives counters that Harris, as well as most people in the old plantation areas, did not pronounce the final r's in words. In terms of Harris' own "r-less" dialect, the final r on *brer* would not be pronounced: "The ER spelling, therefore, does not suggest a constricted sound to a native of the 'r-less' areas. Harris actually meant the same pronunciation by his spelling **BRER** that Mencken meant by his spelling **BRUH**, namely [br ə] or perhaps [br ʌ]."[63] This example also underscores the importance of furnishing readers with a key to decode any unconventional usages. In the case above, we see how confusion results when the "rules of transformation" underlying a projection are not known to readers.

As Ives readily admits, literary dialect cannot give as detailed a phonetic or subphonetic representation as can a special phonetic code such as the IPA. If the literary dialect tries to represent too many features, the difficulty in reading it might severely try the reader's patience. Yet Ives finds that literary dialect can "generally indicate a difference in phonemes, or rather a difference in the distribution of a particular phoneme in the word stock of the dialect." In addition, literary dialect can indicate social gradation between characters and regional differences on the "vulgate" level. Besides indicating these pronunciation features, a writer can use literary dialect to represent "unconventional morphology, local expressions, and local names for things."[64]

In spite of Ives' helpful advice on how to use literary dialect responsibly, one recent critic of literary dialect ignores this advice, choosing to repeat Ives' criticisms of incorrect dialect representation. In "Ritin' Fowklower Daun 'Rong: Folklorists' Failure in Phonology," Dennis R. Preston objects to folklorists' widespread use of literary dialect on several grounds. Preston's charges, if not examined carefully and refuted, might prevent some folklorists from attempting to represent dialect. We must then digress for a moment to answer them.

In surveying and categorizing the English-speaking folklore texts published in the *Journal of American Folklore* in the 1970s, Preston found that 35 out of the 45 folklore texts contained literary dialect. After analyzing these 35 texts, Preston claims that folklorists tend to be "linguacentric," since they respell the speech of Blacks and Appalachians more than that of others.[65] Yet a careful examination of the data Preston presents does not support his claim. His Table I, which he cites to support his charge, directly contradicts his interpretation. According to Table I, only 3 articles contained Appalachian texts, and these are listed under the heading, "No Spelling Changes." His claim about Black texts rests on a misuse of statistics. Instead of giving the percentage of respelled texts for a group measured against the total number of texts published of that group, Preston compares the number of respelled texts per group.

For example, since 14 Black texts were respelled and this number is larger than the 3 "Other U.S." texts which were respelled, then according to Preston, folklorists respell Black speech more than others. Yet a comparison of Tables I and II shows that a high percentage of this "Other U.S." speech is respelled. For example, in Table II, Preston shows 3 "Other U.S." texts as respelled. It is not clear what groups or states comprise this category, since Preston fails to define the composition of the dialect categories in Table II. But looking at Table I, I infer that at least New England, New Jersey, and the Northwest must belong to this group. Since these areas are categorized under "spelling changes," then 3 out of 3 or 100 percent of "Other U.S." texts are respelled. From these figures, we can only conclude that folklorists were just as likely to respell "Other U.S." speech as they were to respell Black speech, since 100 percent of the texts collected in both groups were respelled. Like his claim about Appalachian speech, Preston's claim about Black speech does not withstand scrutiny.

Preston's second attack on literary dialect rests on premises that strike at the heart of any attempt to translate performance to print. These premises hold that not only is print incapable of representing performance features, but that to depart from standardized conventions by respelling words devalues the character of the speaker being represented. Preston begins his article with the assertion that "Writing is a poor, secondary system when compared to speech. No tone or quality of voice can be represented; no helpful and delightful accompanying body language is seen; and no dramatic or embarrassing pauses or rapid tempo can be provided."[66] This statement is belied by such writers as Charles Dickens, William Shakespeare, Mark Twain, and William Faulkner, who manage to capture the speech rhythms, tones, and dialects of a variety of speakers. Barre Toelken's method of describing gestures and audience responses in brackets within a text, István Sándor's use of photographs to convey performance gestures, and Dennis Tedlock's use of typography and layout to convey paralinguistic features, show that folklorists can translate many performance features to print.[67]

Preston goes on to argue that "English has been spelled for so long, and we literates have read it for so long in one shape, that its very appearance has taken on significance beyond the message." Due to this metacommunicative power of print, Preston finds "it difficult to think of a respelling (except such trivial, nonattributed ones as *nite*) that I do not feel to be critical of the speaker." This criticism, he continues, is generally "in the direction of *lower social status, lack of education, illiteracy, boorishness,* or *thuggishness,* or *rusticity* (though I know that all these 'criticisms' are open to romantic interpretations)" [my italics]. The only evidence that Preston cites to show that others share his objections to respellings is an appeal to an alleged "folk fact": "Even the most intelligent and well-trained reader cannot avoid that response, for secondarily, I would argue that such responses constitute a folk fact of literate responses."[68]

If Preston's claim about literate responses to literary dialect is correct, then a good many intelligent scholars and writers must be attempting to denigrate the people about whom they write. Yet it is difficult to believe that scholars such as William Labov, Geneva Smitherman, Roger Abrahams, Edith Folb, and Claudia Mitchell-Kernan, all of whom use literary dialect to represent elements of Black speech,[69] seek to devalue the character of their informants. Indeed, some scholars seem to appreciate Black dialect so much that they represent their own Black dialect through respellings. Geneva Smitherman, for example, in numerous instances in her book, uses respellings to represent her own Black speech. In one example she writes, "On no level is this aesthetic more strikingly revealed than in the language of the new black poetry: the poets bees not only tappin the reservoir of the black cultural universe but doing so in the Black Idiom."[70]

Not only scholars, but Black writers use literary dialect to represent Black speech patterns. And this conscious choice to represent Black speech comes not out of any devaluation, but from positive pride in their culture, or simply a desire to capture the sounds and rhythms of Black speech. Writers such as Mari Evans, Sonia Sanchez, Carolyn Rodgers, Nikki Giovanni, Donald L. Graham, Betty Gates, Gerald W. Barrax, Sterling A. Brown, Langston Hughes, to name but a few, represent a wide range of Black speech patterns, from the simple respellings of *gonna, li'l,* or *yo,* to attempts to represent intonation and emphasis through typography, as in "looooken so cooool" or "aint gonna let no in/junction turn me round," or "yo mom ahh yo maaa yo mommmmmmmmmmmmUHma."[71] Many highly literate scholars and poets, then, consciously employ literary dialect out of genuine appreciation for the dialect and people they are trying to study or represent.

What are we to make of claims such as Preston's, that using literary dialect lowers readers' esteem of the speakers being represented? Certainly those who believe that only one standard dialect should be spoken or written by properly educated persons may turn up their noses at any speech which deviates from their standards of correctness. But folklorists should not hamper their demands for linguistic accuracy simply because some readers hold biased attitudes toward speech usage. Perhaps one reason Preston says that respellings make him critical of the speaker is that he ascribes negative valuations to dialects which differ from those spoken by an educated, middle-class. Perhaps Preston views lower social status, lack of education, and illiteracy negatively, since he lists these characteristics among those criticisms which respellings imply for him. No doubt another source of Preston's dislike of respellings is a belief that the print medium is static and incapable of development, and only subject to deterioration. Yet such a belief that English orthography is fixed and "correct" overlooks a long history of changing conventions, not only with English spelling, but with writing itself. Before the rise of the English "doctrine of correctness" espoused by the 17th and 18th century grammarians, English orthography was highly variable.[72] And at one time, the early Greeks had only a rudimentary system of punctuation and no word division. These conventions which we take for granted today had to be invented.[73]

If we accept the premise that both the print medium and the spoken medium are elastic, and are used variably by different persons in various times and places, then no fear of violating so-called "correct" rules should bother textmakers. As folklorists, our job is to record the speech we hear as accurately as possible, not to worry about offending the taste of some literates who cling to a static view of written language.

Another means of representing pronunciation features with natural language is to preface the text with a general guide to pronunciation. Rather than physically changing the spelling of a word, the textmaker can provide the readers with the information to transpose certain sounds as they read.

In addition to indicating dialect features, natural language can be used to project paralinguistic and kinesic features. As in literary dialect, spelling changes can be used to indicate drawn out syllables such as "ba-ad" or "woooooooooowe." Vocal segregates such as "uh-huh" can be spelled. Vocalizations and voice qualities can be described in descriptive phrases modifying the utterance. In this excerpt from a performance-centered text, Toelken indicates paralinguistic and kinesic features in parentheses: "'Shilna'ash.' (Yellowman speaking very nasally, through side of mouth, lips unmoving and eyes closed, in imitation of Ma'i)."[74] More extensive descriptions of kinesic action can also be included. Chapter 2 of this work cites an excerpt from one of Mallery's texts which gives a detailed account of a narrator's action and intonation. Mallery's kinesic descriptions are written in the imperative voice, as if he expects the reader to follow the directions and perform: "(1) Close the right hand, leaving the index extended, pointed westward at arms length a little above the horizon, head thrown back with the eyes partly closed and following the direction—'Away to the West.'"[75]

If natural language description is to be useful, it must record both molar and molecular actions. Two dangers in using natural language, however, are that recorders might lapse into vague generalities or substitute theoretical generalizations for concrete descriptions. Barker and Wright discuss these problems and suggest some methods for avoiding them. Their cardinal rule for description is to "Give the how of everything the subject does." The how of an action contains the molecular detail differentiating styles of action, and constitutes the first level of description. In contrast to interpretation about behavior or a situation, the first level of description constitutes "running accounts of what a person is doing and of his situation on the level of direct perception or immediate inference." While minor interpretations constituting a second level of description may be useful, Barker and Wright suggest that they should always be bracketed, or in some way set apart from the first level of description. A third descriptive level, which Barker and Wright label technical or professional interpretations, includes generalizations based upon explicit theories, such as "Tom was manifesting repressed aggression against his father." These technical interpretations, say Barker and Wright, should not be included as part of a behavior record simply because they do not concretely and objectively describe the behavior, but rather, generalize *about* the behavior.[76]

In addition to recording pronunciation, paralinguistic, and kinesic features, natural language can describe artifactual and proxemic features as well as details about the aesthetic field. Its strength as a descriptive tool lies in its accessibility and flexibility. The sheer length of natural language descriptions, however, can make them obtrusive. For greater clarity and ease of reading, textmakers can arrange the layout of a page so that modifying descriptions are clearly differentiated from the performer's utterance. Following the layout of dramatic texts, modifying description can be printed in italics, parentheses, or separated from the performer's words in margins or columns. Some type of clear distinction between the actual words used by the performers and the observers' descriptive words must be maintained if the resulting text is to be unambiguous. Imitating the technique of novelists and incorporating description into dialogue tags or a narrative voice may make it difficult to distinguish the performer's narrative from the observer's.

Digital: Analphabetic and Alphabetic Projections

It is easy to see that recording performance features through natural language could greatly increase the length of a text. One of the advantages of notational systems is that their abbreviated form makes recording more compact. Some notational systems, such as that employed by Birdwhistell, utilize both digital and iconic symbols. Here, we will consider the two remaining types of digital notations—alphabetic and analphabetic. David Abercrombie defines these two types of notation as follows: "Alphabetic notations are so called because they are based on the same principle as that which governs ordinary alphabetic writing, namely that of using one single simple symbol to represent each segment. *An*alphabetic notations (meaning notations which are *not* alphabetic) represent each segment by a composite symbol made up of a number of signs put together."[77]

Analphabetic notations are really abbreviated descriptions. Each symbol or letter in the composite represents a component part much as each symbol in a chemistry formula represents an ingredient. Kenneth

Pike's analphabetic phonetic notation (developed in 1943) illustrates the complexities of fully describing spoken sounds. His Functional Analphabetic Symbolism was not developed as a practical notation, but rather to demonstrate the factors constructing a segment of sound. Each letter in the system is the abbreviation for a productive or controlling mechanism. For example, *D* stands for "direction of the air stream," with lower case *e* and *i* abbreviating *egressive* or *ingressive*, respectively.[78] To describe the mechanisms involved in just one vowel sound may take as many as eighty separate characters. The sheer length in describing one sound makes the system useful only for a descriptive label of isolated sounds, not for transcribing connected discourse.[79] An early elocutionary system for describing body movements also utilizes an analphabetic approach. In Gilbert Austin's system, each letter abbreviates a description of the hands, arms, body, head, and feet. To describe a particular movement, letters are linked together in a kind of formula. In this line and the adjoining explanation from Austin's notation of "The Miser and Plutus," we can see how such an analphabetic system is used in a text:

Blf.hf————————a———————— Bfl.br
12. He wrings his hands, he beats his breast.

No. XII. The position of the hands at first is, *both folded horizontal forwards* as expressed in the notation *Bfl.hf.* At the *a* connected by the dash, which signifies *ascending*, the hands are raised up, and at the next notation *Bfl.br.* they are forcibly withdrawn back on the breast.

The above excerpt shows only hand and arm movements. When feet movements are as well written below a line, reading the notation becomes more difficult. In learning the system, one has to memorize letters referring to the placement of arms and legs in an imaginary sphere surrounding the speaker. A humorous illustration of how students responded to this system is seen in the following report of how Jonathan Barber, a disciple of Austin's method, fared with his students: "Evidently Barber was not wholly successful. One morning he found his bamboo sphere on the top of a barber's pole (the sphere was undoubtedly used in teaching Austin's system). Soon Barber resigned. The students found his teaching too mechanical and demanding."[80]

Many of Birdwhistell's kinesic notations are also analphabetic; the letters are mnemonic abbreviations for natural language descriptive terms. For example, R/E stands for right hand to ear; R/f means right hand to forehead. The following analphabetic notation represents a typical male American cigarette grasp in which the right hand is "holding cigarette with 2, 3, 4, 5 crooked and the cigarette held between joint b of fingers 2 and 3: R/12*b*o3*b*3c."[81]

In the third type of digital projection, alphabetic, a separate symbol refers to each classifiable segment. In systems based on the Roman alphabet, the number of symbols must often be augmented, since the 26 characters of the alphabet are not enough. Abercrombie describes in detail how new symbols can be made through using italics, upper and lower case, obsolete letters, numerals, diacritics, letters from foreign alphabets, modifying the shapes of letters, and so on.[82] Some elements of Trager's paralinguistic notational system and Birdwhistell's kinesic system are alphabetic. Commonly used marks for *intonational phonemes*, (superscript numbers—1 for lowest pitch, 4 for highest relative pitch), *terminals* (/↓/, /↑/, and /#/), and *stress* (/′//∧//`//+/) are also alphabetic in principle, and arbitrary.[83]

No doubt the most widely used alphabetic notational system among folklorists is the International Phonetic Alphabet, or IPA. It contains a separate symbol for each phonetic sound. For those who want to capture a speaker's pronunciation as exactly as possible, the IPA is invaluable. Although each symbol is easily learned, it takes extended practice to become a fluent transcriber and reader of IPA. To promote ease in reading, many who use the IPA include standard orthography below the transcription.

Musical notations, most of which are alphabetic in character, have also been used to record paralinguistic features of rhythm, pitch, and volume. Edward Sapir, for example, frequently noted the rhythm and pitch of sung or chanted phrases within his *Wishram Texts* by using musical time signatures, rests, holds, notes, and some dynamic markings. Boas used a similar method in his *Chinook Texts*.[84] Elocutionists such as Joshua Steele and James Rush used musical symbolism for notating pitch, pause, stress, time, and voice qualities.[85] In evaluating Steele's and Rush's approaches from the standpoint of modern knowledge about intonation, Pike says that Steele's analyses suffered from using "units of music which were rigidly fixed and absolute rather than flexible and relative." Pike also criticizes Rush for "too strict a reliance on fixed musical symbolism. . . ."[86]

From the foregoing discussion of digital alphabetic and analphabetic systems, it should be apparent that their utility in making description compact is countered by the effort demanded to become fluent in the reading of a new code. When we recall that recording a performance may entail the combined use of several notational systems, we can quickly see how the decoding chore could become overwhelming. One critic of Birdwhistell's kinesic notations writes that "the system is so detailed that even the youngest user runs the risk of winding up in a geriatric's ward before memorizing all the symbols."[87] While notations may save the textmaker time in transcribing and may be easily read by textmakers who invent their own systems or work daily with them, such notations may

entail more effort from readers who must continually refer to a key
defining the symbols. Although many alphabetic and analphabetic
systems try to use mnemonic devices, the sheer number of symbols
involved makes the decoding task burdensome. Since the symbols bear no
natural connection to their referents, immediate perception is not
sufficient to decode them.

Iconic Projections

   In contrast to the preceding digital projection devices, iconic devices in
some way resemble their referents. Ostensibly the natural resemblance
should make a notational system easier to decode. But, as Abercrombie
illustrates in his discussion of iconic phonetic systems, sometimes the
degree of resemblance is so slight that the symbol's referent is not
immediately apparent. For example, Alexander Melville Bell's system,
published in a book called *Visible Speech: the Science of Universal
Alphabetics*, uses symbols analogous to the mechanisms for producing
speech sounds. For example, /O/ stands for glottis open (aspirate), /I/ for
glottis narrow (voice), /X/ for glottis closed (catch), and / 0 / for super-
glottal passage contracted (whisper).[88] One must, however, learn the
conventions for decoding these signs—they are not readily apparent. Part
of the problem with iconic representations of sound is the difficulty of
visualizing aural phenomena.
   Iconic symbols are frequently used in paralinguistic and kinesic
projections. Perhaps one of the most common iconic signs to indicate
time relationships is the use of blank space between lines or words, with
the amount of blank space varying in proportion to the amount of pause
between words or lines. This type of icon is based on analogy and utilizes
the principle of scanning: "One may create a correspondence between
spatial and temporal messages by scanning, that is, by going through a
spatial structure in a given order."[89] Many poets and writers exploit the
principle of scanning by arranging their words in pause units (or eye
units) that correspond to the pauses in the oral performance. In Ellison's
Invisible Man, Peter Wheatstraw's rapid spiel is indicated by running the
words together, without any space separating them: "In fact,
I'maseventhsonofaseventhsonbawnwithacauloverbotheyesandraisedon-
blackcatboneshighjohntheconquerorandgreasygreens."[90] Many of the
performance-centered texts published in *Alcheringa* use this principle to
represent the rhythmic silences interrupting speech. This use of blank
space to convey time makes use of layout on the page to convey
performance information.
   Other paralinguistic features such as pitch and volume can also be
projected with iconic signs. Borrowing a device used by some

contemporary poets to indicate volume changes, Tedlock represents loud words in capital letters or large print, and soft words in small print.[91] Again, the icon works by analogy—size of letters in proportion to amount of sound. A similar type of coding can be used to indicate relative pitch height. Abercrombie finds the following representation the "most effective" iconic representation of pitch variation: "good ^{af}ter^{no}o$_n$."[92] Although Abercrombie does not say why he finds this method so effective, it seems likely that its effectiveness lies in both the ease of decoding and its simulation of perceptual experience. By fusing letters with pitch levels, the notation imitates the perceptual impression of pitch. Since one does not normally hear pitch as a separate element superimposed on words, but rather as a phenomenon occurring simultaneously with words, this projection method represents perceptual experience more accurately. Tedlock, as well as other textmakers and poets, has used this technique for recording intonations. A variant iconic means of notating intonation is to run a line through words indicating their pitch level: "The weather is lovely." Pike discusses this type of continuous-line notation and its variations in detail.[93] As is readily apparent, the continuous-line notation does not have the perceptual immediacy of printing the words and letters at varying levels on the page.

Iconic projections are frequently used in recording body motions. The most iconic of all printed codes is the photograph, which can convey a detailed likeness in an immediately perceptual mode. István Sándor uses a sequence of photographic shots of the narrator of a tale, with each shot representing a major shift in narrative gestures.[94] Sketches, such as Scheflen uses in his texts of psychological therapy sessions, can also serve the folklorist. Scheflen's sketches, made from film recordings, depict the entire bodies of the participants and their major interactional movements, such as posture or stance shifts, and revealing interpersonal gestures.[95] Still less iconic than photographs or drawings are pictographs, such as those which Birdwhistell uses. Birdwhistell's pictographs vary in the degree to which they bear an immediate likeness to their referents. For example, these symbols " ⌒⌒ *side-wise look,* ⌣ *smile,* ⌣⌣ *toothy smile,*" bear a closer resemblance than these: " Δ_s *curled nostril,* ⊺ right shoulder forward, and ⌒⌒ *focus on auditor.*"[96] The iconic base of some of Birdwhistell's notations is so tenuous as to serve only a mnemonic function after the symbol's meaning has been learned.

Total Impact of Projections

Most of the iconic and digital projection devices have been developed for recording only one instrumentality, such as phonetics, paralinguistics, or kinesics. A performance, however, is a multichanneled medium. Consequently, symbols for individual channels must be combined to represent a performance. Yet a performance is much more than a simple sum of codes. Each of the linguistic, paralinguistic, and kinesic elements in a performance interact with, combine, and modify each other, and all of them influence and are influenced by aesthetic field elements, such as the physical and psychological setting and cultural norms of interaction and interpretation.

Further, each projection device we have considered incompletely or partially symbolizes its referent. The most iconic device, a photograph, records only a semblance of three dimensions and motion, and from only one angle of vision. A paralinguistic notation of a triple arrow / ⬆ / to indicate a high-pitched falsetto only indicates a relative difference in pitch; it does not symbolize the exact tone in the performance. Considering the shortcoming of printed projections, it is clear that a text only approximately records a performance. An unavoidable "untranslatability" inheres in the transmutation of breathing, moving, three-dimensional life to the static, flat plane of paper. Only through a counter-transmutation, in which a person activates the printed symbols, breathes life into the page through embodying and performing the text, can a semblance of the integral presence of the original performance be restored. As Tedlock argues, a translation of oral poetry must be judged "not on the basis of its acceptability as silent written literature, but on the basis of how it sounds, when read aloud, how it strikes ears that have been reeducated to the subtlety and richness of the spoken word."[97]

To encourage a faithful reperformance of the original aesthetic transaction, the textmaker must consider the total impact of the completed text. Not only must individual projections be clear, but so must the grouping and arrangement of projection devices. The appearance of the printed matter itself may invite or repel readers, or signal them to approach the material with certain preconceptions. For example, different literary genres tend to have characteristic patterns of layout on the page. These conventions work as a form of metacommunication, telling readers what genre they are about to read so that they may approach it with the appropriate frame of mind. To clarify the importance of the metacommunicative impact of the printed layout, Jonathan Culler advocates taking an excerpt of journalistic prose from a novel and arranging it on the page as a poem: "The properties assigned to the sentence by a grammar of English remain unchanged, and the different meanings which the text acquires cannot therefore be attributed to one's knowledge of the language but must be ascribed to the special conventions for reading poetry which lead one to look at the language in new ways, to make relevant properties of the language which were previously unexploited, to subject the text to a different series of interpretive operations."[98]

Culler's experiment with rearranging prose suggests a similar one with the arrangement of verbal art texts. If a poetic, rhythmic performance is presented in a traditional prose format, or arranged into tiny component parts which disguise large rhythmic patterns, the reader may not perceive important qualities or patterns. Part of the impetus behind the widespread use of poetic and dramatic conventions among textmakers publishing in *Alcheringa* seems to be an awareness that such conventions precondition the reader to approach folklore with attention to its aesthetic qualities.

CONCLUSION

This discussion of the signals and channel capacity of performance and print provides a rational basis for selecting *what* to record and *how* to record it. Since the textmaker must be knowledgeable about linguistic, paralinguistic, kinesic, artifactual, proxemic, tactile, and olfactory communication, we have discussed concepts from these areas applicable to textmaking. In addition to recording the words of a performance, textmakers must be aware of the suprasegmental phonemes and paralinguistic features. Trager's work on paralinguistics, as well as Martin's thorough synthesis of perceptually-based paralinguistic research, can provide textmakers with a taxonomy of descriptive categories. In kinesics, the structural linguistic and naturalistic observation models provide the greatest contributions to describing performance. Birdwhistell's findings on the interdependence of kinesics and language and his parakinesic categories help in the analysis of body motion. Barker and Wright's philosophy of behavioral description points to the need for intersubjective interpretation and inferential description. Their concepts of molar and molecular levels of behavior clarify the descriptive task.

Analyzing the receptor medium provides the textmaker with an understanding of the underlying digital and iconic signs composing notational and descriptive systems. I introduced the term "projection" to refer to the various graphic means to record a performance. This term calls attention to the rules of transformation by which performance features are encoded in print.

In the digital category of projections, natural language description has the broadest applicability. It is an effective tool for representing pronunciation, paralinguistic, kinesic, artifactual, and proxemic features, as well as other characteristics of the aesthetic field. Two dangers in using natural language, however, are that recorders might lapse into vague generalities or substitute theoretical generalizations for concrete descriptions. To avoid these dangers, textmakers should concentrate on the first level of description and give the *how* of actions by providing molecular detail. Minor interpretations constituting a second level of description may be useful, but they should be set apart from the first descriptive level. Technical interpretations or theorizing *about* the performance should not be included in the performance text. One drawback of natural language description is that it can greatly increase the text's length.

An advantage to digital analphabetic and alphabetic projections is that their abbreviated form makes recording more compact. Yet this utility in making description compact is countered by the effort to read a new code fluently. Since these symbols bear no natural connection to their referents, immediate perception is not sufficient to decode them.

In general, iconic projections are more readily perceptible. They are useful in recording paralinguistic and kinesic features. Yet, even the most iconic of all projections, the photograph, only partially records its referent. An unavoidable "untranslatability" inheres in the transmutation of three-dimensional, breathing, moving life to the static, flat plane of paper. Only through a countertransmutation, in which a person breathes life into the printed page through embodying and performing the text, can a semblance of the integral presence of the original performance be restored. To encourage a faithful reperformance of the original aesthetic transaction, the textmaker must consider the total impact and metacommunication of the printed page. The appearance of the printed matter itself may invite or repel readers.

Now that we have analyzed the two media of translation, we are ready to consider some general principles for translating performance to print.

6

Principles of Translating Performance

In the preceding chapters, we have laid the groundwork for a theory of the performance-centered text. With the contention that a text style should grow out of a theoretical understanding of the nature of folklore, the intended audience's capacity to read the text, and the characteristics of the source and receptor media, we have examined these areas in detail. In identifying the four characteristics of an adequate text, we found that the chief difficulty lies in conveying the original form of the performance without sacrificing the audience's ability to comprehend its sense and spirit. From applying information theory concepts, we discovered that the print medium is a restricted channel, and that to avoid overloading the text with too much information, it must be "adjusted" in some way. Here, we will consider different ways in which performance may be translated to print, and suggest some general principles for making a performance-centered text.

First, we will consider four different approaches to creating equivalences in form and content: formal vs. dynamic equivalence, and analytical vs. perceptual equivalence. After clarifying the necessary orientations toward equivalency, I will suggest a methodology for making the performance *report* of the aesthetic field, and the performance *record* of the aesthetic transaction. Let me stress that in this section, I am proposing general translation principles. Each folklore performance, as a unique artistic experience, presents unique problems which cannot be solved by a mechanical application of rules. Just as it is impossible to prescribe one method that will work for the oral interpretation of every work of literature, it seems dubious that a universal notational system or text style will meet the demands of the many and varied folklore performances. "Translation," I. A. Richards once said, is "probably the most complex type of event yet produced in the evolution of the cosmos."[1] Given the complexities of translation, I believe, with Nida, that they can hardly be solved by a simple set of rules.

The ideal, perfect translation, according to Steiner, would be an exact repetition, a total counterpart of the original work.[2] But crossing media, cultures, and languages makes such perfection unobtainable. Translation, as all communication, involves an inevitable loss, addition, or skewing of information.[3] Despite these difficulties, genuine translation strives to equalize by creating equivalences in form and content. Much of the controversy among translators revolves around different approaches to achieving equivalence. In the translation of artistic verbal performance to print, we can identify four different poles, or orientations toward equivalence: formal vs. dynamic equivalence, and analytical vs. perceptual equivalence. All folklore texts, as we will see, can be placed on a continuum between these four poles.

FORMAL AND DYNAMIC EQUIVALENCE

The first two poles, formal and dynamic, refer to the emphasis placed either on the source culture or the receptor culture. Nida identifies these two poles as basic orientations in translation. They seem to have particular relevance to folklore translations, as the following discussion illustrates.

Formal Equivalence

In an effort to let readers understand the customs and expressions of the source culture, the formal-equivalence translation often tries to reproduce idioms literally. In Nida's definition of formal equivalence, note the emphasis placed on understanding the source culture: "Formal equivalence focuses attention on the message itself, in both form and content. In such a translation one is concerned with such correspondences as poetry to poetry, sentence to sentence, and concept to concept. Viewed from this formal orientation, one is concerned that the message in the receptor language should match as closely as possible the different elements in the source language. This means, for example, that the message in the receptor culture is constantly compared with the message in the source culture to determine standards of accuracy and correctness."[4] The strictest formal-equivalence translation is an interlinear, or gloss translation, in which corresponding receptor words are printed directly underneath the source words. Since no attempt is made to render the translation into appropriate receptor syntax, the interlinear translation is difficult to read. Many ethnographic translations strive for formal equivalence and include numerous footnotes to explain unfamiliar customs and expressions. In recognition of the difficulty in perceiving the sense and spirit of a tale translated interlinearly, ethnographic texts often include a so-called "free" translation alongside the interlinear one. While the free translation arranges the message into the syntax of the receptor language, it still strives to retain source culture expressions by explaining the full meaning in footnotes. The addition of explanatory notes reflects the information theory concept that a message must be lengthened when transmitted through a constricted channel.

Dynamic Equivalence

In contrast, the dynamic-equivalence translation "does not insist" that the receptor "understand the cultural patterns of the source-language context in order to comprehend the message." Aiming at "complete naturalness of expression," it tries "to relate the receptor to modes of behavior relevant within the context of his own culture. . . ." Oriented more toward the receptor's response than to the source message, the dynamic translation emphasizes producing an equivalent effect. Nida describes such a translation as one in which a bilingual, bicultural person can justifiably say, "That is just the way we would say it."[5]

A Range Between Poles

It is easy to see that folklore texts can be arranged in a continuum between these two poles. The translated Indian texts of Sapir and Boas, printed with both interlinear and free translations, and accompanied by notes explaining foreign customs, aim toward formal equivalence. Popularized versions of Indian tales, however, may take great liberties with the original form and content in an effort to seem more "natural" to their readers. Opening and closing formulae may be replaced or omitted, scatological or sexual references blunted or bowdlerized, and repetitions removed. Pressures to suit the public's taste may influence the accuracy of academic texts as well. In one Indian text published by the Bureau of American Ethnology in 1919, the textmaker, Truman Michelson writes, "It may be noted that at times the original autobiography was too naive and frank for European taste; and so a few sentences have been deleted."[6]

Intralingual folklore translation, such as texts of Appalachian or Black folklore, also range from dynamic to formal equivalence. For example, Alan Jabbour and Carl Fleischhauer's folklore texts of the West Virginia

Hammons family strive toward formal equivalence. They retain all vocalizations, even false starts and continual repetitions of "he said." These texts are published with a phonograph record, so one can verify their accuracy. Although the endless repetitions of "he said" which punctuate the narratives are foreign to literary canons of good writing, Jabbour and Fleischhauer find them indicative of Appalachian storytelling style. The phrase not only serves as a rhetorical period, but "it often functions as a stylistic reminder that the narrative is to be taken not as a fanciful creation of the teller but as an accurate report of information passed along from the telling of another."[7] On comparing the Hammons family texts to Leonard Roberts' collection of Appalachian tales, it seems apparent that Roberts has removed typical oral features. His versions contain no false starts, vocalized pauses, or repetitions of "he said."[8] Roberts' texts seem to have been edited to fit the conventions of written style and thus may be termed more dynamic than formal.

In discussing formal and dynamic equivalence, Nida focuses chiefly on the linguistic level of discourse. Yet we can extend these two orientations to cover nonlinguistic performance features as well. A text which records the paralinguistic and kinesic features as they are performed in the source culture strives for formal equivalence, while a text which substitutes these features with gestures or tones native to the receptor culture aims for dynamic equivalence. To translate dynamically a mideastern "burp" of satisfaction over a meal to an Anglo-American culture, one might substitute a polite "sigh" of satisfaction. Or to translate dynamically a pointing lip gesture, common in some cultures, one might replace it with a pointing finger. These substitutions of functionally equivalent gestures have the advantage of being immediately comprehensible to the receptor culture. But they make it impossible to learn exactly how gestures were used in the original performance.

Toward Formal Equivalence

Clearly, the formal-equivalence orientation best serves the interests of the performance approach. Since a major concern among performance-centered folklorists is to discover the culturally unique styles of performance in distinct groups, this goal can hardly be served through texts which substitute functional equivalents, or omit elements which are foreign to the receptor culture's canons of taste. Yet the formal-equivalence orientation can result in obscure literalism if the textmaker forgets the goals of making sense, conveying the spirit and manner of the original, achieving a natural and easy form, and striving for an equivalent response. Unfamiliar cultural concepts and style can quickly make the text difficult to comprehend if care is not taken to present these elements with explanatory notes. When translating between languages, inevitable compromises must be made. For example, to translate the Zuni word *lapappowanne* literally, one would say, "a headdress of macaw tail-feathers worn upright at the back of the head." Yet if one is also trying to translate the line length and pacing of the original, one may have to shorten the translated phrase to "macaw headdress," and footnote or otherwise explain the full meaning.[9]

ANALYTICAL AND PERCEPTUAL EQUIVALENCE

Since there are at least two different ways in which a formal-equivalence text may be made, we must introduce two additional types of equivalence: analytical and perceptual. The differences in these two text styles are epitomized in the contrasts between Barker and Wright's concept of "inferential description" and Birdwhistell's positivistic, structural description.

Analytical Equivalence

In an analytical-equivalence translation, the textmaker separates or dissects the performance into component parts so that the resulting text displays its structural units. Texts made by Birdwhistell, Scheflen, and Pittenger, Hockett, and Danehy exemplify this analytical presentational form. Although none of their texts are records of artistic verbal performance, their attention to contextual and nonverbal features makes them a potential model for the translation of verbal art. Brandon-Sweeney's folklore text utilizing Birdwhistell's kinesic notations sets a precedent for an analytical verbal art text.

In all of these representative analytical texts, behavior is segmented into discrete units and presented in levels above the words. Pittenger, Hockett, and Danehy, for example, print phonemic and paralinguistic notations in levels above a transcript of the utterance in ordinary spelling. Birdwhistell follows this method, but adds a third, kinesic level. Scheflen discusses in detail a methodology for analyzing and transcribing filmed transactions into structural units. He advocates plotting horizontal rows on a time graph with the movements of each separate body part "including the head as a whole, one for the brows, one for the eyelids, one for the eyes, and so on to the mouth, upper torso, arms, hands, pelvis, legs, and feet."[10] In the analytical-equivalent text, no attempt is made to represent the performance in an equivalent perceptual form. Consequently, the text lacks the immediate, sensuous, intuitive, intrinsic, and preanalytic qualities of an aesthetic transaction.

Perceptual Equivalence

In contrast to the analytical orientation, the perceptual-equivalence text goes beyond the analytical to the perceptual form perceived by participants in an aesthetic transaction. Based on the theory that verbal art differs from other modes of spoken communication in its qualitative features, the perceptual-equivalence text strives to translate these distinctive and defining qualities. Unlike an analytical focus, which seeks knowledge by dissecting an entity into component parts, perceptual focus entails a "seizing or grasping" of meaning. Many of the perceptual qualities of a performance do not lend themselves to analytical segmentation. Perceptual qualities such as softness and brightness are multisensory, says Berleant, "appearing to touch, taste, smell, sound, and sight."[11] The continuous rather than discrete nature of such multisensory features makes them difficult to reduce to alphabetic, structural units, according to Tedlock:

> But the dimensions of the speaking event that were screened out by
> alphabetic treatment . . . , simply do not lend themselves to
> structuralist treatment. Such features are *continuous* rather than
> *discrete*. It may be that the /a/ of the linguists is not an /e/, and that
> the subject is not the object, so that we are here dealing with discrete
> entities that can be arranged in a closed system. But how long does a
> silence have to be to be profound? How loud is loud? At what point
> does pitch stabilization become chant? When does an annoyed tone
> become an angry one, or irony become sarcasm? Such qualities are
> not discrete entities and find no secure place in a mechanical scheme,
> but they do make changes in the *meaning* of what is said.[12]

Clearly, these perceptual qualities to which Tedlock refers demand the type of inferential description advocated by Barker and Wright. The following excerpts from Toelken's text of a Navaho tale aptly illustrate the inferential description of perceptual qualities: "[audience: amusement, heavy breathing to avoid open laughter]; [audience: mild amusement]; (normal conversational tone, perhaps a bit more slowly pronounced than usual); (. . . long pauses between sentences, as if tired); (far more slowly, almost drowsily); (admonishing tone, very slowly delivered)."[13]

Tensions Between Analytical and Perceptual Equivalence

Both the analytical and perceptual orientations hold attractions for the performance approach and seem to place the textmaker in a double bind.

The structural linguistic methods underlying current analytical texts of communicative transactions correspond to the performance approach's structuralist roots in sociolinguistic theory. Through an analytical isolation of emic performance codes, the analyst might be able to construct a grammar of performance within a speech community and ultimately compare this grammar with that of other communities. Yet if a performance is more than the sum of its communicative codes, as I have argued it is, then a purely analytical approach may not be sufficient to differentiate a performance of a tale from a report of a tale. Conversely, the perceptual orientation, in its endeavor to record the performance's qualitative, perceptual form, is attractive because it seeks to preserve the ontological form of performance for further study and enjoyment. Since, however, a perceptual text demands inferential description, it seems to threaten the objective pose of scientific description by acknowledging the need for intersubjective interpretation. Implicit in this apparent double bind between analytical and perceptual orientations is a clash between intuitionist and positivist approaches to meaning.

Yet I believe we can resolve this double bind in favor of a perceptual-equivalence orientation, if we incorporate certain analytical procedures into a textmaking methodology. E. D. Hirsch's concept of "corrigible schemata" provides a useful model for making a perceptual-equivalence translation. Hirsch introduces the idea of corrigible schemata to mediate a major schism in hermeneutical theory between two philosophical camps: intuitionism and positivism. The intuitionist position argues that "meaning is finally specified and made definite by a communion with the author's intention." This philosophy is based on the premise that "the letter must be an imperfect representation of meaning." The intuitionist argues that, "It is a matter of empirical fact that the same linguistic form can and does sponsor different interpretations; consequently it must also be a matter of empirical fact that interpretation does always transcend the letter in some respect." In contrast, the positivist argues that "meaning is specified by a refined understanding of linguistic rules and norms." In its newest form, positivist interpretation "has been much refined and expanded until the description of a verbal strategy takes into account the entire linguistic context, including the whole implicit code that lies behind the verbal strategy."[14]

Hirsch believes that both of these positions, in their extreme forms, are inadequate. The intuitionist position "encourages oracular, priestlike pronouncements on the one side, and rebellious subjective individualism on the other." Although the positivist looks for meaning in rule-governed linguistic forms, Hirsch shows that description of linguistic form depends in crucial respects on a prior understanding of the text's meaning: "It may be supposed that stylistics as an enterprise is supposed to assist and confirm interpretation, but in crucial respects stylistics can only exist *ex post facto* to interpretation. For, when the words of a text are interpreted in two different ways (no matter how subtle the differences), they will display two different styles, which is the reason, presumably, why stylistics experts disagree among themselves as much as do the intuitionists." The intuitionist and positivist positions, Hirsch contends, do not account for "two elementary and central facts about interpretative and linguistic change": "our intuitions are open to correction, and our rules and conventions are open to change. . . . The intuitionist cannot explain how or why we come to revise an interpretation. The positivist cannot explain how the rules can change, or how we could know that they change."[15]

Mediation: Corrigible Schemata and Perceptual Equivalence

To bridge the gap between these interpretive poles, Hirsch introduces an interpretive model based on Piaget's notion of corrigible schemata. Hirsch uses the word schema to refer to a hypothesis, genre, or typification used in coming to know any phenomenon. He argues that we approach a new phenomenon with a certain hypothesis, or expectation of its nature and attributes. Since the actual encounter with a phenomenon may confirm, deny, or refine the initial schema, Hirsch calls schemata "corrigible." His model is similar to Heidegger's emphasis on preunderstanding, but involves a self-correcting, validating component: "Unlike one's unalterable and inescapable preunderstanding in Heidegger's account of the hermeneutic circle, a schema can be radically altered and corrected. A schema sets up a range of predictions or expectations, which if fulfilled confirms the schema, but if not fulfilled causes us to revise it."[16]

This "making-matching, constructive-corrective process" inheres in all aspects of verbal interpretation and thought, argues Hirsch. The universality of corrigible schemata suggests that *"the process of understanding is itself a process of validation."* This model of interpretation as corrigible schemata accounts for the central facts of interpretive and linguistic change, left unaccounted for in the intuitionist and positivist camps: "Yet these basic and central facts about language-change are not in the least problematical when understanding is conceived of as a validating, self-correcting process—an active positing of corrigible schemata which we test and modify in the very process of coming to understand an utterance."[17]

Hirsch's model of corrigible schemata helps clarify a procedure which I believe must underlie the making of a perceptual-equivalence text. Some cultural bias and blindness is impossible to avoid, whether one is making an analytical or perceptual-equivalence text. Since the performance approach aims to understand the culture-specific patterning of verbal art, however, it places a premium on accurate recordings from an emic perspective. If investigators unconsciously impose their own aesthetic tastes and concepts on the material they are recording, they may obscure integral elements of the performance. Consequently, in making a perceptual-equivalence text involving inferential description, the textmaker must make sure the inferences made are based on emic perceptions. In interpreting the situational, perceptual meaning of a voice quality or particular gesture, the textmaker must beware of imposing a meaning from his own culture. A gesture such as "wagging the head" may be a sign of derision in one culture, while in the textmaker's culture it might only indicate disapproval or negation.

Acquiring the perspective of the participants involves building an initial corrigible schema of the performance tradition. The components of Hymes' ethnography of speaking model (setting, participants, ends, act sequence, key, instrumentalities, norms, and genre) can provide an initial set of investigatory points.[18] Through becoming familiar with different ways of speaking in a community, and the norms, keys, and instrumentalities appropriate to or typical of them, the textmaker's sensitivity to heightened, intensified artistic communication will grow. Experience with performances will confirm or modify the initial schema. Textual records will aid in the constructive-corrective process as they permit the textmaker, as well as other researchers, to reexamine textual evidence and compare it to ethnographic descriptions and interpretations. Making this first corrigible schema, which can be called "learning the performance tradition," provides the textmaker with the initial preunderstanding needed to participate fully in the aesthetic transaction.

The actual process of making the textual translation involves another construction of a corrigible schema. This schema involves a comparison of the textual form to the video or film form, and continual validation of the text through performing it. Repeated viewings of the film will undoubtedly reveal features which the textmaker missed or observed only dimly in the live performance. To avoid overlooking details, the textmaker may devise a systematic method for recording separate levels of the performance. On one viewing, for example, the textmaker may record only posture shifts. On a second, one might concentrate on hand and arm movements, and so on. Yet the analytical, dissective stage is only a means to an end and should not terminate the translation process. The textmaker must seek a presentational form that embodies the perceptual form of the performance. Through performing the text and having others perform it, the textmaker can learn if his or her translation makes sense, conveys the spirit and manner of the original, has a natural and easy form, and produces a similar aesthetic transaction.

Evidence of current textmakers using such a constructive-corrective process is revealed in some of the recent changes Tedlock has made in his practice of translating Zuni performances. Realizing the importance of conveying immediacy, Tedlock has changed his practice of leaving Zuni onomatopoeic words untranslated: "In *Finding the Center,* I left Zuni onomatopoeia untranslated wherever I preferred its sound to that of the English alternative, but I have since come to the view that an onomatopoeic word helps give a story immediacy, an immediacy that would be lessened by the sudden intrusion of a foreign word in the translation."[19]

In order for a text to record verbal art as performance, then, and not some other mode of communication, the textmaker must strive for formal and perceptual equivalence. Actual translation choices of how to project a performance must grow out of the nature of the particular performance being translated. Yet certain principles can be suggested to aid the textmaking process.

MAKING THE PERFORMANCE REPORT

As we saw in Chapter 4, the performance-centered text consists of two parts: a record of the aesthetic transaction and a report of the aesthetic field. Since, as Bauman has argued, artistic communication requires a shared understanding of the aesthetic conventions being employed,[20] it is important to provide readers with an understanding of these aesthetic conventions before they confront the textual record. An accompanying report describing the aesthetic field, the rules of transformation governing the projection devices, and performance features which could not be incorporated into the text, is as important as the record itself. A performance report makes it possible to provide the cultural and linguistic redundancy needed to widen the reader's capacity to appreciate the aesthetic transaction. The report serves the vital function of lengthening, or adjusting the performance to accomodate it to the receptor medium and culture.

Regrettably, many of the currently published performance-oriented texts give only partial, perfunctory reports. A thorough report could be modeled on Hymes' ethnography of speaking model, and describe the setting and scene, participants, ends, act-sequence, key, instrumentalities, norms, and genre.

In suggesting Hymes' model, I do so because its components function in a manner similar to Aristotle's rhetorical *topoi,* or topics. They can serve to remind the textmaker of those significant dimensions of the performance event to observe. Yet no system of categories can substitute for genuine awareness and involvement with a performance event. Thus, these categories should not be applied mechanically as ends in themselves, but as reminders of important aspects of a performance.

Setting and Scene

The report of the physical setting should furnish details on the time of day, season, physical locale, and arrangement of space. Hall's proxemic categories (discussed in Chapter 4) provide points to consider. Describing the psychological scene in which the performance occurred is especially important. Was the performer coerced into performing and in a hurry to get it over with, or was he or she eager to entertain the audience? Were there tensions among the participants? Did they feel uncomfortable being recorded? Did the psychological scene change as a result of the performance? The textmaker's ability to accurately interpret the psychological mood of the participants will be aided by a familiarity with the culture's characteristic nonverbal clues for indicating psychological states.

Participants

In reporting details about the participants, the textmaker should include information about audience members as well as the performer. Since the textmaker's presence as a participant influences the performance, he or she should be sure to include information about his relationship and interactions with the participants. Describing the participants' ages, educational background, occupations, and interrelationships can provide invaluable information for later studies. Information about how the performer learned the tale, what he or she considers important in a good performance, and how he or she interprets its meaning can aid in studying performance traditions. Descriptions of the performer's physical appearance, habitual voice set and body base, and any artifacts used in the performance can help readers envision the concrete details of the performance. Photographs might be useful in illustrating these details.

Ends and Act Sequence

Through interviewing participants, the textmaker can report on the public purposes or private goals (ends) which the performance serves. Reporting the act sequence of the aesthetic transaction itself should not be necessary if the text records the complete narrative. But reporting the acts immediately preceding and following a performance may be crucial in understanding how the performance is used and understood by participants.

Key and Instrumentalities

Discussing how the performance is keyed and how the instrumentalities, or channels, are used can provide readers with necessary information to perform the text. Here, the textmaker can include details about performance style that he or she could not record in the text. For readers to understand the pacing and tone of a chant, for example, a comparison to a similar sounding chant in the readers' culture might be helpful. In translating a Zuni prayer, for example, Tedlock reports that the performance resembles "the effect of a rapid paternoster."[21] Toelken describes the pacing of a Navaho performer's style by comparing it to the pacing of a stand-up comedian in a night club.[22] When such clues are not provided, it may be almost impossible for readers to understand what the performance should sound like. In the preface to a Zuni text, Tedlock acknowledges that "a number of people have told me of their difficulty in deciding just what these stories should finally sound like. . . ." He then gives a reference to his readers' performance tradition which provides a better clue to the general key of the stories: "the reader should not sound like someone making a speech (unless a character in the story is making a speech), but like someone telling a story at the hearthside."[23]

Key to Projections

Along with reporting the performance's keys and instrumentalities, the textmaker should explain how he or she has attempted to translate these. Certainly, any unusual projection devices must be explained if the reader is to know how to perform them. To clarify the importance of explaining the rules of transformation underlying projections, it might help to conceive of the text operationally, as an abstract model of the original performance. The physical presence of projections on the page is an abstraction, a partial representation of the original performance. The material text, then, is the function of some projections into print of the aesthetic transaction. Yet only when the material, physical print symbols are further transformed through a reconstructive performance, is the translation of performance completed. The "integral presence" of verbal art is finally restored through a second, interpretive performance whose degree of equivalence to the original depends greatly on the performer's understanding of the printed projections.

Norms and Genre

Since a formal-equivalence text of a cultural group different from the readers' will undoubtedly record unfamiliar customs, concepts, and interaction patterns, a report explaining these foreign elements is imperative. By describing the norms of interaction and interpretation of the performance situation and the verbal art, the report can prepare readers to engage in an aesthetic transaction. For example, Bahamian "old stories," or folktales, are marked by a characteristic norm of interaction: audience participation patterns built around the use of the expletive "Bunday." A narrator uses "Bunday" to open and close a story, to call for the audience's attention, for emphasis, for pause, and sometimes to riddle with the audience.[24] Certainly, readers unfamiliar with the various functions of "Bunday" may be confused by its appearance in so many different places in a story.

Through delineating all of the above points, the textmaker will undoubtedly discover how the performance fits into the community's own framework for categorizing or naming performance. By reporting the native genre or speech act name, if any, later comparisons can be made among texts of the same genre.

MAKING THE PERFORMANCE RECORD

In making the record of the aesthetic transaction, the textmaker, like Ferlinghetti's acrobatic poet, is "constantly risking absurdity."[25] The simultaneous goals of formal and perceptual equivalence place great tensions on the textmaker. Pulled between two media, performance and print, and frequently two cultures, he or she must effect a delicate balance. On one hand, the textmaker desires to represent the original performance as faithfully, as completely, as possible. On the other, he or she knows that if "every little movement" were recorded, the text would be unreadable, and translation would fail. Thus, selecting what and how to record becomes paramount, and necessarily involves critical and aesthetic judgment. Steiner's four hermeneutic steps of translation: trust, penetration, embodiment, and restitution, coupled with the translating principles we have already discussed, can serve as a framework for making the textual record.

Trust

In order to translate the aesthetic transaction, the textmaker must first *experience* the aesthetic transaction. The understanding which translation reveals, says Steiner, begins with an act of trust.[26] The translator must surrender himself to the performance, experience it, savor it, enjoy it. This initial aesthetic experience and the subsequent ones which ensue in the many viewings of the video or film recording, will form a standard against which to measure the text. Only by first experiencing the performance's perceptual, qualitative features, will the textmaker know what he or she must strive to record.

Penetration

"After trust comes aggression," says Steiner. "The second move of the translator is incursive and extractive." This dissective, penetrative, analytical step leaves "the shell smashed and the vital layers stripped."[27] Since, as we have seen, the textmaker must select what to record, he must locate the patterns, the vital structure of the work. The simultaneity, density, and fluidity of the performance signals call for many viewings and a systematic method of analysis. The peculiarities of different performances will suggest varying analytical procedures. But I can offer some suggestions based on my experience with translating "Stagolee" (see Chapter 7).

First, make both a video (or film) recording and an audio recording. Attention must be given to the placement of recording equipment so as to catch important participants and actions. To discuss the technicalities of making a good video or film recording is beyond the scope of this work.[28] Transcribe a rough draft of the words of all participants and any other noises heard on the tape, and make several copies to work with. Nida says that careful translators do not translate meaning in a word-for-word fashion, but rather, translate by "meaningful mouthfuls."[29] Using this concept as a guideline, I have found it best to begin describing the large, easily perceptible, molar actions whose meanings are immediately clear. For example, many performers mime actions and characters using definitive iconic motions. All of these large iconic actions, such as pulling an imaginary gun, riding an imaginary horse, shaking hands, knocking on a door, swaggering, pleading for mercy, imitating an explosion, dealing cards, playing the guitar, and so on, can be readily noted on the draft.

But since molar descriptions alone do not reveal style, on subsequent viewings the analyst must search for the molecular actones which give the molar actions qualitative form. For example, in "Stagolee," when the performer first imitates pulling a .44 out of his left pocket, he does it with a cocky flair by simultaneously shifting his weight and jutting his right hip out. Using similar actones gives this same cocky air, enriched with sexual overtones, to the line "Now when the women heard him a-shuck the blues on the guitar, he could have whichever one he laid his eyes on." As he mimes playing a guitar, he swings his hip out to the right three times, on the words *shuck, blues,* and *guitar.*

In subsequent viewings, one can note progressively smaller movements. Examining the performer's stance shifts throughout can reveal important rhythmic and structural patterns. In my first experience with the performance, I was aware of a strong rhythmic pattern, but could not tell how it was constructed. After marking the stance shifts, I found that the performer regularly pivoted from left to right, and regularly tilted forward and backward. These motions constituted a basic rhythmic grid, over which other rhythmic patterns were laid. Separate analyses of arms and hands, facial expressions, and eyes will reveal how movements emphasize, punctuate, and counterpoint the spoken narrative.

On another draft, one can follow a similar procedure analyzing paralinguistic features. Again, starting with easily perceptible vocal characterizers, such as whispering or sobbing, and proceeding to smaller vocal qualities, such as intensity, pitch height, and extent, and voice qualities, such as gutteral sounds or articulation control, one can note paralinguistic features. Whether one chooses to record any or all of the suprasegmental phonemes is a matter best left to the individual nature of the performance and the patience of the textmaker. Recording intonational phonemes may be too many nits to pick without becoming a nitwit. The terminal junctures, however, are more easily discernible.

Embodiment and Restitution

If the process were to end at this second step, the result would be an analytically-equivalent text. We would, indeed, be left with a broken shell. The appropriative comprehension of analysis disrupting the "integral presence" of the performance must now be counterbalanced with the steps of embodiment and restitution.[30] Embodiment, in our case, means choosing what to project and locating appropriate projection devices in the receptor medium. Restitution, the act of restoring the integral presence of the performance by a second, interpretive performance, must be used in the process of choosing projections. Steiner's description of the final hermeneutic step of restitution shows its importance in the paradigm of translation: "The final stage or moment in the process of translation is that which I have called 'compensation' or 'restitution.' The translation restores the equilibrium between itself and the original, between source-language and receptor-language which had been disrupted by the translator's interpretative attack and appropriation. The paradigm of translation stays incomplete until reciprocity has been achieved, until the original has regained as much as it had lost."[31]

In the task of translating performance, however, I believe the act of restitution is not simply a final step, but must accompany the act of embodiment, in a dialectical constructive-corrective process. In choosing projection devices, one must continually evaluate the decisions through performance. The second corrigible schema comes into play here, as the textmaker compares his or her own performance (or that of others) to the video recording and the qualities present in the original aesthetic transaction. This dialectical process of embodiment and restitution confirms George Quasha's definition of translation as an activity "which strives in the structure of its behavior to *re-perform*, within the materials of one's own language, the possibilities and special realizations which exist in a foreign work."[32]

All of the analytical segmentation should make it easier for the textmaker to discern important stylistic patterns and qualities. Knowing the limits imposed by overloading the text with too much information, one must search for the essential patterns which give the performance its aesthetic form. Through an inferential shuttling back and forth between the molar and molecular levels, the textmaker can synthesize the fragments into perceptual units. This task will be easier in highly redundant performances. Frequently, verbal art involves many repetitions and formulaic passages on the linguistic level which may be matched by accompanying paralinguistic and kinesic repetitions. Each character in a story, for example, usually has an identifying voice, posture, and body movements. Similarly, a performer may have an economical performance style using a small set of repeated movements. Scheub's analysis of the aesthetic patterning of the body in oral narrative performances provides an excellent source for the textmaker at this stage.[33] Scheub describes various ways in which body movements are patterned, and how they function aesthetically.

From examining the different ways in which print can record performance features, the textmaker should be in a better position to choose projections. The most immediately perceptible projections are the iconic devices with a strong degree of resemblance to their referents, and natural language description.

The exact way in which projections should be arranged on the page must grow out of the nature of the particular performance. One approach, that illustrated in the final chapter, makes use of margins, underlining, italics, and other projection devices in a systematic way. Molar kinesic movements can be described through natural language placed in the right margin. These molar movements accompany all of the underlined words in the discourse. Molecular movements, which usually accompany only a few words, can be indicated directly beneath the words which they accompany. Molar paralinguistic features which modify an entire line or lines can be placed in italics in the left margin. Smaller molecular paralinguistic features, such as a rasp, or an elongated vowel, can be recorded with the word on which they occur.

CONCLUSION

In translating performance, the textmaker should strive for formal and perceptual equivalency. Analytical methods can be incorporated into making a perceptual-equivalent text through constructing corrigible schemata. The first corrigible schema involves learning the performance tradition. The second schema entails comparing the text to the video or film recording, and continual validation through performing the text.

The performance report describes the aesthetic field, explains any unfamiliar projections, and describes performance features which could not be incorporated into the text. A thorough description of the aesthetic field should begin by describing the setting and scene, participants, ends, act sequence, key, norms, instrumentalities, and genre.

Making the performance record involves critical and aesthetic judgment. Steiner's four hermeneutic steps of translation: trust, penetration, embodiment, and restitution serve as a framework for making the textual record. In the first step of trust, the textmaker must *experience* the aesthetic transaction of the live performance. This initial aesthetic experience provides a standard to measure the text against. The second step, penetration, refers to the analytical dissective stage in which the textmaker selects what to record. This analytical stage may be systematized by beginning first with describing large, easily perceptible molar actions, and then proceeding to smaller molecular actones which give the molar actions qualitative form.

The third step, embodiment, entails choosing what to project and locating appropriate projection devices in the print medium. The most immediately perceptible iconic and natural language projections are of most use in making a perceptual-equivalent text. This step must be combined with the fourth step, restitution, in a dialectical, constructive-corrective process. Restitution involves an intersemiotic translation from print to performance. Here, the textmaker compares performances of the text to the video or film recording and the qualities present in the aesthetic transaction of the original performance. We will see how these principles can be applied in the final chapter.

7

An Illustration of a Performance-Centered Text

In the previous chapters we have laid the theoretical groundwork for making performance-centered texts. Yet these theoretical principles can only be confirmed by the practice they facilitate. This chapter will include a performance-centered text, discuss how it was made, and compare it to a literary text of the same tale.

To demonstrate how these principles can be applied, it seems best to work with a performance which fully exploits the expressive potential of voice and body. The performance tradition of the Afro-American "toast," a type of narrative monologue, is especially attractive for this purpose. Folklorists who have collected toasts frequently comment on their rich performance style. Abrahams writes that "toasts are devices to call attention to performance abilities," and Jackson stresses that "toasts are not recited, they are acted; the teller does not just say a toast, he performs it."[1] Yet while attention has been focused on the importance of performance style to this genre, no performance-centered texts of toasts have been published.[2]

This toast performance was videotaped in an undergraduate class on the study of Black literature through performance. In the first assignment, in which students were asked to perform folklore from their own oral traditions, one student gave an excellent performance of a well-known toast, "Stagolee." His performance was so creative and stimulating that half the class were on their feet shouting approval and roaring with laughter. Although this first performance was not recorded on videotape, seeing it convinced me that it would be a challenge to record in print. Three months later, the student again performed "Stagolee" for the class, so that I could videotape it.

The performer, James Hutchinson, first heard a friend perform this version of "Stagolee" during a high school lunch break. Hutchinson listened to his friend perform several times and asked him to write down the words. His friend gave him a handwritten version and told him that the story originated from Julius Lester's book, *Black Folktales*.[3] Hutchinson never looked at Lester's version, but learned the tale from watching his friend perform and reading the manuscript. Thus, Hutchinson's performance is the result of a curious interplay between oral and written sources of transmission. Julius Lester credits his literary version of "Stagolee" to versions he heard circulating orally, so the first source of the transmission was oral. In transmitting the tale through print, however, Lester changed many features characteristic of oral style. In performing Lester's version, Hutchinson's friend must have deleted certain literary trappings and added characteristic performance features. Unfortunately, the manuscript version no longer exists, so it is impossible to see what changes the friend made, or how Hutchinson's performance compares to the manuscript. But it is possible, from the following performance report and record, to compare Hutchinson's performance to Lester's text and thus get a look at the changes made when a written folktale re-enters oral tradition.

THE REPORT

The aesthetic field of this performance extends beyond the specific performance event to include the larger performance tradition of "Stagolee" tales and songs. Before focusing on the specific performance event, the report considers the larger performance tradition. Then, the specific performance event and instrumentalities are discussed. The report ends with an explanation of the projections used in the text.

Performance Tradition

Among Black Americans, "Stagolee" is a popular folk hero whose escapades are chronicled in both song and narrative. Stagolee is a bad man, an outlaw, sometimes referred to as a "ba-ad nigger"[4] who defies authority, often wantonly killing and raping. Many versions of both songs and toasts include a notorious fight between Stagolee and another bully named Billy Lyons. While gambling, Billy and Stag have a fight over Stagolee's Stetson hat. Often Billy pleads with Stagolee not to kill him, mentioning that he has a wife and children to support. But Stagolee calmly shoots Billy with his forty-four, rapes his wife, or his mother, and ends up in Hell, terrorizing the Devil. "Stagolee" narratives range from obscene versions told among men to milder versions told among women and children.

Although today folklorists rank Afro-American narratives such as "Stagolee" "at the very highest level of achievement in terms of poetic and narrative values,"[5] for many years this tradition escaped the attention of professional folklorists. No doubt the obscene nature of many versions kept them from being widely published, or attracting the attention of folklore scholars. Since Roger Abrahams' pioneering work on toasts, *Deep Down in the Jungle,* appeared in 1964, however, many toasts have been published and scholarly debate continues over their form and meaning.[6] It is not my intention to rehearse all of the literature on toasts here, but rather to focus only on those issues relevant to an understanding of this particular rendition of "Stagolee."

A major issue, still unresolved, concerns how toasts, as a genre, should be defined and named. The reader of Abrahams' collected toasts will note that they are rhymed, usually in balanced, four-stress lines arranged in rhyming couplets: "She said, 'Who did this crime, may I ask you, please?'/I said, 'Me, bitch, and they call me Stackolee.' " Abrahams says that the "couplet provides the basic structural unit of the toast in most cases."[7] Before we conclude that all toasts employ a rhymed poetic form, however, we must note that other collectors have published so-called "prose" versions which their informants also call "toasts."[8] Whether or not these unrhymed versions should be termed "prose," however, is a point we will return to below. While Hutchinson's version is unrhymed, it has a pronounced rhythmic structure more akin to free verse poetry than to prose.

The definition problem becomes further complicated when we learn that many performers do not use the term "toast," but call their narratives "jokes."[9] The performer of the version recorded here was not familiar with the term "toast," but called his narrative a "joke." Yet these narratives differ from typical American joke structure. While jokes build to a punch line and "have one point, one discharge, the toast often has several."[10] Commenting on the different forms and names given to "toasts," David Evans contends that "it would be impossible to construct an inclusive native generic definition, and even an analytical definition would be difficult, or else it would be extremely generalized and not particularly useful." I agree with Evans' conclusion that the best we can do is "only describe the range of characteristics of what our informants call 'toasts' and collect and publish as many textual examples as possible."[11]

Although Hutchinson calls his version a "joke," and although he does not use rhymed couplets, his performance is similar enough in structure and performance style to be categorized under the analytical generic term "toast." From examining the text of his performance, we can see the following features in common with the larger toast-telling tradition. As mentioned above, toasts are characterized by a distinctive performance style. The performer is, in a real sense, on-stage, striving to hold and entertain an audience. Jackson compares the toast to a kind of street-theater involving only one performer at a time. Those persons "who can say the lines but cannot act them get little opportunity to perform, because they are boring." Jackson reports that performers use voice changes involving differences in stress, accent, and clarity of articulation for the various personae.[12] Abrahams describes a similar theatrical style. Characterizing one performer's style as "very theatrical," Abrahams says, "He used as many dramatic devices as possible, changing voices for different characters or varying situations, utilizing the full range of his voice's pitch and intensity, and he would speed up and slow down at will." In characterizing the performance style of toasts in general, Abrahams writes, "Performing was performing, and there was no attempt by the teller to confuse the reader by introducing pieces that seemed to involve casual speech. Voice pitch and other elements of vocal production were, for each performer, different in a very important way from his usual manner of speaking, whether through utilization of a wider range of pitch levels and loudness, great emphasis on story line or its embroidery, or simply sheer rapidity of narration."[13] Confirming Abrahams' remarks, Labov, Cohen, and others, write that "toasts are delivered in a rhetorical style which is quite different from ordinary speech." The "whole style is far from casual, with meter emphasized, and special voice qualifiers, such as falsetto, used."[14]

In addition to a theatrical delivery style, toasts have other distinctive stylistic features. Hutchinson's version has the typical thematic structure of other "Stagolee" tales and employs some of the recurring clichés. The fight with Billy Lyons, the descent to Hell, and the defeat of the devil are common themes. Details such as Stagolee's forty-four and his Stetson hat are common clichés. "Stagolee" toasts frequently contain a high percentage of dialogue, and Hutchinson's version is no exception. Although Hutchinson does not employ rhymed couplets, he uses another characteristic rhythmic feature—the balanced line. Abrahams says that toast lines are often balanced conjunctionally, paratactically, or appositionally. Hutchinson's version employs all these types of balance. His sentences have the same "subject/verb/modifiers" syntax which Abrahams finds typical of toasts.[15]

Now that we have described some of the key features of the performance tradition and located this "Stagolee" performance within it, we will examine the specific characteristics of the performance event.

Performance Event

The performer, James Hutchinson, provided information on how he learned "Stagolee," why he and his friends told it, and what he considers

necessary in a good performance of "Stagolee."[16] Hutchinson was twenty-
one years old, a student at the University of Texas, and a native of
Houston. He is the youngest of six children and describes himself as the
only actor in the family. Everyone in his family praised him for his acting
ability. In sixth grade, he played the role of Rumplestiltskin in a school
play. In tenth grade, Hutchinson "got into drama" when he realized that
"nothing is done to its fullest unless I do it."

It was difficult for Hutchinson to pinpoint when he first heard
"Stagolee." He remembers hearing a song version on the radio as a young
child, and said he heard his older brothers performing "Stagolee" when
he was about six years old. Hutchinson describes the version his brothers
performed as "more or less like Uncle Remus," "fit for a child," and
"much more calmed down." When Hutchinson was in the ninth and
tenth grades, he and his friends, both male and female, would perform
"Stagolee" and other "jokes" during the school lunch break, outside. He
first heard this version of "Stagolee" during this period and learned most
of the lines from hearing his friend perform. It was then that he had his
friend write down the words for him.

When Hutchinson was asked if he could remember whether he tried to
copy his friend's performance delivery in any way, he said he picked up
his friend's hand gesture of tapping his forefingers on his chest for the
line "I gonna take care of your wife." Hutchinson changed his version
from the manuscript, explaining that he cut out some parts to make it
"not as violent," and "not as harsh." He said that he "wanted it to be
more like a tale." He has heard more obscene versions of "Stagolee," but
says he would not tell such versions in an audience with females. When
he performs only for his male friends, he "jives it up" by throwing in
"some curse words." Hutchinson said he would not perform the version
of "Stagolee" he told in class for his parents, who disapprove of
"Stagolee" stories. When asked why his parents disapprove, he said that
they dislike the word "nigger." Hutchinson estimates that since he
learned "Stagolee," he has performed it about twenty times, and that each
time, he adapts it to his audience. The first time he performed for the
class, Hutchinson said he was nervous and tried to "jazz it up." On the
second performance, he "tried even more to jazz it up, so that the audience
would see something different."

Hutchinson said that he and his friends like "Stagolee" because they
identify with Stagolee; "his coolness" makes him attractive. What makes
a "Stagolee" performance good? "It's the performer who makes it good,"
Hutchinson said and continued, "A good performance of 'Stagolee'
requires relaxing and performing the characters as you and the audience
see them." Since Hutchinson narrates "Stagolee" in third-person, I asked
what type of person he thinks the narrator is. He replied that when he

says the narrative lines, he believes he is someone who believes in Stagolee, "one of his followers."

Hutchinson's performance was videotaped during a regular class meeting in late May, 1977. Out of the thirty-four students in the course, only six were white. During this course called Oral Interpretation of Black Literature, the students were expected to give several performances. By the end of the semester when Hutchinson performed, students were accustomed to performing and comfortable being recorded on video. Many of the students were friends, and the convivial mood of the class tended to compensate for the sterile, institutional, fluorescent-lit, windowless classroom.

In the videotaped interaction immediately preceding Hutchinson's performance, the participants began to assume performer and audience roles. This preparatory interaction provides a sample of Hutchinson's casual, nonperformance speaking style, which enables us to better appreciate the contrast between artistic verbal performance and routine speech. We scheduled the performance to begin the class session. While we waited for the last stragglers to arrive, I videotaped Hutchinson getting ready to perform. The students talked among themselves and to Hutchinson. The audience sat in their chairs in the typical large semicircle used for most of the class performances. As Hutchinson put on his microphone, someone hissed "sh!,sh!" and the class quieted down considerably. In the following transcript, Hutchinson talks in a quiet, low voice and occasionally laughs nervously. In contrast to his flamboyant performance movements, his gestures are subdued, his posture consistently straight.

Student:	Sh! Sh! (making a "hushing" sound)
Hutchinson:	Don't do that. Wait till I think of it first. (gestures for a student to come into the class) Are you ready?
Fine:	Yeah.
Hutchinson:	Want to leave the door open?
Fine:	Yeah.
Hutchinson:	Can I close the door?
Fine:	Yeah.
Male student:	(taunting James) Oh, why do you want to close the door? Shoot!
Hutchinson:	(gives the student a dirty look, walks over and closes the door). I don't remember it. (laughs nervously) Right here's fine? (nervously fools with microphone cord around his neck) If I forget it, y'all don't laugh. (hitches up his pants) You ready now?

(bows head and drops hand to his side for a second before
beginning "Stagolee")

By the time Hutchinson bowed his head, the audience was quiet and
attentive, ready for a performance.

Before discussing how the accompanying text was made, let me briefly
explain the camera positions. In the planning stages, I considered ways to
capture all of the audience, as well as the performer, on video. To do so
would have involved using two cameras, one focused on the performer
and the other on the audience. In order to view the tapes simultaneously,
the tapes could either be specially edited onto a split screen, or shown on
two monitors. If they were shown on split screen, however, all of the
figures would be reduced in size, making it difficult to observe expressive
details.

Although the class was accustomed to seeing performers videotaped,
the presence of an additional camera trained on the audience might have
proved disruptive. From observing Hutchinson's "Stagolee" performance
earlier in the semester, it was certain that the audience would play a
relatively passive role and that the only person assuming responsibility
for performance would be Hutchinson. The microphone would pick up
the audience's verbal reactions, and in an effort to get at least a few of the
audience members' faces into the frame with Hutchinson, the students
were asked to extend one side of their normal semicircle seating
arrangement to run along Hutchinson's left. The camera, positioned
downstage to Hutchinson's right and at an angle, revealed almost a three-
quarter view of the performer, and four or five audience members. A
medium-close shot recorded Hutchinson's body from the knees up,
providing more expressive detail than a long shot.

Analysis of Instrumentalities

Although this description of the analytical process follows the general
order in which I examined the performance, the process was by no means
as orderly as it may appear. Sometimes while concentrating on describing
one feature, I would hear or see another feature that had escaped my
notice. And each repetition of the tape helped refine and correct earlier
perceptions. Throughout the analytical process, it was often necessary to
imitate the voice and action on the screen. Some of Hutchinson's
movements, such as his stylized, "cool" imitation of running, involved so
many different movements that only by performing the movements
myself could I literally feel how to describe them. Often, I tested these
descriptions by asking other persons to describe a particular tone or
movement.[17]

Once the videotape had been made, a separate audio tape recording was
used in transcribing the initial rough draft. I spelled the words as I heard

them—"wantcha" for "wants you," "git" for "get," and "hoss" for "horse." Since my own dialect is standard Mid-western American English, the literary dialect spellings should be interpreted against this norm. I also indicated special sounds such as clapping and sighing, and recorded audience responses in brackets. Then I began the process of analysis described in Chapters 5 and 6.

Beginning with the videotape, I first described the larger parakinesic categories of body base, body set, and stance. From observing Hutchinson's typical nonperformance behavior in the class, I knew that his normal, everyday body base was heavyset, male, healthy. He dressed in simple, conservative clothes, normally stood straight, and used gestures that were unobtrusive but appropriate to conversational interactions.

In contrast to his typical body base, Hutchinson's varying body sets reveal his flexibility as a performer. A key way in which he effects these changes is through shifting his stance. He gives each character, Stagolee, Billy Lyons, St. Peter, Death, the Lord, the Devil, and the sexy sister, a distinctive body set. Hutchinson accomplishes these graceful, fluid character changes through an extremely economical, highly patterned system of stances. This small set of basic postures serves as a foundation from which he quickly changes from one character to another by adding modifying actones and paralinguistic features.

Hutchinson's most common stance involves two variations. He frequently stands with his left hand on his hip and his weight on his left foot, either with his right hand held up at about shoulder level to emphasize points, or with his right arm held across his chest, with his hand closed. These two closely related stances occurred so often that I began to abbreviate them as either the hip/hand or the hip/arm stance.

Hip/Hand Stance   Hip/Arm Stance

Figure 6

From these basic positions, Hutchinson constructs many of his characters' poses. Since Stagolee is cool, sexy, and dangerous, Hutchinson accentuates these qualities by leaving his left hand on his hip, while shifting his weight to make his right hip jut out. This stance with one hip jutting out is similar to what Benjamin Cooke calls a "player stance." The "player" differs from the pimp by having a lot of lady-friends for pleasurable rather than financial reasons.[18] Hutchinson's use of this stance reinforces Stagolee's traditional reputation as a ladies' man. To imitate a stereotyped stance for a sexy woman, Hutchinson only has to slightly change the hip/hand stance, by shaping his right arm like a swan's neck, with his wrist hanging limp. For a variation of this sexy female stance, he moves his right hand up to touch his hair, as if primping, raises his left shoulder several times, and sways his hips.

Sexy Woman Stances

Figure 7

Hutchinson frequently uses the hip/arm stance for both Stagolee and the Lord. Since he portrays these two characters as almost evenly matched in strength, he often uses the hip/arm stance to give them a similar commanding, self-assured posture. When imitating the Lord, however, Hutchinson does not jut out his hip; consequently the Lord's stance does not convey the same sexuality as Stagolee's. To further differentiate Stagolee from the Lord, Hutchinson commonly uses a loud, deep voice for the Lord, and a low, usually calm, sometimes breathy voice for Stagolee.

It is interesting to note the correspondence of the hip/hand stance with a similar stance used in Kongo oratory and sculpture. According to Robert Farris Thompson, "This ancient, most important attitude, is reserved for women and men of high rank, signalizing, variously, the channeling, summoning, or arresting of power at moments of crisis or ceremonial urgency. It is a gesture which, slightly modified, re-emerges among the strongly Kongo-influenced blacks of Haiti where, significantly, it is called 'the Kongo pose.'" Without further research, whether the hip/hand stance used by Hutchinson is connected to the African Kongo pose can be only a matter of conjecture. Yet the similarity between the poses suggests that just as verbal motifs might be traced to their historical-geographical origins, so might nonverbal gestures and stances. Only when more folklore texts record nonverbal features will this type of research be feasible.[19]

Another basic stance frequently superimposed on either the hip/hand or hip/arm stances involves bending the torso either forward or back. In the opening description of Stagolee, Hutchinson leans back, which automatically throws his chin up and his chest out. This posture is particularly appropriate for Stagolee's tough, strong-man personality. In contrast, to portray both Billy Lyons' and Death's cowardly moments, and St. Peter's great age, Hutchinson bends forward from the waist. He uses this forward and backward tilt skillfully to emphasize ideas and hold the audience's attention. For example, he bends forward to impersonate St. Peter "a-CHECKIN' out EARTH," but suddenly leans way back when St. Peter spies Stagolee and exclaims "Why Golly!" Sometimes he bends forward several times on a line, emphasizing the key words. In these lines, spoken by Death, most of the forward tilts (marked by ⌐) occur on those words which Hutchinson stresses paralinguistically:

"LOR-R-RD what you TRYIN' to DO—get me KILLED?"
  ⌐   ⌐   ⌐   ⌐ ⌐

A final stance variation, which Hutchinson superimposes on all other stances, involves turning his head (and often his whole body) to look at the audience to his left, at the middle, or to the right of the room. On the rough draft, I marked every turn, discovering that these frequent, regular shifts rhythmically punctuate the performance. Although I later decided against projecting these head turns in the text, let me give an example of how they were used. In the following passage, *L*, *M*, and *R* stand for left, middle, and right head turns, respectively. Notice how the right-to-left shifts in focus help create the impression of Stagolee "checkin' out" his new environment.

    Well, Stagolee walked around checkin' it out.
    L   R

    It was COol.
      M

    Brothers and Sisters had put in WA-LL-to-WALL
                          R   L

      CARpeting⌐

    STER--eo SYS-tem⌐
    R   M

    and BEST of all—AIR conditionin'.
               R   L

These frequent lateral sweeps of the head are sometimes accompanied by turning the whole body to the left or right. The changes in focus seem to reflect Hutchinson's sensitivity to his audience, who surrounded him in a broad semicircle. By continually sweeping the entire audience, he makes eye contact with everyone. In addition, he often turns his head or body during dialogue, which helps distinguish one character from another.

    On subsequent viewings, I noted iconic movements, such as imitating the action of pulling a gun, or dealing cards. Many of Hutchinson's icons are standard, widely recognized pantomimes. For example, to mime playing the guitar, he holds one hand around the neck of an imaginary guitar, while the other hand mimes plucking the strings. To imitate a gun, he uses the typical pointed index finger. In describing such standard icons, it seemed sufficient to simply say "mimes playing guitar."

Hutchinson performed several icons, however, with a pronounced Afro-American style. When Stagolee meets his brothers and sisters in Hell, for example, they greet him not with a typical White American handshake, but with the Black gesture of "giving skin." To imitate this gesture, Hutchinson emphatically and repeatedly alternates slapping his left palm on his right palm, and then his right palm on his left palm. This forceful, emphatic style of "giving skin" resembles what Cooke describes as "emphatic skin": "For example, if you really agree with someone and you want to accentuate this agreement more than usual, you might use some emphatic skin. In this case, the arm might be raised quite high and brought down with a great deal of exaggerated force; the contact is usually palm-to-palm in this situation. Although the contact seems to be hard, it is actually a quick, crisp movement."[20]

Hutchinson's way of miming Stagolee's walk also reflects Black style. One of his imitations of Stagolee's walk resembles what Cooke calls a "catting walk," designed "to attract attention and admiration, especially from females."[21] Cooke compares this walk to the strutting of a peacock, and I simply describe it in the text as a strut. To perform the strut, Hutchinson swings his arms in a slow, exaggerated rhythmic way, his knees bend as his heels hit the ground first, giving a slight spring to the walk; and he leans back, throwing his chest and chin up. The use of this strut on the line "HE decided HE wasn't gonna WORK for the white folks," appropriately suggests Stagolee's proud nature, while at the same time hints at his sexual attractiveness and power.

Hutchinson uses a different style of walk, what Cooke terms a "cool walk"[22] when Stagolee walks around Hell "checkin' it out." This walk involves the same springy step of the strut, but the arm swing is not as exaggerated, nor does he throw his chest and chin up.

A third type of stylized pose, Hutchinson's imitation of Stagolee running, seems to epitomize Stagolee's coolness. To perform this pose, Hutchinson freezes in the first step of a run, jumping down on his right foot while pulling both bent arms back, and snaps his fingers on both hands. Bringing both arms back, he throws his chest out. This running pose, as well as the above stylized icons, seems appropriate to Stagolee's identifying trait—his concern for style and "coolness." As Jackson says, Stagolee is "all style." He "seems more anxious to display his badness or his 'coolness' than attain any particular goal or end."[23]

After describing the large icons, I looked at smaller hand and arm movements and facial expressions. Hutchinson's hand and arm gestures were used for emphasis, or, to indicate a direction. Most of his hand gestures were the same vertical chopping motions used for emphasis in most conversational speech. While in the hip/hand stance, he accompanies his speech with his right hand performing the typical chopping movements used to emphasize words. Occasionally, he uses both hands in this same chopping motion. I decided to refer to these basic emphasizing hand gestures as simply "right hand emphasis" or "both hands emphasis." When he adds a pointing index finger to an emphasizing gesture, I wrote, "points right finger in emphasis." In one instance, Hutchinson uses a special variation of the chopping hand emphasis to indicate the amount of time Stagolee "lived on." In the following lines, he moves his right hand to the right, as if parting space, each time he brings it down in a chopping motion with the word "on."

> WELL, Stagolee lived ON and ON,
> and ON and ON,
> and ON-an-ON-an-ON.

To describe this type of emphasis, I wrote "right hand emphasis, parts space."

Once the significant body movements had been noted, I turned to the audiotape to work with linguistic and paralinguistic features. Here again, the pre-performance tape of Hutchinson's speaking made it easier to note the difference in pronunciation features and paralinguistic qualities used in performance. Hutchinson employed certain dialect pronunciations and words which he did not normally use in the classroom. For example, in the performance he omits the "*r*" on door ("Stagolee knocked on the do'.") but prior to the performance, he retains the final "*r*" when he asks, "Can I close the door?" In performance, many of his postvocalic *r*'s are deleted, as in such words as "po'ch," "fo'ty fo'" and "befo'." Yet Hutchinson does not consistently delete the postvocalic "*r*" in performance; for example, he says "sure," not "sho" and says "horse" once instead of "hoss." His lack of consistency in this feature suggests that he is consciously stylizing his speech rather than speaking out of habit. Pronunciations such as *"a-checkin' "* (checking), *"gonna"* (going to), *"coulda"* (could have), *"chillun"* (children), *"hoss"* (horse), *"git"* (get) and *"jest"* (just) were not normally part of Hutchinson's classroom speech. His well-modulated, medium low voice, manifested no unusual voice qualities or vocal characterizers. But in performance, he skillfully uses falsetto, rasp, stress, and other voice qualities and vocal characterizers.

By comparing the tape to the initial rough draft, definite pauses could be detected which were not apparent in the prose layout of the first draft. During each audition of the tape, I marked a slash wherever a pause could be detected clearly. After checking these pauses several times, I retyped the draft into a poetic layout. In this new form, each major pause occurs at the end of a line.

After listening to the pauses, it was apparent that traditional punctuation marks could not accurately represent the different types of terminal junctures which Hutchinson uses. In addition to the common fall in pitch associated with the end of declarative sentences, Hutchinson either slightly retains the pitch level on the final phoneme, or slightly raises it. To mark these junctures on the page, I used a dash for the retained pitch level, and a rising horizontal line for the rising pitch. For the numerous falling pitch junctures, I used punctuation marks appropriate to the grammatical structure. Thus, all commas, periods, and exclamation points represent falling pitch junctures. None of these stops, however, indicates the same length of pause as the line ends. Since the question mark is normally associated with a rise in pitch, it is used in place of the rising vertical line whenever the sentence is composed as a question and ends with a rising pitch.

It was quite evident that Hutchinson skillfully patterns the terminal junctures for rhetorical purposes. In the following passage, we can see how the rising junctures are not implied by the syntax. Consequently, if we did not represent them with a special mark, the reader would have no way of recognizing their occurrence.

> Now he coulda done anything in the WOR-LD
>   but that to StagoLEE⌐
> Stagolee looked over at him⌐
> Gave him that E--vil evil EYE⌐
> And Billy got to pleadin'.

After the pauses and terminal junctures were marked, I began to examine the remaining paralinguistic features. It was easy to discern the vocal characterizers of sobbing, whimpering sighs, and shouting. While the voice qualities, too, were easy to recognize, it was sometimes difficult to find appropriate descriptive words to convey their qualities. In order to find a suitable term, I often performed the line myself, imitating Hutchinson's delivery in order to interiorize the attitude. In difficult cases, friends gave their impressions of how a line was said. For example, in the following sentence, Hutchinson changes the forceful delivery of the first three lines to what can best be described as "hip" or "cool." Part of the "cool," "hip," quality stems from the way Hutchinson lowers and softens his voice, and throws his hip out.

> With a guiTAR on his SHOULder⌐
> a deck of CARDS in one Pocket—
> and a
> Fo'ty-fo' in the other.

Part of the performance's rhythmic structure comes from the special emphases which Hutchinson uses. To make it easy to see these stresses on the page, all heavily stressed words or syllables are typed in caps. Many of the stresses are not the simple linguistic stresses stemming from the syntax. Rather, Hutchinson seems to use these special stresses to build rhythm, create suspense, and emphasize attitudes and emotions. In marking the frequent falsetto pitches and rasps, I saw that these features often occurred on stressed words. In addition, the stresses are frequently accompanied by a gesture, which further emphasizes the word.

Hutchinson also stresses words by elongating vowels. His use of these elongated vowels (represented on the page by hyphens) sometimes alters a word's meaning, as in the word "ba--ddest." When the vowel is elongated, *bad* reverses its typical meaning to "very good, extremely good."[24] In another case, Hutchinson compresses two different meanings into one by combining an elongated vowel with a rise in pitch:

WELL, Stagolee took off STRAI-$^{-ght}$ for Hell.

As Hutchinson says "STRAI-$^{-ght}$," he looks up, with his hands clasped in prayer. This nonverbal gesture and the rise in pitch point upward, in the direction of Heaven. Thus, he loads the word "straight" with the meaning straight up to Heaven. By suddenly shattering this implied meaning through lowering his voice, dropping his head and looking down as he says, "for Hell," he adds an effective counterpoint to the line. Some of the elongated vowels, such as in "Ma--n" function too as another indicator of Hutchinson's conscious use of Black English, or what Claude Brown terms "Spoken Soul": "No matter how many 'man's' you put into your talk, it isn't soulful unless the word has the proper plaintive, nasal 'maee-yun.'"[25]

After describing the kinesic and paralinguistic features, I examined olfactory, tactile, proxemic, and artifactual features. Although Hutchinson does not use any real scents, costumes, or props, he imaginatively suggests their presence. He actually sniffs the air, as if smelling the barbecue cooking in Hell, and mimes the existence of objects such as cards, a guitar, the devil's pitchfork, a gun, a bow and arrow, and a horse. To portray the devil's long tail vividly, he points his arm behind him, as if indicating its length. His use of tactile communication is also revealed in the kinesic descriptions. To show Stagolee checking out Hell, Hutchinson uses gestures of metaphorically "touching" his surrounding environment. As Stagolee sees the wall-to-wall carpeting and stereo system, he pushes the palms of each hand out as if feeling his surroundings. Although Hutchinson never touches any of the audience, by touching parts of his own body (thumping his chest, clapping hands,

snapping fingers, and so on), he endows the performance with tactile
sensations.

Hutchinson's use of space helps define his performance as more
theatrical than interpersonal. He maintains a social and public distance
with a range of eight feet, from the persons on his left, and up to twenty
feet from those on his right. The various descriptions of his movements
reveal a full use of the space immediately surrounding him; his
movements are within about a three-foot radius in all directions.

The important stylistic features of the performance became clear after
close analysis of the videotape. Hutchinson uses basic stances, icons,
rhythmic pauses and stresses, falsettos and rasps, rising and sustained
terminal junctures, elongated vowels, and elements of Black English,
artistically and gracefully. We will consider the aesthetic impact of these
stylistic features when we compare Hutchinson's performance to Lester's
literary version of "Stagolee." The following section contains a brief
explanation of the projections used in translating this performance to
print.

Key to Projections

In deciding how to project the performance, the principles set forth in
the preceding three chapters provided guidelines. I wanted the finished
text to make sense, convey the spirit of the performance, be natural and
easy to read, and create a similar aesthetic response. Aware of the dangers
of overloading the text with too much information, I tried to avoid
introducing too many unfamiliar symbols. All of the projections used are
either iconic symbols or natural language. Like the analytical process, the
process of choosing projections involved constant checking and
correction.

In recording the kinesic and paralinguistic features, I gave primacy to
the major features such as the stances, icons, and vocal characterizers, and
added only those actones which further stylized or affected the
significance of a movement or sound. For the most part, the molar kinesic
movements appear in the right margin and accompany all of the
underlined words in the discourse. The subordinate molecular details are
placed directly below the words they accompany. The large
paralinguistic features, spanning a line or lines, such as the vocal
characterizers and qualifiers, appear in the left margin. Smaller features,
such as a falsetto or rasp, or an elongated vowel on only one word, are
recorded with the word on which they occur.

Repetitive stances, or particularly complex movements requiring an
explanation too long to fit comfortably alongside the discourse, required
an abbreviated description, such as "stylized running pose." The asterisk

with this abbreviation refers the reader to the accompanying report for a detailed explanation.

Before listing the projections and explaining how to interpret them, let me briefly mention the features which are only partially translated, or left untranslated. A real factor influencing what could be clearly projected was the space limitation imposed by the size of the page and type. Only so many words fit easily in the margins. In the cases in which a line contains both the narrator's voice and a different voice for a character, it is difficult to describe both voices in the margin to the left.

This difficulty can be overcome, however, by simply prefacing the record with a general description of the narrator's typical way of talking. Throughout the story, for example, Hutchinson narrates in what can best be described as a general conversational key similar to the type used in many American joketelling or storytelling situations. That is, while playing the role of the narrator, he does not assume any special characterizations, such as that of an old man or a drunk. He modifies this conversational norm, however, with many qualities, such as crisp articulation, drawl, a matter-of-fact tone, forceful or confidential tones, volume changes, and so on. Since these modifying qualities are so important to the aesthetic patterning of the performance, they are always recorded in the margin. Since space does not always permit recording the general conversational norm as well, readers should remember that any words such as softer, lower, or forceful to the left of narrator lines modify the general conversational key. In cases in which the narrator and a character speak on the same line, only the character's voice qualities and characterizers are described, leaving readers to assume the general conversational key for the narrator's lines.

Experiments with the notation of linguistic intonational and stress phonemes proved that these molecular details, if recorded fully, would overload the text and obscure the more important paralinguistic stresses, falsettos, and rasps. While Hutchinson's linguistic suprasegmental intonational and stress patterns seem typical of standard English practice, the paralinguistic intonations and stresses reflect conscious artistry. If the reader performs the paralinguistic features marked in the text, the linguistic intonational and stress phonemes should take care of themselves.

Finally, a myriad number of molecular movements such as eye blinks, position of fingers within gestures, or occasional handling of the microphone cord are not translated. Such detail would overwhelm readers and contribute little to the perception of stylistic patterns.

In the following list, the projections appear in the left column, and their explanation appears in the right.

Paralinguistic Features

words in left margin	Indicates vocal characterizers and voice qualities. A word followed by a dash indicates that the feature continues until the next description. Words without dashes apply only to the line to the right.
"crisp"	Indicates clipped, stacatto-like articulation.
↑ ↟ ↟ ↟	Indicates four degrees of falsetto. / ↑ / is slight; / ↟ / is extreme.
↑⁻ ⁻↑	When more than one word is said in falsetto, these symbols bracket the falsetto passage.
～～～～	Indicates a rasp, or harsh, gutteral, grating quality.
ALL CAPS	Indicates words said with greater emphasis or stress.
ris^{ing} letters	Indicates a rise in pitch on those letters.
hyphens between letters in a word	Indicate that the preceding vowel is held longer than usual. The longer a sound is stretched, the more hyphens appear.
end of line	Indicates a major pause of about three-quarters of a second. Lines followed by audience response have slightly longer pauses. Indented lines are used when a line is too long for the page; pause only at the end of the indented line.
commas, periods, exclamation marks within a line	Indicate a barely perceptible pause. Do not pause nearly as long as at the end of a line.
question mark	Used only for questions with a rising pitch at the end. Questions delivered with a falling or sustained pitch are marked by falling or sustained juncture symbols.

/ ⌐ / or /?/	Indicates rising juncture; pitch on last phoneme rises slightly.
/—/	Indicates sustained juncture; pitch of last phoneme is retained.
/./ /,/ & /!/	Indicates falling juncture; pitch of last phoneme falls or fades away.

Kinesic Features

words in right margin	Describes movements that occur with the underlined words in the line to the left.
words in rt. margin followed by dash—	The movements immediately preceding the dash and following the preceding semi-colon continue for the next line.
(- - -)	Indicates the same movements as the line above.
hip/arm stance	Left hand on hip, right arm across chest with hand closed. See Figure 6.
hip/hand stance	Left hand on hip, right hand held up at shoulder level to emphasize points. See Figure 6.
left hand on hip, rt. arm forms swan neck to side	See Figure 7. A stereotyped stance for a sexy woman.
strut	Leans back throwing his chest and head up; swings arms in a slow exaggerated rhythmic way; bends knees as his heels hit the ground, giving a slight spring to the walk.
stylized "cool" walk	Involves the same springy step of the strut, but the arm swing is not as exaggerated nor does he throw his chest and chin up.
stylized running pose	Freezes in the first step of a run, jumping down on his right foot while pulling both bent arms back and snapping fingers on both hands.
arms crooked	Arms bent, akimbo; fists closed.

rt. hand emphasis both hands emphasis	Typical vertical chopping motions used to emphasize speech.
rt. hand emphasis, parts space	Vertical chopping motion moving to the right, as if dividing space.
emphatically slaps alternating palms 6 times to mime "giving skin"	An Afro-American gesture for greeting, agreement, and approval.
words beneath the discourse	These gestures occur with the words above them. They often occur to modify a longer stretch of action described in the rt. margin. For example, as Hutchinson mimes playing the guitar (described in the rt. margin), he swings his hips on certain words (described beneath the words).
/ ⟍ / or / ⟋ /	Iconic symbols for backward or forward torso tilts. The more pronounced the tilt, the more curved the symbol. A tilt continues for the entire line, unless otherwise marked. Assume a straight posture on lines without tilt marks.

THE RECORD

The following record of "Stagolee" was performed by James Hutchinson in Austin, Texas, in May, 1977. As a translation of artistic verbal performance, the text is only complete when readers restore the integral presence of the original through performance. Before performing the text, readers should read the accompanying report of the aesthetic field and familiarize themselves with the projections used.

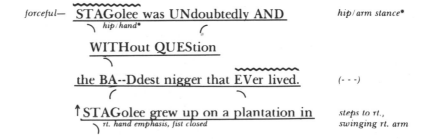

GEORgia;

and by the ↑TIME he was <u>TWO</u>,

holds up 2 fingers on rt. hand, lt. hand on hip

↑<u>HE</u> decided ↑<u>HE</u> wasn't gonna <u>WORK</u>

struts to rt.

<u>for the white folks.</u>

<u>UM--MM</u>

juts out lower lip, waves rt. palm in negation, lt. hand on hip

<u>HE LEFT.</u>

sharply extends rt. arm and finger, pointing rt. lt. hand on hip

<u>With a guiTAR on his SHOULder</u>

slings imaginary guitar over lt. shoulder, lt. hand on hip

<u>a deck of CARDS in one POCKet</u>—

confidently pats rt. hip pocket, lt. hand on hip

hip, cool softer, lower <u>and a</u>

lt. hand on hip, rt. arm down; throws rt. hip out—

<u>Fo'ty-fo' in the other.</u>

—pulls imaginary gun from lt. pocket, holds gun near hip, rt. arm down

conversational— Now when the ↑<u>WO</u>men heard <u>him</u>

<u>a-SHUCK the BLU--ES</u>
   hip swing   *hip swing*

<u>on the GUItar</u>

mimes playing guitar

HE <u>could have whichever one he laid his</u>
    shakes rt. hand

lt. hand still up from holding guitar neck

<u>EYES</u> on.
points rt. finger in emphasis

<u>and when he needed MONey he could</u>—

rt. arm outstretched, palm up, lt. arm down

<u>play ↑CARDS.</u>

deals imaginary cards to audience

crisp— <u>And when ↑ANybody got in his way,</u>

rt. hand emphasis, lt. arm down*

HE had his FO'ty-fo'.
juts rt. hip out — *rt. arm down; mimes pulling gun from lt. hip pocket—*

HE was REAdy. — *—holds gun; rt. hand emphasis*

conversational— ↑Now on this ONE particular occasion — *hip/hand stance**

STAGolee was playin' cards with Billy

LYons,

and ↑NATurally Stagolee was jest takin'
both hands emphasis

ALL of Billy Lyons' money. — *hip/arm stance*

emphatic— BILly got mad. — *furrowed brow; both hands clinched, down at sides*

He JUMPED UP and

a-KNOCKED Stagolee's Stetson HAT
claps outstretched hands

off his HEAD⌒ — *hip/arm stance*

and-uh HUGHGH-PEW! SPIT in it! — *hip/arm stance*
clears throat, mimes spitting, both hands on hips

confidential, softer— Now he coulda done anything in — *hip/hand stance—*

the WOR-LD but that to StagoLEE⌒ — *(- - -)*

Stagolee looked over at him⌒ — *struts 1 step; assumes hip/arm stance—*

1/2 step higher crescendo gave him that E--vil evil EYE⌒ — *(- - -) narrows 1 eye, juts out chin*

faster And Billy got to pleadin', — *fists clinched at chest*

loud, almost sobbing— "PLEASE Mr. Stagolee, — *fingers interlocked as in prayer, upturned eyes—*

I've got a wife and three chillun! PLEASE!" — *(- - -)*

[chuckles]

lower— Stagolee say,

hip/hand, rt. hip out—

"Well, that's cool—"

(- - -) slight shrug of shoulder, eyes down, holds tight-lipped frown after "cool"

[loud laughter]

crisp— "because the LORD'S gonna take care of
eyes up, throws rt. hand up, shakes it

hip/hand stance

your CHILlun,

and I gonna take care of your WIFE."
thumps chest with fingers

holds tight-lipped smile, eyebrows up, hip/hand stance

[laughter]

matter of fact— That's JEST what he did.

hip/hand; rt. hand points in emphasis

He BLEW Billy Lyons away.
flings rt. hand up in air

hip/hand

cheerful— WELL, later on that DAY Stagolee went over

to Billy Lyons ↑HOUse.

lt. hand on hip, rt. arm down

He KNOCKED on the do'.

knocks rt. hand in air as he stamps rt. foot on floor three times, lt. hand on hip

Mrs. Lyons come to the do'.

pulls rt. hand back to open door, lt. hand on hip

rapidly He say, "My name is Stagolee
taps chest, rt. fingers

your husband's dead the Lord's
thumbs out at hips   *points up,*

gonna take care of your chillun
rt. finger

and I'm movin' in."
taps chest, rt. fingers

[chuckles]

both hands out as if to silence objections—

truthful Jest what he did.

(- - -) cocks head

188

[laughter]

conversational—
drawls the   WELL, Stagolee lived <u>ON</u> and <u>ON,</u>   *rt. hand emphasis,*
word "ON"—   *clasps both hands at chest*   *parts space—**

and <u>ON</u> and <u>ON,</u>   *(- - -)*
(- - -)

and <u>ON</u>-an-<u>ON</u>-an-<u>ON</u>.   *same, rapidly*
(- - -)

<u>Well that was his BIG mistake.</u>   *hip/hand stance*

<u>You</u>   see, Stagolee lived so <u>LO--ng,</u>   *hip/arm stance—*

<u>till he started attractin' attention from up</u>   *(- - -)*

<u>in Heaven.</u>

<u>One day old St. Peter was jest</u>   *lt. hand on hip*

<u>a-CHECKin' out EARTH</u>
right hand cups brow as if searching

<u>and he noticed a NIGger SITtin'</u>   *lt. hand on hip*
               points arm down and out

<u>down there on the PO'CH.</u>

nasal twang   "WHY GOLly! <u>That look like</u>   *hip/arm*
   arms crooked

<u>STAGolee Jones!"</u>
looks again

conversational— SURE enough!   *flings rt. hand up,*
                                            lt. hand on hip

<u>St. Peter went over and checked it</u>
walks to left; bends over imaginary book,

<u>out in the book</u>
pointing finger—

STAGoLEE—<u>WA---Y past due.</u>   *leans back,*
(- - -)   *pointing*
                                              outstretched arm
                                              and finger

[laughter]

St. Peter went over and talked with the Lord.   *hip/hand, points in emphasis*

nasal twang— "Now LORD, 'ERE'S this NIGger down

there in Fatback Georgia,   *hip/hand, shaking pointing finger—*

by the name of StagoLEE—   *(- - -)*

↑Now Lord, that nigger's jest way   *folds arms across chest*

past due!"

[laughter]

deep, loud "We-ll⌐ call Death."   *snaps rt. fingers, hip/arm, frowns*

high, twang "Want me to call Death Lord?"   *fists closed at chest*

[laughter]   *looks exasperated, calls over right shoulder*

shouts, deep "DEATH! HEY, DEATH!"   *hip/arm stance*

very high, toothless falsetto "🌲 Yessuh, Lord 🌲"   *shuffle walk, head bent to left shoulder, limp lt.*

[laughter]   *wrist held to chest, head bobbing, almost spastic*

gruff, deep "What took you so long!"   *hip/arm stance*

toothless falsetto "🌲 Lord, you don't know how folks is   *same shuffle walk*

a-dyin' now days. 🌲"

[laughter]

deep, forceful— "Well, LOOK.   *hip/arm stance, emphasizes by shaking pointed finger—*

There's a NIGger down there in Fatback   *(- - -)*

Georgia by the name of StagoLEE.   *(- - -)*

190

deep, forceful I wantcha to go down there and GIT him.''   *(- - -) hip/arm stance*

high toothless falsetto "↑⁻YESsum Lord.⁻↑"   *same shuffle walk*

conversational— Death got on his big white horse and <u>rode on</u>   *mimes riding. lt. hand holds reins in front, rt. hand hits rear of horse, 3 rapid pelvic thrusts*

<u>down to Earth.</u>

[chuckles]

↑<u>Well Death got down there about</u>   *hip/arm stance*

<u>twenty minutes LAter,</u>

Stagolee was still sittin' on the porch

shuckin' some
hip swing

<u>BLUES on the GUItar.</u>   *mimes playing guitar*
hip swing　　*hip swing*

<u>Stagolee looked up—</u>   *still holds guitar, disbelieving expression caused by slight head turns—*

crescendo <u>saw this BI--G old white HO--SS</u>⁄   *(- - -)*

crescendo <u>with this LI--ttle old WHI--TE MA--N</u>⁄   *(- - -)*

crescendo <u>dressed in this LO--NG old WHITE</u>   *(- - -)*

<u>SHEE--T</u>⁄

loud, surprised Stagolee say, <u>"MA--N, we NEVer had no</u>

<u>KLANS in the DAYtime befo'!"</u>   *steps back in surprise, both hands emphasis*

[laughter]

conversational ↑Anyway, Death come RIDin' up to   *lifts leg up and over, dismounting* the porch and got off

toothless falsetto — "↑̄Is you STAGolee JONES? ̄↑" — *rt. hand emphasis, lt. arm down at side*

conversational — "Yeah, that's me (laughs nervously)" — *taps chest with rt. fingers, lt. arm down*

toothless falsetto — "↑̄ I'm Death. Come with me ̄↑." — *beckons with rt. arm, walks half step to left*

louder — "You who?" — *lt. arm down, rt. hand closed across chest*

[laughter]

raspy, very forceful — "I'm DEATH. Now come on, nigger!" — *arms crooked in front,* hands closed, thumbs up*

calm disbelieving — "You Death, huh?" — *lt. arm down, rt. hand closed across chest*

raspy, very forceful — "Now I AIN'T got all DAY—so COME on!" — *bends forward emphasizing underlined words, arms crooked*

soft — ↑̄STAGolee looked at the little man ̄↑ — *both arms down, juts rt. hip out*

crescendo — ↑̄REACHED in his POCket ̄↑— *rt. arm down, lt. hand mimes gun, holds at hip level—*

↑̄PULLED out his forty-four ̄↑—

crescendo — let one of them BULlets fly past Death's EAR— *—pushes thumb down on hammer of gun*

rapid, low, loud — DEATH wasn't NO time in gettin' away — *mimes riding horse, same as above, but twice as fast-6 rapid pelvic thrusts*

from THERE.

[laughter]

conversational — Death got back up in heaven — *hip/hand stance*

loud sobbing raspy — "LOR-R-RD what you TRYIN' to DO—get — *trembling crooked arms and hands*

me KILLED?"

192

[laughter]

"You know that NIGger like to SHOT me!"   *same trembling*
points rt. finger   *gestures*

[chuckles]

(exasperated sigh) Lord say,   *juts out rt. hip, lt.*
hand on hip, rt.
arm down,
frowns—

deep, loud "You WANT SOMEthin' DONE,   *(- - -) points rt.*
finger to
DO it yourself!"   *emphasize*

(clap, clap) The Lord called for his mighty
claps outstretched hands

thunderbolt,   *points rt. finger*
up over head

crescendo looked DOWN   *lowers head; arms*
at sides

crescendo took AIM   *mimes pulling*
large bow and
arrow—

very loud POW!!!   *(- - -) hands open,*
arms fly up,
jumps back

matter-of-fact— That was the end of Stagolee.   *tosses rt. hand up*
to chest, lt. arm
down

[laughter]

Jest can't mess with the Lord.   *crosses himself*
with rt. hand, lt.
arm down

[laughter]

conversational— WELL, Stagolee took off ST^RAI--^ght
looks up, hands clasped in prayer

for Hell.
looks down, head drops

He's about thirty miles away he coulda   *lt. arm down, rt.*
hand emphasis

(sniff sniff) SMEL--L the barbecue
sniffs loudly

a-COOKin' <u>anda,</u>
⌒ *snaps fingers on hands*

1/2 step higher   HEA--R the juke box a-PLAYin'⌒   *swings hips*

STAGolee <u>got</u> to <u>RUNnin'</u>.   *stylized running pose,* snaps fingers*

<u>When he got</u> there the
both hands emphasis

<u>brothers and sisters</u> came to the door
rt. hand emphasis

from <u>EVerywhere</u> to greet him.
⌐ *both hands emphasis*

emphatic, loud—   "WELL now STAGolee WHAT'S GOin'

on STAG! GIVE me some <u>of dat</u>   *emphatically slaps alternating palms 6 times to mime "giving skin."**

<u>HEY STAG</u>!"

[laughter]

"<u>WHAT</u> took <u>YOU</u> so long to get <u>down</u>   *hip/arm stance, smile*
rt. hand emphasis

<u>here</u>."

[laughter]

soft, crisp—   Well, <u>Stagolee walked around checkin'</u>   *stylized "cool" walk**

<u>it out.</u>

<u>It was COol</u>   *both hands emphasis*

Brothers and Sisters had put in WA-LL-to-
pushes rt. open palm to rt. front at chest level

WALL CARpeting⌒
pushes lt. open palm to lt. front, at chest level

1/2 step higher   STER--eo SYS-tem⌒
⌐ *same gestures, but at eye level*

194

breathy on | and BEST of all—AIR conditionin'. | *lt. arm down*
"conditionin' " | *fans face with open rt. hand* |

[strong laughter]

low, breathy Well Stagolee say, "Uh, — *hand on hip, rt. arm down—*
sexy voice
while talking
to the hey, this is nice!" — *(- - -)*
Sister—

He say, "Come here. Uh. — *lt. hand on hip, turns head, looks over rt. shoulder; small beckoning gesture with lowered rt. hand*

who's that right over there?"
raises eyebrows, points with thumb on lowered rt. hand

high, breathy One of the sisters say, "Oh, Baby uh! — *lt. hand on hip, rt. arm forms swan neck to side**
sexy voice on
Sister's
lines— THAT'S the DEVil." — *same sexy pose*

"Who is that again?" — *both arms down*

pleasurable " ⭡uh! THAT'S the DEVil ⭡uh!" — *same sexy pose*
whimper on
"uh."
"Wh-what seems to be his problem?" — *lt. hand on hip, rt. arm down*

coughs out "h- ⭡ He haven't learned to cope with us
"He"
— *lt. hand on hip, rt. hand primps hair, sways seductively, raising left shoulder several times*
pleasurable niggers yet ⭡⁻ uh-huh-uh ⁻⭡."
whimper on
"uh-huh-uh."

Stagolee went over to him, — *steps to right-front, swinging arms*

this LITtle bittie old RED man with

crescendo his LITtle red leoTAR-D⌐ — *holds closed hands to chest, disgusted look*

crescendo this LO--NG TA--IL⌐ — *points lt. arm back to left, looks back to left*

crescendo this BIG black PITCH ⭡ fork⌐ — *rt. hand raises imaginary pitch fork, disgusted look, lt. arm down*

soft Stagolee say, "Hey,   hip/hand,
                                                              pointing in
                                                              emphasis—

you got your pitch fork   (- - -) looks down
                                                              at devil

                                                              lt. hand mimes
and I got my forty-fo'.   pulling gun out of
  taps chest with rt. fingers   pocket—

                                                              (- - -) holds
Let's GO a round!"   pointed gun near
                                                              hip, rt. hand in
                                                              pocket

↑⁻Death ain't say nothin'⁻↑.   rt. hand in pocket,
                                                              lt. hand closed at
                                                              chest—

↑⁻He jest looked at him all PITiful⁻↑.   (- - -) looks up,
                                                              fearful expression

rapid ↟⁻Stagolee say, "Well, that's COol⁻↟.   raises brows, shifts
                                                              weight, drops
                                                              hands to sides

very loud Cause I'M gonna RUN HELL ALL BY   furrows brow
forceful   *thumps chest with thumbs*   *waves palms in front, as if saying no*

MYself!"

                                                              brows up,
matter-of-fact And that's JEST what he did.   hip/arm stance;
                                                              drops head and
                                                              arms at the end

[applause, yea, yea]

THE PERFORMANCE-CENTERED TEXT AND
THE LITERARY TEXT: A COMPARISON

Now that we have seen a performance-centered text of "Stagolee," we should be able to better appreciate the aesthetic patterning of Hutchinson's performance. Such performance-centered texts can provide data for a variety of research questions (see Chapter 1). To illustrate the advantages of performance-centered texts, let us briefly consider the immediate questions arising from the origin of Hutchinson's performance in Julius Lester's literary text.

In literate cultures such as ours, literary and oral traditions exist side-by-side and often cross-fertilize each other. Many novels and short stories, for example, originate from folk stories; conversely, written literature, ranging from *Genesis* to poetry such as Robert W. Service's "Cremation of Sam McGhee," circulates orally. Several collectors of Black toasts mention that some of their informants learned their versions from manuscripts or books, yet no published studies examine how the written versions change in performance.[26]

No doubt, the lack of performance-centered texts is one reason for the absence of comparative studies of the oral and written versions of toasts. Without a record of the nonverbal, paralinguistic, and contextual features of a performance, it is difficult to do more than make generalizations, such as the performer dramatizes characters, or uses his voice and body effectively. Since we have a performance-centered text of "Stagolee" and know its origin in Lester's literary version, we are in a prime position to explore what happens when a literary text enters a performance tradition. Although the comparative data in these two texts is rich enough for a long, exhaustive analysis, this discussion will be limited to a brief examination of the major differences in content and form.

One of the most striking features about the two different texts is that while many of the phrases in Hutchinson's version are often exact or very close copies of Lester's words, Hutchinson's version is about five times shorter than Lester's. Hutchinson's text contains only 853 words, compared to Lester's 4,224. Part of the cause of this greater economy stems from the omission of four themes present in Lester's text: gunning down a new white sheriff who tries to arrest him, surviving a second white sheriff's attempt to hang him, a description of his funeral and resurrection, and his ascent to heaven. Yet these four themes contain only 1,756 words, and even after subtracting them, Lester's version remains almost three times as long as Hutchinson's. Thus, other causes than omission of themes contribute to the economy of the oral version.

The chief source of Hutchinson's greater economy lies in the deletion of Lester's long, elaborated descriptions. Apparently, Lester must assume his audience has little familiarity with the traditional characterizations of Stagolee and Billy Lyons, since he elaborates their reputations before showing their confrontation in the bar. In the following excerpt from Lester's text, the underlined words are those which Hutchinson quotes exactly from Lester. Broken lines indicate closely paraphrased words. This example typifies the way Hutchinson takes essential action from the story, omitting elaborations:

> Well, this one time, Stagolee was playing cards with a dude they called Billy Lyons. Billy Lyons was one of them folk who acted like they were a little better than anybody else. He'd had a little education, and that stuff can really mess your mind up. Billy Lyons had what he called a "scientific method" of cardplaying. Stagolee had the "nigger method." So they got to playing, and, naturally, Stagolee was just taking all of Billy Lyons' money, and Billy got mad. He got so mad that he reached over and knocked Stagolee's Stetson hat off his head and spit in it.[27]

Instead of including Lester's long character sketches and descriptive passages which continually interrupt the action, Hutchinson either summarizes action or directly portrays it through dialogue. For example, when Death first appears in his performance, Hutchinson does not use any words to describe him. Rather, he speaks in a toothless falsetto and shuffles like a decrepit, slightly spastic, old man. In contrast, one of Lester's longest elaborations is his character sketch of Death. Lester inserts 326 words describing Death between the Lord's lines "HEY, DEATH! HEEEEY, DEATH!" and "What took you so long, Death?" Although it would take too much space to quote this passage in full, one paragraph provides a clear example of Lester's style of elaboration used throughout the tale. Notice the frequent topical allusions to Vietnam and bureaucratic structure:

> Now Death was laying up down in the barn catching up on some sleep, 'cause he was tired. Having to make so many trips to Vietnam was wearing him out, not to mention everywhere else in the world. He just couldn't understand why dying couldn't be systematized. He'd tried his best to convince God either to get a system to dying or get him some assistants. He'd proposed that, say, on Mondays, the only dying that would be done would be, say, in France, Germany, and a few other countries. Tuesday it'd be some other countries, and on like that. That way, he wouldn't have to be running all over the world twenty-four hours a day. But the Lord had vetoed the idea. Said it sounded to him like Death just wanted an excuse to eventually computerize the whole operation. Death had to admit that the thought had occurred to him. He didn't know when he was going to catch up on all the paper work he had to do. A computer would solve everything. And now, just when he was getting to sleep, here come the Lord waking him up.[28]

Why does Hutchinson's version omit four themes and so much descriptive detail? Since the intermediary manuscript version no longer exists, we cannot tell how much detail Hutchinson's friend omitted. But as Hutchinson said, he cut out some parts of the manuscript to make it "not as violent," "not as harsh," and "more like a tale." Certainly, since

Hutchinson performs for friends familiar with the Stagolee tradition, he has no need to go into detail telling who Stagolee and Billy Lyons are. As in the toasts published by Abrahams and Jackson, Hutchinson gets right to the fight between Billy Lyons and Stagolee, without long character sketches. Perhaps the four missing themes were omitted to intensify the major action and tighten Lester's somewhat unwieldy tale. The omitted sheriff themes serve only to build up Stagolee's reputation; they do not advance the plot to the change in fortune when Stagolee meets his superior, the Lord. Similarly, the omitted themes about Stagolee's burial and his trip to heaven delay the denouement—Stagolee's triumph over the Devil.

Still other reasons may be responsible for the omission of so much detail. Some of the details which Lester introduces clash with the traditional folk view of Stagolee, or are simply inconsistent. For example, in one of the themes which Hutchinson omits, Lester describes Stagolee as being "always respectful to women," and says that "generally, he made a good husband, as husbands go."[29] Yet Stagolee, in most versions, is noted for his disrespectful actions toward women.[30] Details such as Stagolee's refusal to buy "war bonds" in the same story with references to Vietnam, are inconsistent and confusing.[31] By omitting this detail, Hutchinson aligns his version with the performance tradition. Other versions of Stagolee are comparatively short, and comprised of action and dialogue rather than long descriptive passages.

So far, we have discussed the major omissions from Lester's text. But Hutchinson does more than simply shorten the text; he fundamentally changes its written style to an oral style more in keeping with the performance tradition. His changes include replacing the written style of handling dialogue with an oral style closer to Black speech patterns; changing prose lines to well-balanced, rhythmic, poetic lines; adding dialogue to scenes; incorporating ideophones; using pitch patterns to create suspense; and using body movements in highly patterned, rhythmic, and symbolic ways.

Lester's text reflects a literary style of attributing dialogue lines by following the quoted material with "he said." In contrast, Hutchinson follows a characteristic Black oral style of preceding dialogue lines with "he say." For example, Lester writes, " 'We ain't never had no Klan in the daytime before,' Stagolee said,"[32] while Hutchinson says, "Stagolee say, 'MA--N, we NEVer had no KLANS in the DAYtime befo'!'"

Just as Hutchinson changes the dialogue tags to a more natural performance style, he changes many of Lester's long, rambling sentences into a more rhythmical, balanced style. One of the characteristics of toast performances, according to Labov, and others, is that toasts are "recited in a rhythmic, slightly 'rifting' style."[33] Hutchinson's balanced lines, achieved through a combination of parallel constructions and rhythmic stresses and pauses, seem much easier to recite rhythmically than Lester's. Many of the lines are balanced paratactically or conjunctionally. In the following excerpts from the two texts, we can see how Hutchinson rearranges syntax and adds pauses and stresses to change Lester's prose style into poetry. I have placed the syllable count to the left of Hutchinson's lines to reveal the syllabic balance. As the suspense builds, the lines increase in length by one syllable.

> Now on this particular day, Stagolee was sitting on the porch, picking the blues on the guitar, and drinking. All of a sudden, he looked up and saw this pale-looking white cat in this white sheet come riding up to his house on a white horse. "We ain't never had no Klan in the daytime before," Stagolee said.[34]

(18) Stagolee was still sittin' on the porch shucking some BLUES on the GUItar.

(5) Stagolee looked up—

(6) saw this BI--G old white HO--SS⌒

(7) with this LI--ttle old WHI--TE MA--N⌒

(7) dressed in this LO--NG old WHITE SHEE--T⌒

(17) Stagolee say, "MA--N, we NEVer had no KLANS in the DAYtime befo'!"

As the preceding excerpt indicates, Hutchinson also uses a rising pitch pattern to build suspense. He uses a similar pitch pattern seven times throughout the tale for the same purpose.[35] In each case, the pattern forms a *gradatio*, a figure which advances from one statement to the next until a climax has been reached.[36] Perhaps the similar climactic and pitch patterns in his descriptions of Death and the Devil account for his accidental substitution of Death for the Devil in the last scene. A few lines after Hutchinson describes the devil as,

> this LITtle bittie old RED man with his LITtle
>   red leoTAR-d⌒
> this LO--NG TA--IL⌒
> this BIG black PITCH ↑fork⌒

he says, "↑‾Death ain't say nothin'‾↑."

Using rising pitch patterns is but one way in which Hutchinson makes his performance vivid and sensuous. He adds ideophones and other sound imitations, such as pretending to spit, snapping his fingers, clapping his hands, and stomping his foot on the floor to create the sound of Stagolee knocking on the door. In addition, he adds vivid dialogue and descriptions which are not part of Lester's text.

Hutchinson's description of the devil in a little red leotard with a long tail and big black pitch fork is not found in Lester's text. Nor does Lester's version include a sexy sister in Hell. While Hutchinson emphasizes Stagolee's role as a "player" by appropriately having him ask "one of the sisters" about the Devil, Lester's Stagolee addresses his questions to the general populace of Hell:

> After he'd finished checking it out, he asked,
> "Any white folks down here?"
> "Just the hip ones, and ain't too many of them.
> But they all right. They know where it's at."
> "Solid." Stagolee noticed an old man sitting over
> in a corner with his hands over his ears.
> "What's his problem?"
> "Aw, that's the Devil. He just can't get himself
> together. He ain't learned how to deal with niggers yet."[37]

Another clear example of Hutchinson's addition of vivid detail and dialogue can be seen in the Billy Lyons scene. Lester's version contains no reference to Stagolee giving Billy the "E--vil evil EYE," yet this detail is particularly appropriate to Stagolee's calm, cool, but mean nature. Just a hateful look from Stagolee is enough to make Billy plead for his life. While Lester simply reports that Stagolee "went off to Billy Lyons' house and told Mrs. Billy that her husband was dead and he was moving in,"[38] Hutchinson dramatizes the scene by adding direct discourse:

> He KNOCKED on the do'.
> Mrs. Lyons come to the do'.
> He say, "My name is Stagolee your husband's dead
>   the Lord's gonna take care of your chillun
>   and I'm movin' in."

We have examined some of the linguistic and paralinguistic changes which Hutchinson uses to transform a long, rambling, literary version to a highly economical, rhythmical, and vivid poetic account. Yet we have not discussed a final and extremely important contributing factor to the aesthetic structure of Hutchinson's performance—his body movements. In the analysis of instrumentalities, we discussed the economical way he changes characters by varying basic stances, his icons, and his particularly Afro-American movements. Now, let us briefly consider the aesthetic impact of these kinesic features.

Hutchinson's bodily characterization of Stagolee helps reinforce one of the most admired characteristics of Stag, his "coolness." When we examine all of the gestures used in portraying Stagolee, we can see how controlled, calm, and subtle they are. For example, Stagolee threatens

Billy Lyons with his eyes, not words or fists. Whenever he draws his gun, he holds it close to his pocket rather than stretched out in front of him. While staring Death in the face, Stagolee remains calm, simply shaking his head in disbelief. Rather than taking fright and running from Death, Stagolee simply steps back in surprise. Indeed, Stagolee's most vigorous action is his "run" toward Hell. But as we described earlier, this run is quite stylized and cool, performed with snapping fingers. When Stagolee gestures to the sexy sister, he keeps his hands down at his side, using very subtle beckoning and pointing gestures.

No doubt these subtle gestures, which contrast so greatly with the expansive movements of the other characters, contribute to the overall impression of Stagolee's cool nature. One of the largest laughs from the audience occurs when Stagolee replies to Billy's dramatic plea for his life with the simple words, "Well, that's cool—." Part of the humor evoked by this line seems to lie in the contrast in nonverbal actions between Billy and Stagolee. Hutchinson has Billy sob, bend forward, look up, and fold his hands in prayer. In contrast, Stagolee shrugs, looks down at Billy, calmly stands in the hip/hand stance, and wears a tight-lipped frown as he says, "Well, that's cool—."

In addition to enriching Stagolee's characterization, Hutchinson uses body movements as part of the rhythmic structure. The frequent head turns, combined with the basic hip/hand and hip/arm stances, and the forward and backward tilts, provide a basic rhythmic grid from which all of the other nonverbal images emerge. In discussing the significance of such patterned movements, Scheub writes that they "provide the regular grid against which the images are performed, and are crucial to the experience of the message of the performance. These movements provide a rhythmic context for the experiencing and development of the images; they shape the external form of the performance and are most significant and functional aesthetically. They are the flow from which the images are particularized, a flow which in its nonverbal character unites artist and audience, tying them emotionally, much as music and dance do."[39]

One way in which the nonverbal rhythmic grid functions aesthetically is to build anticipation in the audience. As the nonverbal patterns begin to emerge, the audience's attention is captivated by the attractiveness of the patterned repetitions. This attention is perceptual, immediate, and sensuous; as Scheub says, it is "not a conceptual anticipation, it is an anticipation that is felt. . . ."[40] Once a rhythmic grid is established, any deviations from the basic patterns immediately stand out. For example, part of the power behind Hutchinson's imitation of Stagolee's run and his "giving skin" to his brothers and sisters in Hell seems to lie in their difference from so many of the icons that are built out of the hip/arm or hip/hand stance.

A final aesthetic function of the nonverbal rhythmic grid lies in its effect on the perception of narrative time. Hutchinson's plot progresses rapidly, with few, if any, digressions or interruptions. The performance itself runs about five minutes. Yet perceptually, the story seems longer. The continual repetitions of the same basic stances, even though new modifying actones and words occur with them, seem to work against the progression of time. Explaining this phenomenon, Scheub writes, "The almost identical repetition of image-sequences plays havoc with the audience's experience in real time. We keep arriving back at point A, it seems."[41]

CONCLUSION

In this chapter we have discussed some of the most apparent differences in the aesthetic patterning of an oral and literary version of "Stagolee." As we can see from this performance-centered text, the greater economy of Hutchinson's performance is somewhat paradoxical. While his version uses only one-fifth as many words as Lester's, each word in his performance is enriched, fleshed out, made immediate and sensuous through the complex interactions of word, voice, and body.

Yet, if this performance had been recorded in a traditional text format, following either the ethnolinguistic or literary models identified in Chapter 2, we would not be able to appreciate its artistic design. None of the rhythmic pauses, stresses, and stances would be preserved, nor would his vivid characterizations. Without the performance-centered text, a critic comparing Hutchinson's version to Lester's might conclude that Hutchinson's version is simply shorter and less interesting stylistically. Without a record of Hutchinson's dynamic paralinguistic and kinesic style, it would be impossible to distinguish clearly between characters, or perceive the humor evoked nonverbally. Without a performance-centered text, a critic might assume that because Hutchinson's version does not have rhymed couplets, it is prose. Yet we have seen a number of rhythmic devices which clearly make Hutchinson's version poetic. Thus, the performance-centered text permits readers to appreciate more of the integral presence of artistic verbal performance.

This illustration of a performance-centered text will serve as a fitting conclusion to this work if it demonstrates that texts can be made to present a fuller and more accurate record of artistic verbal performance. The definition of the text as an intersemiotic translation should make scholars studying verbal art aware that texts which neglect to record nonverbal and contextual features have missed a vital part of the aesthetic transaction. Although folklorists have increasingly realized the importance of recording more of these performance features, the apparent complexities of recording so many simultaneously occurring features no doubt cause many to avoid the task. Yet as I have argued here, the complex problems of recording performance can be systematically attacked through following a translation approach based on an analysis of folklore as performance, the problems of audience, and the characteristics of the source and receptor media. If textmakers follow the translating principles proposed here, we can expect the folklore texts of the future to go beyond a simple transcription of words to a fuller record of the qualitative nonverbal and contextual dimensions of performance.

Certainly, future performance-centered texts will take many different forms as textmakers experiment with the resources of the print medium. And as more performance-centered texts are made, the principles proposed here will no doubt be refined and new principles developed. Not only folklore performances, but performances of literary works and speeches can be translated to print, and as the number of performance-centered texts increases, empirical knowledge about performance will grow. Through fuller and more accurate texts, both interpreters and folklorists can expand their research into the ground rules of performance, performer competence, the sociology and psychology of the performer, performance as social interaction, and the aesthetics of performance.

But performance-centered texts can do more than provide research data. They can enable persons who might not otherwise be able to experience the verbal art of a culture to more fully appreciate its integral, aesthetic presence. To demonstrate this point, let me relate a recent experience. For the final assignment in an oral interpretation of folklore class, students were asked to research the performance tradition of an American Indian tribe and perform a text, trying to recreate an appropriate performance context and style. One student chose Toelken's performance-centered text of a Navaho coyote story.[42] She feared that the audience would not be able to relate to the Navaho humor in the narrative, and consequently, used an onstage audience to play the role of the Navaho audience members whose laughter and reactions were recorded in the text. To her surprise, her performance of Coyote's nasal, whining voice, as well as other performance features recorded in the text, delighted the classroom audience. They reacted in much the same way Toelken described the Navaho audience reacting. When the student read the text silently, she could not perceive the irony and humor resulting from the interactions of plot with voice and body. But through performing the text, the translation process came full circle, and the integral presence of the verbal art was restored.

Notes

1. Introduction

1. When referring to the field of interpretation or interpreters, I mean the field of oral interpretation and oral interpreters.
2. Notational practices of elocutionists will be discussed in Chapter 5, as part of a larger discussion on problems of notating performance. See Katherine Loesch, "Empirical Studies in Interpretation: The Text," *Western Speech* 33 (1969): 250-268 for a review of interpretation research concerned with prosodic descriptions of texts, most of which is limited to "the essential sound level of poems." Loesch found only one descriptive study on interpretive performance as performance *per se,* Seymour Chatman's "A Study of James Mason's Interpretation of 'The Bishop Orders His Tomb,'" *The Oral Study of Literature,* ed. Thomas O. Sloan, pp. 94-132, which describes intonational and paralinguistic features of a performance.
3. Following William Bascom's well-accepted definition of folklore as "verbal art," I will use the words folklore and verbal art interchangeably. See William H. Bascom, "Verbal Art," *Journal of American Folklore* 68 (1955): 245-52.
4. MacEdward Leach, "Problems of Collecting Oral Literature," *PMLA* 77 (1962): 335.
5. Dell Hymes, "Folklore's Nature and the Sun's Myth," *Journal of American Folklore* 88 (1975): 359.
6. Dennis Tedlock, "On the Translation of Style in Oral Narrative," *Journal of American Folklore* 84 (1971): 114-15.
7. Richard Bauman, "Verbal Art as Performance," *American Anthropologist* 77 (1975): 298. The performance approach is described in detail in Chapter 3. Throughout this work, the use of the word performance refers to artistic verbal performance, unless otherwise specified.
8. J. Barre Toelken, "The 'Pretty Language' of Yellowman: Genre, Mode and Texture in Navaho Coyote Narratives," *Genre* 2 (1969): 211-12.
9. Linda Dégh, *Folktales and Society: Storytelling in a Hungarian Peasant Community,* trans. Emily Schossberger: p. 53.
10. Tedlock, "On the Translation of Style in Oral Narrative," and *Finding the Center: Narrative Poetry of the Zuni Indians,* trans. Dennis Tedlock.
11. *Alcheringa: Ethnopoetics* 1 n.s. (1975): 2.
12. Hymes, "Folklore's Nature," pp. 356, 359.
13. Hymes, "Breakthrough Into Performance," pp. 19, 69.
14. Ibid., p. 13.
15. Stith Thompson, "Folktale," *Funk and Wagnalls Standard Dictionary of Folklore, Mythology, and Legend,* 1, ed. Maria Leach, p. 408, as cited by Daniel J. Crowley, *I Could Talk Old-Story Good: Creativity in Bahamian Folklore,* p. 2.
16. Archer Taylor, *The Black Ox,* in *Folklore Fellows Communications* No. 70 (1927): 10-11, as cited by Crowley, same as above.

17. For a detailed discussion of this devolutionary view of the deterioration of folklore from an earlier state of purity, see Alan Dundes, "The Devolutionary Premise in Folklore Theory," *Journal of the Folklore Institute* 6 (1969): 5-19.

18. Claude Lévi-Strauss, "The Structural Study of Myth," *Journal of American Folklore* 68 (1955): 430, as cited by Tedlock, "On the Translation of Style in Oral Literature," pp. 120-21.

19. Dan Ben-Amos and Kenneth S. Goldstein, "Introduction," *Folklore: Performance and Communication*, p. 4.

20. For more on the relationship between speech and music see William Bright, "Language and Music: Areas for Cooperation," *Ethnomusicology* 7 (1963): 26-32; and Marcia Herndon, "Analysis: The Herding of Sacred Cows," *Ethnomusicology* 18 (1974): 248.

21. See Clifford Geertz, "Blurred Genres: The Refiguration of Social Thought," *American Scholar* 49 (Spring 1980): 165-79.

22. Arnold Berleant, *The Aesthetic Field: A Phenomenology of Aesthetic Experience*.

23. Roman Jakobson, "On Linguistic Aspects of Translation," *On Translation*, ed. Reuben A. Brower, p. 233; and Eugene A. Nida, *Toward a Science of Translating*, p. 4.

24. Nida's major theoretical work used in this study is *Toward a Science of Translating*, same as above; George Steiner, *After Babel: Aspects of Language and Translation*.

25. Ray L. Birdwhistell, *Kinesics and Context: Essays on Body Motion Communication*; Roger G. Barker and Herbert F. Wright, *Midwest and Its Children: The Psychological Ecology of an American Town*.

26. E. D. Hirsch, Jr., *The Aims of Interpretation*, pp. 21-34.

27. Dell Hymes, "Models of the Interaction of Language and Social Life," *Directions in Sociolinguistics*, eds. J. J. Gumperz and Dell Hymes, pp. 35-71.

28. Steiner, pp. 296-303.

29. Julius Lester, *Black Folktales*, pp. 78-135.

30. Wallace Bacon, "The Dangerous Shores a Decade Later," *The Study of Interpretation: Theory and Comment*, ed. Richard Haas and David Williams, p. 223.

31. Thomas O. Sloan, "Oral Interpretation in the Ages Before Sheridan and Walker," *Western Speech* 35 (1971): 147-54; Beverly Whitaker, "Research Directions in the Performance of Literature," *Speech Monographs*, 40 (1973): 238-42; Leland Roloff, "The Field of Interpretation: Instructive Wonder," *Interpretation Division Newsletter* (Spring 1973): 7-8; and David W. Thompson, "Teaching the History of Interpretation," *Speech Teacher* 22 (1973): 40.

32. Jean Haskell Speer, "Folklore and Interpretation: Symbiosis," *Southern Speech Communication Journal* 40 (1975): 365-376; Edwin Cohen, "The Role of the Interpreter in Identifying the Concept of Folk," *Western Speech* 37 (1974): 170-175; Elizabeth C. Fine and Jean Haskell Speer, "A New Look at Performance," *Communication Monographs* 44 (November 1977): 374-389.

33. See Lee Hudson, "Beat Generation Poetics and the Oral Tradition of Literature;" Hilda-Njoki McElroy, "Traditional Wit and Humour in Pan-African Drama," Patricio Lazaro, "A Survey of Approaches in Philippine Oral Literature Scholarship," and Thomas J. Turpin, "The Cheyenne World View as Reflected in the Oral Traditions of the Culture Heroes, Sweet Medicine and Erect Horns;" and Jean Haskell Speer, "Folkloristics and the Performance of Literature."

34. "The Phenomenon of Performance," Doctoral Honors Seminar, Northwestern University, 1973.

35. "Breakthrough Into Performance: Research Implications," a program sponsored by the Research and Interpretation Divisions of the Speech Communication Association, presented at the 1976 SCA Convention.

36. Janet Bolton, "Response," *The Study of Oral Interpretation: Theory and Comment*, p. 90.

37. Ibid.

38. Beverly Whitaker, "Evaluating Performed Literature," *Studies in Interpretation*, II, ed. Esther M. Doyle and Virginia Hastings Floyd, p. 269.

39. The following discussion of the first four areas of research stems from "A New Look at Performance" by Elizabeth C. Fine and Jean Haskell Speer, see note 32, above.

40. Bauman, "Verbal Art as Performance," p. 299.

41. Speer, "Folkloristics and the Performance of Literature."

42. These variables are from Dell Hymes's SPEAKING model in "Models of the Interaction of Language and Social Life", pp. 35-71.

43. Hymes, "Breakthrough Into Performance," p. 18, defines "true performance" as performance that is full, authentic, or authoritative, when "standards intrinsic to the tradition in which the performance occurs are accepted and realized."

44. Toelken, "The 'Pretty Language' of Yellowman."

45. István Sándor, "Dramaturgy of Tale-Telling," *Acta Ethnographica: Academiae Scientarium Hungaricae* 16 (1967): pp. 303-38.

46. Berleant, p. 10.

47. Ibid., p. 13. Berleant defines aesthetic facts as "rather highly probable *statements* about these events, especially general statements, that have been arrived at by carefully examining those situations in which aesthetic phenomena occur."

48. Ibid.

49. Ibid.

50. Ibid., p. 14.

51. Ibid.

52. For a bibliography of such studies, see Bauman, "Verbal Art as Performance."

53. Abrahams, "Enactments."

54. Hymes, "Folklore's Nature," p. 356.

2. The Development of the Text in American Folkloristics

1. Richard Dorson, ed., *Buying the Wind: Regional Folklore in the United States*, p. 1.

2. Richard Bauman and Roger D. Abrahams with Susan Kalcik, "American Folklore and American Studies," *American Quarterly* 28 (1976), pp. 1-2.

3. Alan Dundes, "The American Concept of Folklore," *Journal of the Folklore Institute* 3 (1966), p. 228.

4. For a detailed discussion of the split between the anthropological and literary folklorists, see Michael J. Bell, "William Wells Newell and the Foundation of American Folklore Scholarship." *Special Issue: American Folklore Historiography*, in *Journal of the Folklore Institute* 10 (1973), pp. 7-22.

5. Dundes, p. 229.

6. Benjamin Colby and James Peacock, "Narrative," *Handbook of Social and Cultural Anthropology*, ed. John J. Honigmann, p. 616.

7. William R. Bascom, "Folklore and Anthropology," *The Study of Folklore*, ed. Alan Dundes, p. 33.

8. Virginia Hull McKimmon Noelke, "The Origin and Early History of the Bureau of American Ethnology, 1879-1910," Diss. University of Texas at Austin, 1974, pp. 68-69.

9. John Wesley Powell, "Report of the Director," *First Annual Report of the Bureau of American Ethnology*, p. xv.

10. Noelke, p. 58.

11. George Gibbs, "Instructions for Research Relative to the Ethnology and Philology of America," *Smithsonian Miscellaneous Collections* 7, No. 160, p. 14.

12. Powell, *Introduction to the Study of Indian Languages, with Words, Phrases, and Sentences to Be Collected*, 2nd ed., pp. vi, 62-63.

13. Powell, "Report of the Director," *Second Annual Report of the Bureau of American Ethnology*, pp. xx.

14. Ibid., xxix-xxx.

15. J. O. Dorsey, A. S. Gatschet, and S. R. Riggs, "Illustration of the Method of Recording Indian Languages," *First Annual Report of the Bureau of American Ethnology*.

16. Powell, "Report of the Director," *Second Annual Report*, p. xx.

17. Thomas A. Burns, "Folkloristics: A Conception of Theory," *Western Folklore* 36 (1977):114.

18. Powell, "Sketch of the Mythology of the North American Indians," *First Annual Report*, pp. 22-23.

19. Powell, "Limitations to the Use of Anthropologic Data," *First Annual Report*, p. 82.

20. See Dundes, "The American Concept of Folklore," pp. 241-42, who argues that early anthropological folklorists treated folklore as a product of the past.

21. Melville Jacobs, "Folklore," in *The Anthropology of Franz Boas*, ed. Walter Goldschmidt, *Memoirs of the American Anthropological Association*, No. 89, p. 123.

22. Noelke, p. 208.

23. Robert H. Lowie, *The History of Ethnological Theory*, p. 132.

24. Franz Boas, "The Documentary Function of the Text," Letter to Professor

Holmes, Bureau of American Ethnology, 1905, in *The Shaping of American Anthropology 1883-1911: A Franz Boas Reader,* ed. George W. Stocking, Jr., pp. 122-23.

25. Report of Committee of American Anthropological Association, "Phonetic Transcription of Indian Languages," *Smithsonian Miscellaneous Collections* 66, No. 6 (1915):1-15. Other members of the Committee were P. E. Goddard, E. Sapir, and A. L. Kroeber.

26. Boas, "The Central Eskimo," *Sixth Annual Report of the Bureau of American Ethnology,* pp. 648-49.

27. Idem., *Chinook Texts,* pp. 116-17.

28. Jacobs, "Folklore," p. 135, gives Boas credit for writing "meritoriously about style at a time when many decades of research had still not produced satisfactory statements about style in non-Western oral literatures."

29. Melville J. Herskovits, *Franz Boas: The Science of Man in the Making.*

30. Ibid., pp. 89-90, 67-88. Functionalist theories of folklore analyze the roles or functions which folklore plays in a culture.

31. Ibid., p. 93.

32. Hilary Henson, *British Social Anthropologists and Language: A History of Separate Development,* pp. 17-18.

33. Garrick Mallery, "Sign Language Among North American Indians Compared with that Among Other Peoples and Deaf Mutes," *First Annual Report of the Bureau of American Ethnology,* p. 289.

34. Ibid., p. 396.

35. Ibid., p. 399.

36. Ibid., pp. 508, 518.

37. David G. Mandelbaum, "Editor's Introduction," *Selected Writings of Edward Sapir in Language, Culture and Personality,* ed. David G. Mandelbaum, p. vi.

38. Edward Sapir, ed., *Wishram Texts, together with Wasco Tales and Myths,* collected by Jeremiah Curtin, Publications of the American Ethnological Society, II, pp. 139, 134,142-43.

39. Sapir, "Song Recitative in Paiute Mythology," *Selected Writings of Edward Sapir,* ed. David G. Mandelbaum, p. 466.

40. Sapir, "Abnormal Types of Speech in Nootka," *Selected Writings of Edward Sapir,* ed. David G. Mandelbaum, p. 179.

41. Richard Bauman, "Linguistics, Anthropology, and Verbal Art: Toward a Unified Perspective, With a Special Discussion of Children's Folklore," *Linguistics and Anthropology,* ed. Muriel Saville-Troike, p. 15.

42. Dan Ben-Amos and Kenneth S. Goldstein, eds., "Introduction," *Folklore: Performance and Communication,* pp. 2-3.

43. Bronislaw Malinowski, *Coral Gardens and Their Magic II: The Language of Magic and Gardening,* pp. 7-8.

44. Ibid., pp. 36, 30.

45. Ibid., p. 26. See also Malinowski's *Myth in Primitive Psychology,* p. 35.

46. Ibid., pp. 249-50, 318.

47. Bauman, "Linguistics, Anthropology, and Verbal Art," p. 17.

48. Bauman and Abrahams, p. 8.

49. Herbert Halpert, "American Regional Folklore," in "Folklore Research in

North America: Reports of the Committee on Research in Folklore, 1945-
46," *Journal of American Folklore* 60 (1947):356-357.

50. Ibid., pp. 359-60.
51. Ibid., p. 359.
52. See Stith Thompson, "Folktale," *Funk and Wagnalls Standard Dictionary
of Folklore, Mythology, and Legend,* 1, ed. Maria Leach, p. 408; and Archer
Taylor, *The Black Ox* in *Folklore Fellows Communications* 70 (1927), pp.
10-11, both cited by Daniel J. Crowley, *I Could Talk Old-Story Good:
Creativity in Bahamian Folklore,* pp. 1-2.
53. Stith Thompson, *The Folktale,* p. 410.
54. See for example, Frank Cushing, *Zuni Folk Tales.*
55. Halpert, pp. 360-61.
56. Dorson, "Print and American Folk Tales," *California Folklore Quarterly* 4
(1945):208-210.
57. William O. Hendricks, "Linguistics and Folkloristics," *Linguistics and
Adjacent Arts and Sciences,* in *Current Trends in Linguistics,* Vol. 12, ed.
Thomas A. Sebeok, p. 661.
58. Ladislav Matejka, "Postscript. Prague School Semiotics," *Semiotics of Art,*
eds. Ladislav Matejka and Irwin A. Titunik, p. 266.
59. Ferdinand de Saussure, *Cours de linguistique generale* (Geneva: 1916); see
Course in General Linguistics, trans. W. Baskin.
60. See Edward Stankiewicz, "Structural Poetics and Linguistics," *Linguistics
and Adjacent Arts and Sciences,* ed. Thomas A. Sebeok, pp. 638-639 for
further discussion.
61. See Josef Vachek, *The Linguistic School of Prague,* pp. 34-36.
62. See Jan Mukarovský, "Poetic Reference," *Semiotics of Art,* p. 157; and
Matejka, "Postscript," pp. 275-276.
63. Mukařovský, "Poetic Reference," p. 158.
64. Matejka, "Postscript," pp. 270-71.
65. Bauman, *Verbal Art as Performance,* p. 11. For an earlier version of this
work, see "Verbal Art as Performance," *American Anthropologist* 77
(1975):290-311.
66. Mukařovský, "Standard Language and Poetic Language," *A Prague School
Reader,* trans. Paul L. Garvin, p. 19.
67. Roman Jakobson, "Closing Statement: Linguistics and Poetics," *Style in
Language,* ed. Thomas A. Sebeok, pp. 353, 355, 356-57. Jakobson refers to
Bühler, but never mentions Mukarovský's work.
68. Ibid., p. 369.
69. Roman Jakobson and P. Bogatyrev, "Die Folklore als besondere Form des
Schaffens," *Donum Natalicium Schrijnen.*
70. E. Ojo Arewa and Alan Dundes, "Proverbs and the Ethnography of
Speaking Folklore," *American Anthropologist* 66, part 2 (1964): p. 71. For
more on the links between the Prague School and the ethnography of
speaking, see John J. Gumperz and Dell Hymes, eds., *Directions in
Sociolinguistics,* p. 540.
71. Petr Bogatyrev, "Semiotics in the Folk Theater," *Semiotics of Art,* p. 46.
Other applications of semiotics to folklore are found in Bogatyrev's
"Costume as Sign," *Semiotics of Art,* pp. 13-19; "Folk Song from a

Functional Point of View," *Semiotics of Art*, pp. 20-32; and "Forms and Functions of Folk Theater," *Semiotics of Art*, pp. 51-56.

72. Albert B. Lord, *The Singer of Tales*.
73. See Roger Abrahams, "Folklore and Literature as Performance," *Journal of the Folklore Institute* 8 (1972):75-94 and Elli Köngäs Maranda, "Theory and Practice of Riddle Analysis," *Toward New Perspectives in Folklore*, eds. Américo Paredes and Richard Bauman, pp. 51-61.
74. Bauman, *Verbal Art as Performance*, p. 38.
75. Clifford Geertz, "Blurred Genres: The Refiguration of Social Thought," *The American Scholar* 49 (Spring 1980): 168.
76. To discuss all the strands of influence on the performance approach would lead astray from our focus on textmaking. A comprehensive bibliography of influences on the ethnography of speaking published in Appendix I of John J. Gumperz and Dell Hymes, eds., *Directions in Sociolinguistics*, serves as well as a guide to influences on the performance approach.
77. Roger Abrahams, "Introductory Remarks to a Rhetorical Theory of Folklore," *Journal of American Folklore* 81 (April-June 1968):144-145.
78. Brian Sutton-Smith, "The Expressive Profile," *Toward New Perspectives in Folklore*, pp. 80-92; Joseph Doherty, "Towards a Poetics of Performance," Manuscript; Dell Hymes, "Breakthrough Into Performance," *Folklore: Performance and Communication*, eds. Dan Ben-Amos and Kenneth S. Goldstein, pp. 11-74; Bruce A. Rosenberg, "Oral Sermons and Oral Narrative," *Folklore: Performance and Communication*, pp. 75-104.
79. Victor Turner, *The Ritual Process*; James L. Peacock, *Rites of Modernization*; Clifford Geertz, "Deep Play: Notes on the Balinese Cockfight," *The Interpretation of Cultures*, pp. 412-453.
80. Geertz, "Blurred Genres," p. 169.
81. Gregory Bateson, "A Theory of Play and Fantasy," *Steps to an Ecology of Mind*, pp. 177-193.
82. Bauman, *Verbal Art as Performance*, pp. 9-16; Barbara A. Babcock, "The Story in the Story: Metanarration in Folk Narrative," *Verbal Art as Performance*, p. 68.
83. Erving Goffman, *The Presentation of Self in Everyday Life, Encounters,* and *Interaction Ritual*. Dell Hymes, "Breakthrough into Performance," p. 18; Barbara Kirshenblatt-Gimblett, "A Parable in Context," p. 120; Bauman, "Differential Identity and the Social Base of Folklore," *Toward New Perspectives in Folklore*, p. 34.
84. Goffman, *Frame Analysis*, pp. 40-82.
85. Bauman, *Verbal Art as Performance*, p. 16.
86. Bauman and Joel Sherzer, "The Ethnography of Speaking," *Annual Review of Anthropology* 4 (1975):95-96.
87. Hymes, "Models of the Interaction of Language and Social Life," *Directions in Sociolinguistics*, pp. 35-71.
88. These include: John J. Gumperz and Dell Hymes, eds., *Directions in Sociolinguistics*; W. Bright, ed., *Sociolinguistics*.
89. Hymes' address, "The Contribution of Folklore to Sociolinguistic Research" is published in *Toward New Perspectives in Folklore*, pp. 42-50. He mentions work by Alan Lomax, *Folksong Style and Culture*; Abrahams,

"Introductory Remarks to a Rhetorical Theory of Folklore;" Abrahams, "A Performance-Centered Approach to Gossip," *Man*, 5 (1970):290-301; Dan Ben-Amos, "Analytical Categories and Ethnic Genres," *Genre*, 2 (1969):275-301; and E.Ojo Arewa and Alan Dundes, "Proverbs and the Ethnography of Speaking Folklore."

90. Hymes, "The Contribution of Folklore to Sociolinguistic Research," p. 47.

91. Richard Bauman and Joel Sherzer, eds., *Explorations in the Ethnography of Speaking*.

92. Ruth Benedict, *Zuni Mythology*, Vol. I., p. xxxiii. Benedict had her informants narrate in English, which obviously affected their performance style. In addition, she edited their tales so as to not retain "their inadequate English in the translation" (I, p. xxvii). She neglects to record any details about the performance situation.

93. Paul Radin, "The Literature of Primitive Peoples," *Diogenes* 12 (1955):2-4.

94. Melville J. Herskovits and Francis J. Herskovits, *Dahomean Narrative: A Cross-Cultural Analysis*, pp. 9-10.

95. Bascom, "Folklore and Anthropology," pp. 32-33.

96. Bascom, "Verbal Art," *Journal of American Folklore* 68 (1955):245-52.

97. C. F. Voeglin, "A Modern Method for Field Work Treatment of Previously Collected Texts," *Journal of American Folklore* 67 (1954):16, 19. For other attempts to improve the ethnolinguistic text, see Charles F. Hockett, "Translation Via Immediate Constituents," *International Journal of American Linguistics* 20 (1954):313-15; C.F. Voeglin, "Multiple Stage Translation," *International Journal of American Linguistics* 20 (1954):271-80.

98. Jacobs, "Folklore," p. 124.

99. Jacobs, *The Content and Style of an Oral Literature; The People Are Coming Soon*.

100. Jacobs, *Clackamas Chinook Texts*, Indiana University Publications of the Research Center in Anthropology, Folklore, and Linguistics, Nos. 8 and 11.

101. Jacobs, *The Content and Style of an Oral Literature*, p. 2.

102. Ibid., pp. 3-5.

103. Francis Lee Utley, "Conflict and Promise in Folklore," *Journal of American Folklore* 65 (1952):112-15.

104. Dorson, "Standards for Collecting and Publishing American Folktales," *Journal of American Folklore*, 70 (1957):53.

105. Ibid., pp. 54-57.

106. William Hugh Jansen, "Classifying Performance in the Study of Verbal Folklore," *Studies in Folklore*, ed. W. Edson Richmond, pp. 110-11.

107. Dorson, "Oral Styles of American Folk Narrators," *Style in Language*, ed. Thomas A. Sebeok, pp. 27-51. Dorson was also influenced by John Ball's "Style in the Folktale," *Folk-lore* 65 (December 1954): 170-72, which argues for collectors to portray the "dynamic relationship among style, story, teller, audience, and culture." Dorson's interest in performance style continued in his *Negro Folktales in Michigan*.

108. MacEdward Leach, "Problems of Collecting Oral Literature," *PMLA* 77 (1962):335-36.

109. Horace P. Beck, "MacEdward Leach—1896-1967," *Keystone Folk Quarterly* (Fall 1967):195.
110. Kenneth S. Goldstein, *A Guide for Field Workers in Folklore*, pp. 5-6. The earlier folklore handbooks of George L. Gomme, C. S. Burne, and Sean O. Suilleabhain devoted only marginal space to a general methodology of fieldwork. Rather, they emphasized detailed informant questionnaires and definitions of folklore materials.
111. Ibid., pp. 5-9.
112. Ibid., pp. 91-93.
113. Arewa and Dundes, "Proverbs and the Ethnography of Speaking Folklore," pp. 71, 72.
114. Ibid., pp. 73, 70.
115. Alan Lomax, *Folk Song Style and Culture*, pp. viii, xi.
116. Ibid., p. 223.
117. Alan Dundes, "Texture, Text, and Context," *Southern Folklore Quarterly* 28 (1964), pp. 254-57.
118. Ibid., pp. 265, 255.
119. Ibid., p. 255.
120. Linda Dégh, *Folktales and Society*, p. 53.
121. The quotation is from the published version of this paper, Dan Ben-Amos, "Toward a Definition of Folklore in Context," *Toward New Perspectives in Folklore*, p. 13.
122. See Bauman, "Introduction," *Toward New Perspectives in Folklore*, pp. xi-xii.
123. Roger Abrahams, "Introductory Remarks," pp. 144-45.
124. Robert Georges, "Toward an Understanding of Storytelling Events," *Journal of American Folklore* 82 (1969):316, 327-28.
125. Barbara Kirshenblatt-Gimblett, "A Parable in Context," *Folklore: Performance and Communication*, pp. 105-30; Roger Abrahams, "A Performance-Centered Approach to Gossip," *Man* 5 (1970):300; Abrahams, "Folklore and Literature as Performance," *Journal of the Folklore Institute* 8 (1972):75.
126. Bauman, "Introduction," *Toward New Perspectives in Folklore*, p. xi; Richard Bauman and Joel Sherzer, eds., *Explorations in the Ethnography of Speaking;* Dan Ben-Amos and Kenneth S. Goldstein, eds., "Introduction," *Folklore: Performance and Communication*, p. 4.
127. Bauman, "Verbal Art as Performance," pp. 290, 293.
128. Dennis Tedlock, "On the Translation of Style in Oral Narrative," *Journal of American Folklore* 84 (1971):114-33; and *Finding the Center: Narrative Poetry of the Zuni Indians*, trans. Dennis Tedlock.
129. Dell Hymes, "Models of the Interaction of Language and Social Life," pp. 35-71.
130. Tedlock, *Finding the Center*, pp. xix.
131. Ibid., pp. xxi-xxii.
132. Ibid., p. xxii.
133. Ibid., p. xxiv.
134. Jerome Rothenberg, ed., *Shaking the Pumpkin: Traditional Poetry of the Indian North Americas*, p. xxiii; and Rothenberg, "Total Translation: An

Experiment in the Presentation of American Indian Poetry," reprinted from *Stony Brook* 3/4 (1969) in George Quasha, "New Aspects of Translation," *The World of Translation*, p. 220.

135. *Alcheringa: Ethnopoetics* 1 n.s. (1975):2. The journal ceased publication in 1980.

136. Harold Scheub, "Translation of African Oral Narrative-Performances to the Written Word," *Yearbook of Comparative and General Literature* 20 (1971):28, 21, 32, 36.

137. Dell Hymes, "Folklore's Nature and the Sun's Myth," *Journal of American Folklore* 88 (1975):345-69.

138. Tedlock, "Toward an Oral Poetics," *New Literary History* 8 (Spring 1977):507-19.

139. Hymes, "Discovering Oral Performance and Measured Verse in American Indian Narrative," *New Literary History* 8 (Spring 1977):453-54.

140. Hymes, "Folklore's Nature," p. 360.

141. Hymes, "Reading Clackamas Texts," *Traditional American Indian Literatures*, ed. Karl Kroeber, pp. 117-59. My comments on this article appear in my book review of *Traditional American Indian Literatures*, *Journal of American Folklore* 96 (1983):225-27.

142. Richard Dauenhauer, "Notes on Swanton Numbers 80 and 81," *Journal of American Folklore* 94 (1981):363-64.

143. J. Barre Toelken, "The 'Pretty Language' of Yellowman: Genre, Mode and Texture in Navaho Coyote Narratives." *Genre* 2 (1969):211-35.

144. Barre Toelken and Tacheeni Scott, "Poetic Retranslation and the 'Pretty Languages' of Yellowman," *Traditional American Indian Literatures*, p. 70.

145. *Ibid.*, pp. 92-93.

146. Beverly Brandon-Sweeney, "Kinesics and Its Interpretation," *Folklore Annual of the University Folklore Association* 4/5 (1972-73):23-51.

147. Harold Scheub, "Body and Image in Oral Narrative Performance," *New Literary History* 8 (1977):345-68; V. Hrdličková, "Japanese Professional Storytellers," *Genre* 2 (1969):179-210.

148. István Sándor, "Dramaturgy of Tale-Telling," *Acta Ethnographica: Academiae Scientarium Hungaricae* 16 (1967):314.

149. Linda Dégh and Andrew Vazsonyi, "Legend and Belief," *Folklore Genres*, ed. Dan Ben-Amos, pp. 100-101, 108.

150. Harvey Sacks, "An Analysis of the Course of a Joke's Telling in Conversation," *Explorations in the Ethnography of Speaking*, pp. 337-53.

151. Jan Harold Brunvand, *Folklore: A Study and Research Guide*, p. 79.

152. Dorson, "Print and American Folk Tales," p. 210.

153. D. K. Wilgus, "The Text is the Thing," *Journal of American Folklore* 86 (1973):244.

3. The Performance Approach: Implications for the Text

1. Richard Bauman, *Verbal Art as Performance*, p. 11.

2. Archibald MacLeish, "Ars Poetica," *Collected Poems, 1917-1952*, pp. 40-41.

3. This definition, typical of a narrow view of communication, is taken from David W. Johnson, "Increasing Your Communication Skills,"

Interpersonal Communication in Action, eds. Bobby R. Patton and Kim Griffin, p. 13.

4. For an example of a contemporary transactional view of communication see Jesse G. Delia, "Constructivism and the Study of Human Communication," *Quarterly Journal of Speech* 63 (February 1977): 66-83.
5. Bauman, *Verbal Art as Performance,* p. 11.
6. Ibid., p. 10.
7. Ibid., pp. 7-8.
8. Roger Abrahams, "Introductory Remarks to a Rhetorical Theory of Folklore," *Journal of American Folklore* 81 (April-June 1968): 144-45.
9. Roger Abrahams, "In and Out of Performance" and "Enactments."
10. Dell Hymes, "The Contribution of Folklore to Sociolinguistic Research," *Toward New Perspectives in Folklore,* eds. Américo Paredes and Richard Bauman, p. 50.
11. Hymes, "Folklore's Nature and the Sun's Myth," *Journal of American Folklore* 88 (1975): 352.
12. Hymes, "Breakthrough Into Performance," *Folklore: Communication and Performance,* ed. Dan Ben-Amos and Kenneth Goldstein, pp. 13, 18.
13. Hymes, "Folklore's Nature and the Sun's Myth," p. 353.
14. Dan Ben-Amos, "Toward a Definition of Folklore in Context," *Toward New Perspectives in Folklore,* ed. Américo Paredes and Richard Bauman, pp. 10-11.
15. Dennis Tedlock, *Finding the Center: Narrative Poetry of the Zuni Indians,* trans. Dennis Tedlock, p. xvi.
16. Bauman, *Verbal Art as Performance,* pp. 16-22.
17. Hymes, "Breakthrough Into Performance," pp. 13, 18.
18. Hymes, "Folklore's Nature and the Sun's Myth," p. 352.
19. See Hymes, "Folklore's Nature and the Sun's Myth," p. 352 and Bauman, *Verbal Art as Performance,* p. 8.
20. Abrahams, "In and Out of Performance," pp. 13-14.
21. See Hymes, "Models of the Interaction of Language and Social Life," *Directions in Sociolinguistics,* ed. J. J. Gumperz and D. Hymes, p. 60.
22. Bauman, *Verbal Art as Performance,* p. 28.
23. Ibid., p. 38.
24. Ibid., p. 40.
25. Barbara Kirshenblatt-Gimblett, "A Parable in Context," *Folklore: Performance and Communication,* ed. Dan Ben-Amos and Kenneth Goldstein, pp. 105-30.
26. Bauman, *Verbal Art as Performance,* pp. 44-45.
27. See Gary H. Gossen, *Chamulas in the World of the Sun: Time and Space in a Maya Oral Tradition,* p. x.
28. Abrahams, "A Rhetorical Theory of Folklore," pp. 148-49.
29. Ruth Finnegan, "What is Oral Literature Anyway?" *Oral Literature and the Formula,* ed. Benjamin A. Stolz and Richard S. Shannon, pp. 158-59; quoted by Roger Abrahams, "License to Repeat and Be Predictable," p. 4.
30. Abrahams, "License to Repeat and Be Predictable," p. 3.
31. Bauman, *Verbal Art as Performance,* pp. 26-31.
32. Ibid., p. 31.

33. See David H. Smith, "Communication Research and the Idea of Process," *Speech Monographs* 39 (August 1972): 174-82 for a review of the backgrounds to processual approaches to communication.

34. Larry D. Browning and Robert Hopper, "How Messages Get to Mean—Influences in a Bureaucratic Organization," p. 2.

35. Ibid., pp. 3-4.

36. See Gary H. Gossen, *Chamulas in the World of the Sun* and "Chamula Genres of Verbal Behavior," *Toward New Perspectives in Folklore*, ed. Américo Paredes and Richard Bauman, p. 161.

37. An exception to this statement is Roman Jakobson's communication model in "Closing Statement: Linguistics and Poetics," *Style in Language*, ed. T. A. Sebeok, pp. 350-77. Jakobson's model of the functions of language includes a poetic, or aesthetic function, which Jakobson defines as "focus on the message for its own sake" (p. 356). In this model, however, poetics is defined solely in terms of the formal features of the art object, and performance plays a secondary role: "Meanwhile the truth is simple and clear: 'There are many performances of the same poem—differing among themselves in many ways. A performance is an event, but the poem itself, if there *is* any poem, must be some kind of enduring object.' This sage memento of Wimsatt and Beardsley belongs indeed to the essentials of modern metrics" (pp. 365-66).

38. Meyer H. Abrams, *The Mirror and the Lamp*.

39. Hilde Hein, "Performance as an Aesthetic Category," *Journal of Aesthetics and Art Criticism* 28 (Spring 1970): 381-86.

40. Arnold Berleant, *The Aesthetic Field: A Phenomenology of Aesthetic Experience*, p. 47.

41. Ibid., pp. 31-32.

42. Ibid., pp. 32, 35.

43. See Erving Goffman, *Frame Analysis* and Elizabeth Burns, *Theatricality*, pp. 47-50; 232-33.

44. See Delia, "Constructivism and the Study of Human Communication," p. 70.

45. Berleant, pp. 52, 53.

46. John Dewey, *Art as Experience*.

47. Berleant, p. 66.

48. Ibid., pp. 49, 88, 89.

49. Ibid., pp. 65, 52-53.

50. Ibid., p. 93.

51. Ibid., p. 94.

52. Linguist Kenneth L. Pike, in *Language in Relation to a Unified Theory of the Structure of Human Behavior*, Part I, Preliminary Edition, p. 8, coins the terms "emic" and "etic" (from phonemic and phonetic) to distinguish between two basic standpoints from which to describe human behavior. For a discussion of emic and etic units in folklore study, see Alan Dundes, "From Etic to Emic Units in the Structural Study of Folktales," *Journal of American Folklore* 75 (1962): 95-105.

53. Berleant, *The Aesthetic Field*, pp. 122-24, 44.

54. In their review of the major theories about myth, Melville and Frances

Herskovits, *Dahomean Narrative: A Cross-Cultural Approach,* pp. 81-122, suggest that weaknesses in the theories stem from Euro-American analytical biases of using myths to prove *a priori* theories.

55. Linda Dégh and Andrew Vazsonyi, "Legend and Belief," *Folklore Genres,* ed. Dan Ben-Amos, p. 108.

56. Robert Kellogg, "Oral Literature," *New Literary History* 5 (1973): 57-58.

57. See Bruce Jackson, *"Get Your Ass in the Water and Swim Like Me": Narrative Poetry from Black Oral Tradition,* p. 5.

58. See Kenneth S. Goldstein, "Introduction," *Monologues and Folk Recitation,* ed. Kenneth S. Goldstein and Robert D. Bethke, *Southern Folklore Quarterly* 40 (March-June 1976), for an account of how Service's and other poets' works circulate in oral tradition.

59. Julius Lester, *Black Folktales,* p. viii.

60. Albert B. Lord, *The Singer of Tales,* p. 4.

61. For example, Nelson Goodman, in *Languages of Art: An Approach to a Theory of Symbols,* p. 186, argues that a notational score rather than a performance defines the identity of a musical work.

62. That is, according to the norms of interaction and interpretation for that tradition. See the discussion earlier in this chapter of Hymes' distinction between a report of a performance and an authentic performance.

63. Abrahams, "In and Out of Performance," p. 17.

64. See Bruce Rosenberg, *The Art of the American Folk Preacher,* p. 55; and Jack L. Daniel and Geneva Smitherman, "How I Got Over: Communication Dynamics in the Black Community," *The Quarterly Journal of Speech* 62 (1976): 26-39.

65. Berleant, *The Aesthetic Field,* p. 103-04.

66. Ibid., p. 113.

67. Ibid., pp. 115-16.

68. Ibid., pp. 116, 120.

69. Ibid., p. 126.

70. Ibid., p. 118.

71. See Aristotle's *The Art of Rhetoric,* trans. J.H. Freese, Book I, 1355a-1357b. For a clear discussion of the difference between Aristotle's and Plato's conceptions of rhetoric see Everett Lee Hunt, "Plato and Aristotle on Rhetoric and Rhetoricians," *Historical Studies of Rhetoric and Rhetoricians,* ed. Raymond F. Howes, pp. 60-68.

72. For a discussion of rhetoric and commonsense knowledge see Lawrence W. Rosenfield, "An Autopsy of the Rhetorical Tradition," *The Prospect of Rhetoric: Report of the National Developmental Project,* ed. Lloyd F. Bitzer and Edwin Black, pp. 65-66; and Thomas B. Farrell, "Knowledge, Consensus and Rhetorical Theory," *The Quarterly Journal of Speech* 62 (February 1976): 1.

73. See, for example, Aristotle's discussion of metaphor in *The Art of Rhetoric,* trans. J. H. Freese, in which he argues that metaphors produce the pleasant effect of easy learning; they teach and inform. Aristotle further argues that "all style and enthymenes that give us rapid information are smart" (III.10.2-5), and that similes are less desirable because they are less concise and convey information less rapidly.

74. Berleant, *The Aesthetic Field*, pp. 145, 147.

75. For an illustration of how different textmakers change the form of a tale, examine the texts of the Zuni "Deerboy" tale made by three different anthropologists. See Ruth Benedict, *Zuni Mythology*, I, Columbia University Contributions to Anthropology 21, p. 18; Ruth Bunzel, *Zuni Texts*, Publications of the American Ethnological Society, 15, pp. 108-09; and Tedlock, *Finding the Center*, p. 21.

76. Berleant, *The Aesthetic Field*, p. 139.

77. Rev. J. P. Richards, "Christ is the Answer in this Shipwrecked Age," sermon delivered at the Evergreen Baptist Church, Oakland, California, May 7, 1973.

78. Pike, p. 33.

79. George Mills, "Art: An Introduction to Qualitative Anthropology," *Art and Aesthetics in Primitive Societies*, ed. Carol F. Jopling, p. 96.

80. See Roman Jakobson, "Closing Statement: Linguistics and Poetics," *Style in Language*, pp. 350-77; Abraham Moles, *Information Theory and Esthetic Perception*, trans. Joel E. Cohen; and Umberto Eco, *A Theory of Semiotics*.

1. Intersemiotic Translation from Performance to Print

1. George Steiner, *After Babel: Aspects of Language and Translation*, p. 302.

2. Clifford Geertz, "Deep Play: Notes on the Balinese Cockfight," *The Interpretation of Cultures*, p. 452.

3. Clifford Geertz, "Thick Description: Toward an Interpretive Theory of Culture," *The Interpretation of Cultures*, pp. 6-10.

4. Paul Ricoeur, "The Model of the Text: Meaningful Action Considered as a Text," *New Literary History* 5 (1973):91-117.

5. Ju. M. Lotman, B. A. Uspenskij, et al., "Theses on the Semiotic Study of Cultures (As Applied to Slavic Texts)," *The Tell-Tale Sign: A Survey of Semiotics*, ed. Thomas A. Sebeok, p. 62.

6. Irene Portis Winner and Thomas G. Winner, "The Semiotics of Cultural Texts," *Semiotica* 18 (1975):108.

7. William O. Hendricks, *Essays on Semiolinguistics and Verbal Art*, p. 48.

8. Note that Hendricks, who faults Dundes' definition of text for falsely separating content from its linguistic expression, can be criticized in turn for limiting his concept of text to the linguistic medium, ignoring the nonverbal channels of communication which occur and interact simultaneously with the verbal channel.

9. *Webster's Third New International Dictionary of the English Language, Unabridged*, 1981.

10. Ray Birdwhistell, *Kinesics and Context: Essays on Body Motion Communication*, p. 197.

11. Walter J. Ong, *The Presence of the Word: Some Prolegomena for Cultural and Religious History*, p. 19.

12. Ibid., p. 21.

13. Steiner, pp. 239, 242.

14. See Steiner, pp. 1-48, for a discussion of understanding as translation. Roman Jakobson, in "On Linguistic Aspects of Translation," *On Translation*, ed. Reuben A. Brower, pp. 232-33, says "For us, both as

linguists and as ordinary word-users, the meaning of any linguistic sign is
its translation into some further, alternative sign, especially a sign 'in which
it is more fully developed,' as Peirce, the deepest inquirer into the essence of
signs, insistently stated."

15. Steiner, p. 250.
16. Dennis Tedlock, "On the Translation of Style in Oral Narrative," *Journal of American Folklore* 84 (1971):121.
17. Dell Hymes, "Folklore's Nature and the Sun's Myth," *Journal of American Folklore* 88 (1975):352.
18. Abraham Moles, *Information Theory and Esthetic Perception*, trans. Joel E. Cohen, p. 7.
19. This breakdown of records into written and spoken is suggested by Rulon S. Wells in "Comments to 'Part Five: Metrics,'" *Style in Language*, ed. Thomas A. Sebeok, p. 198, and reiterated by Katherine Loesch, "Empirical Studies in Oral Interpretation: The Text," *Western Speech* 33 (1969):250-68. Loesch defines the text as "any *record* of the poem . . . that registers in a visual notation on the page the words of the poem and their temporal order."
20. As Loesch, above, points out, in English we may expect three types of texts: "1) ordinary written texts . . . 2) phonological texts, either phonetic or phonemic, and 3) texts of either the first or second types to which one or more kinds of further notation have been systematically added—for example, paralinguistic notation, grammatical notation, or notation of implied sensory components" (p. 251n).
21. See Richard Dorson, "Oral Styles of American Folk Narrators," *Style in Language*, ed. Thomas A. Sebeok, pp. 27-51; and Harold Scheub, "Body and Image in Oral Narrative Performance," *New Literary History* 8 (Spring 1977):345-67.
22. Tedlock, pp. 114-33.
23. Jerome Rothenberg, ed., *Shaking the Pumpkin: Traditional Poetry of the Indian North Americas*, p. xxiii.
24. Harold Scheub, "Translation of African Oral Narrative-Performances to the Written Word," *Yearbook of Comparative and General Literature* 20 (1971):28.
25. Lee Roloff, *The Perception and Evocation of Literature*, p. 19.
26. Paul Valéry, "The Course in Poetics: First Lesson," *The Creative Process: A Symposium*, ed. Brewster Ghiselin, p. 99.
27. Roman Jakobson, "On Linguistic Aspects of Translation," p. 233.
28. Eugene A. Nida, *Toward a Science of Translating*, p. 4.
29. Lewis Galantière, "Introduction," *The World of Translation*. Papers delivered at the Conference on Literary Translation held in New York City in May, 1970 under the auspices of P.E.N. American Center, p. x.
30. Steiner, p. 239.
31. Nida, p. 22.
32. In outlining Nida's methodology, I am referring to the approach used in his book, *Toward a Science of Translating*, a more theoretically-oriented work than *The Theory and Practice of Translation*.

33. Richard Dorson, "Standards for Collecting and Publishing American Folktales," *Journal of American Folklore* 70 (1957):53-57.
34. Dell Hymes, "An Ethnographic Perspective," *New Literary History* 4 (Autumn, 1973):200.
35. Ray L. Birdwhistell, *Kinesics and Context;* Robert E. Pittenger, Charles F. Hockett, and John J. Danehy, *The First Five Minutes;* George L. Trager, "Paralanguage: A First Approximation," *Language in Culture and Society,* ed. Dell Hymes.
36. Birdwhistell, p. 314.
37. Scheub, p. 32.
38. J. Barre Toelken, "The 'Pretty Language' of Yellowman: Genre, Mode and Texture in Navaho Coyote Narratives," *Genre* 2 (1969):216.
39. Nida, *Toward a Science of Translation,* p. 162.
40. Ibid., pp. 162-63.
41. Ibid., p. 163.
42. Ibid., p. 164. For earlier statements on the principle of "similar response" see, as mentioned by Nida, Benjamin Jowett, *Preface to the Dialogues of Plato,* 2nd ed.; Alexander Souter, *Hints on Translation from Latin into English,* p. 7; Ronald A. Knox, *On English Translation,* p. 5; and Vladimir Procházka, "Notes on Translating Technique," *A Prague School Reader on Esthetics, Literary Structure and Style,* ed. and trans. Paul L. Garvin, pp. 108-30.
43. See George A. Miller, *The Psychology of Communication: Seven Essays.*
44. Moles, pp. 203-08.
45. Ibid., p. 7.
46. Nida, *Toward a Science of Translating,* p. 126.
47. Ibid., pp. 126, 130.
48. Ibid.
49. Ibid., p. 131. Nida's figures deal with interlingual translation. I have adapted them to apply to intersemiotic translation of performance to print.
50. Ibid., p. 130.
51. Ibid., pp. 131-32.
52. Ibid., p. 131.
53. Tedlock, "On the Translation of Style," p. 117.
54. Idem., "Learning to Listen: Oral History as Poetry," *Envelopes of Sound,* ed. Ronald J. Grele, p. 116; "On the Translation of Style," pp. 131-32.
55. Nida, *Toward a Science of Translating,* pp. 140-41.
56. Tedlock, "Learning to Listen," p. 119.
57. Jean Rouch, "The Camera and Man," *Studies in the Anthropology of Visual Communication* 1 (Fall, 1974):40.

5. Analysis of Source and Receptor Media: Performance and Print

1. Kenneth L. Pike, *The Intonation of American English,* University of Michigan Publications, Linguistics, Vol. I., p. 171.
2. Ibid., p. 170.

3. Ibid., pp. 170-71.

4. Ibid., p. 171.

5. There is still considerable disagreement on how these suprasegmental phonemes should be categorized. For our purposes, Pittenger, Hockett and Danehy's categorization, based on Trager and Smith's widely accepted formulation, is adequate. See Pittenger, Hockett, and Danehy, *The First Five Minutes*, pp. 187-94; and George L. Trager and Henry Lee Smith, Jr., *An Outline of English Structure, Studies in Linguistics: Occasional Papers* 3.

6. Pittenger, Hockett, and Danehy, pp. 191-93.

7. George L. Trager, "Paralanguage: A First Approximation," *Language in Culture and Society*, ed. Dell Hymes, p. 276.

8. Ibid., pp. 276-77.

9. See David Crystal, *Prosodic Systems and Intonation in English;* J.C. Catford, "Phonation Types: The Classification of Some Laryngeal Components of Speech Production," *In Honor of Daniel Jones*, ed. David Abercrombie, pp. 26-37; David Abercrombie, *Elements of General Phonetics*.

10. Howard Rodney Martin, *The Prosodic and Paralinguistic Analysis of Dramatic Speech: A Practical System*.

11. John H. McDowell, "Some Aspects of Verbal Art in Bolivian Quechua," *Folklore Annual of the University Folklore Association* No. 6 (1974), pp. 70-71.

12. David Abercrombie, *Elements of General Phonetics*, pp. 7-9.

13. Albert E. Scheflen, *Communicational Structure: Analysis of a Psychotherapy Transaction*, pp. xi-xii.

14. See Ann Hutchinson, *Labanotation*, and Juana de Laban, "Movement Notation: Its Significance to the Folklorist," *Journal of American Folklore* 67 (1954): 291-95. Although Laban suggests that folklorists may find the system useful, I believe its utility is limited to recording folk dance.

15. Norbert Freedman, "Toward a Mathematization of Kinetic Behavior: A Review of Paul Bouissac's *La Mesure Des Gestes"* (*Approaches to Semiotics*, Paperback Series, 3: The Hague: Mouton, 1973), *Semiotica* 15 (1976): 83.

16. Irmgard Bartenieff and Martha Ann Davis, "Effort-Shape Analysis of Movement: The Unity of Expression and Function," *Body Movement: Perspectives in Research*, ed. Martha Davis, p. 4.

17. Alan Lomax, *Folk Song Style and Culture*, p. 223.

18. Bartenieff and Davis, p. 43.

19. Randall P. Harrison and Mark L. Knapp, "Toward an Understanding of Nonverbal Communication Systems," *The Journal of Communication* 22 (Dec. 1972): 347-48.

20. Roger G. Barker and Herbert F. Wright, *Midwest and Its Children: The Psychological Ecology of an American Town*, p. 199.

21. Birdwhistell, pp. 242, 234, 286.

22. Ibid., pp. 244-45.

23. Ibid., pp. 248, 250.

24. Ibid., p. 251.

25. Ibid., pp. 252-53, 256.

26. Ibid., pp. 258-59.
27. Ibid., pp. 258-59, 261.
28. Ibid., pp. 269-70, 272-74. I have not listed an eighth category, *self-possessed—self-contained* because Birdwhistell says it is a dubious category.
29. Ibid., pp. 276-77.
30. Ibid., pp. 281-82.
31. Ibid., pp. 282-83.
32. Ibid., pp. 169-72.
33. Ibid., p. 293.
34. Scheflen, p. 18.
35. Birdwhistell, pp. 249, 162.
36. Ibid., p. 235.
37. Ibid., pp. 284-88.
38. Roger Poole, "Objective Sign and Subjective Meaning," *The Body as a Medium of Expression*, ed. Jonathan Benthall and Ted Polhemus, pp. 80-81.
39. Ibid., pp. 95, 81.
40. Barker and Wright, pp. 178-79.
41. Ibid., p. 186.
42. Ibid., pp. 205, 201-02.
43. Freedman, pp. 93-94.
44. Barker and Wright, p. 209.
45. Ibid., pp. 196-97.
46. Gregory Bateson, "Problems in Cetacean and Other Mammalian Communication," pp. 372-74.
47. Paul Ekman and Wallace V. Friesen, "The Repertoire of Nonverbal Behavior: Categories, Origins, Usage, and Coding," *Semiotica* 1 (1969): 60n, 68-69.
48. Thomas A. Sebeok, "Six Species of Signs: Some Propositions and Strictures," *Semiotica* 13 (1975): 245-46.
49. Dale C. Leathers, *Nonverbal Communication Systems*, p. 86.
50. V. Hrdličková, "Japanese Professional Storytellers," *Genre* 2 (1969): 195.
51. Edward T. Hall, *The Hidden Dimension*.
52. Regna Darnell, "Correlates of Cree Narrative Performance," *Explorations in the Ethnography of Speaking*, eds. Richard Bauman and Joel Sherzer, pp. 465-66n.
53. Hall, pp. 103-12.
54. Ibid., pp. 116-25.
55. Ibid., pp. 50, 160.
56. *American College Dictionary*, 1966.
57. Umberto Eco, *A Theory of Semiotics*, p. 189.
58. J. M. Lotman, "The Discrete Text and the Iconic Text," *New Literary History* 6 (1975): 334.
59. Loesch, pp. 256-59.
60. This special definition of projection is similar in principle to this *Oxford English Dictionary* definition of the word project: "Hence, to represent or delineate (a figure) according to any system of correspondence between its points and the points of the surface on which it is delineated."

61. Paul H. Bowdre, Jr., "Eye Dialect as a Literary Device," *A Various Language: Perspectives on American Dialects,* eds. Juanita V. Williamson and Virginia M. Burke, p. 180.
62. Sumner Ives, "A Theory of Literary Dialect," *A Various Language,* p. 162.
63. Ibid., p. 159.
64. Ibid., pp. 156, 171.
65. Dennis R. Preston, "'Ritin' Fowklower Daun 'Rong: Folklorists' Failures in Phonology," *Journal of American Folklore* 95 (1982): 305. The following reply to Preston's charges is a shortened and slightly revised version of my article, "In Defense of Literary Dialect: A Response to Dennis R. Preston," *Journal of American Folklore,* 96 (1983): 323-30.
66. Ibid., p. 304.
67. See J. Barre Toelken, "The 'Pretty Language' of Yellowman: Genre, Mode, and Texture in Navaho Coyote Narratives," *Genre* 2 (1969): 211-35; István Sándor, "Dramaturgy of Tale-Telling," *Acta Ethnographica: Academiae Scientarium Hungaricae* 16 (1976): 303-38; Dennis Tedlock, "On the Translation of Style in Oral Narrative," *Journal of American Folklore* 84 (1971): 114-33.
68. Preston, pp. 322-23. See Preston, "'Mowr Bayud Spellin': A Reply to Fine," *Journal of American Folklore* 96 (1983):330-39 for a subsequent attempt to substantiate this "folk fact" of negative attitudes toward respellings. Preston presents the results of a study in which 92 college students in basic writing courses were asked to rank the social status of four speakers based on a conversational transcript in which the speakers used various levels and degrees of standard and nonstandard constructions and respellings. Only one speaker, Speaker #2, used standard constructions, but had some of his speech represented through respellings. Thus, only the attitudes of readers toward the speech of Speaker #2 can support or refute Preston's claim that readers assign lower social status to respelled speech, *per se.* Significantly, 70 of the 92 students ranked Speaker #2 as middle class or above. Only 2 students ranked the speaker as lower class, and only 20 ranked the speaker as lower middle class. Thus, Preston's study seems to confirm the very point he wishes to refute. Over 75 percent of the readers in his study did *not* find that respellings alone indicate lower social status.
69. See William Labov, "Rules for Ritual Insults," pp. 265-314, Roger D. Abrahams, "Joking: The Training of the Man of Words in Talking Broad," pp. 215-40, and Claudia Mitchell-Kernan, "Signifying, Loud-talking, and Marking," pp. 315-35, all in *Rappin' and Stylin' Out: Communication in Urban Black America,* ed. Thomas Kochman; Geneva Smitherman, *Talkin and Testifyin: The Language of Black America* and Edith A. Folb, *Runnin' Down Some Lines: The Language and Culture of Black Teenagers.*
70. Smitherman, p. 180. For other examples see pp. 3, 23, 217, 219, 221, and 233-34.
71. The line "looooken so cooool" is from Sonia Sanchez, "chant for young brothas & sistuhs," reprinted in Smitherman, *Talkin and Testifyin,* p. 181; the line "ain't gonna let no in/junction turn me round" is from Donald L. Graham, "April 5th," in *Understanding the New Black Poetry,* ed. Stephen Henderson, p. 320; and the last line is from Gerald W. Barrax, "The Dozens:

A Small Drama in One Act, One Scene," in *Understanding the New Black Poetry*, p. 360.

72. See Smitherman, *Talkin and Testifyin*, pp. 185-200, for a review of the origins of the "doctrine of correctness."

73. For more on the history of the print medium see L. D. Reynolds and N. G. Wilson, *Scribes and Scholars, A Guide to the Transmission of Greek and Latin Literature*, pp. 5-9.

74. Toelken, p. 216.

75. Garrick Mallery, "Sign Language Among North American Indians . . . ," *First Annual Report of the Bureau of American Ethnology* p. 500.

76. Barker and Wright, pp. 217, 207-08.

77. Abercrombie, p. 112.

78. Pike, *Phonetics: A Critical Analysis of Phonetic Theory and A Technic for the Practical Description of Sounds*, p. 154.

79. Abercrombie, p. 127.

80. Gilbert Austin, *Chironomia or a Treatise on Rhetorical Delivery . . .* , eds. Mary Margaret Robb and Lester Thonssen, pp. 369-71, xvii-xviii.

81. Birdwhistell, pp. 373-75.

82. Abercrombie, pp., 121-22.

83. Pittenger, Hockett and Danehy, pp. 191-92.

84. Edward Sapir, *Wishram Texts*, Vol. 2, ed. Franz Boas, Publications of the American Ethnological Society; Franz Boas, *Chinook Texts*, Smithsonian Institution, Bureau of Ethnology.

85. Joshua Steele, *Prosodia Rationalis, or An Essay Toward Establishing the Melody and Measure of Speech, to be Expressed and Perpetuated by Peculiar Symbols;* James Rush, *The Philosophy of the Human Voice . . . ,sixth ed.*

86. Pike, *Intonation of American English*, pp. 4 5.

87. Leathers, p. 204.

88. Alexander Melville Bell, *Visible Speech: the Science of Universal Alphabetics,* as quoted in Abercrombie, pp. 118-19.

89. Moles, p. 54.

90. Ralph Ellison, *Invisible Man*, pp. 172-73.

91. Tedlock, *Finding the Center.*

92. Abercrombie, p. 131.

93. Pike, *Intonation of American English*, p. 42.

94. Sándor, pp. 303-338.

95. Scheflen, *Communicational Structure: Analysis of a Psychotherapy Session.*

96. Birdwhistell, pp. 329-32.

97. Tedlock, "Toward an Oral Poetics," *New Literary History* 8 (Spring 1977): 516.

98. Jonathan Culler, *Structuralist Poetics: Structuralism, Linguistics, and the Study of Literature*, p. 114.

6. Principles of Translating Performance

1. I. A. Richards, "Toward a Theory of Translating," *Studies in Chinese Thought.* American Anthropological Association, Vol. 55, Memoir 75, p. 250, mentioned in Nida, "A Framework for the Analysis and Evaluation of

Theories of Translation," *Translation: Applications and Research,* ed. Richard W. Brislin, p. 79.

2. George Steiner, *After Babel: Aspects of Language and Translation,* p. 302.
3. Nida, "Principles of Translation as Exemplified by Bible Translating," *Language Structure and Translation: Essays by Eugene A. Nida,* ed. Anwar S. Dil, p. 27.
4. Nida, *Toward a Science of Translating,* p. 159.
5. Ibid., pp. 159, 166.
6. Truman Michelson, "The Autobiography of a Fox Indian Woman," *Annual Report of the Bureau of American Ethnology* 40, p. 295.
7. Carl Fleischhauer and Alan Jabbour, eds., *The Hammons Family: A Study of a West Virginia Family's Traditions,* p. 22.
8. Leonard Roberts, *Sang Branch Settlers: Folksongs and Tales of a Kentucky Mountain Family.*
9. Tedlock, "On the Translation of Style in Oral Narrative," *Journal of American Folklore* 84 (1971): 129.
10. Scheflen, *Communicational Structure: Analysis of a Psychotherapy Session,* p. 319.
11. Berleant, *The Aesthetic Field: A Phenomenology of Aesthetic Experience,* pp. 103-04.
12. Tedlock, "Toward an Oral Poetics," *New Literary History* 8 (Spring 1977): 510.
13. Toelken, "The 'Pretty Language' of Yellowman: Genre, Mode, and Texture in Navaho Coyote Narratives," *Genre* 2 (1969): 215-19.
14. E. D. Hirsch, Jr., *The Aims of Interpretation,* pp. 21-26.
15. Ibid., pp. 21, 23, 34.
16. Ibid., pp. 32-34.
17. Ibid.
18. Dell Hymes, "Models of the Interaction of Language and Social Life," *Directions in Sociolinguistics,* eds. J. J. Gumperz and Dell Hymes, pp. 35-71.
19. Tedlock, "Translator's Introduction," in Walter Sanchez, "The Girl and the Protector," a story translated from the Zuni by Dennis Tedlock, *Alcheringa: Ethnopoetics* n.s. 1, No. 1 (1975): 111.
20. Richard Bauman, "Differential Identity and the Social Base of Folklore," *Toward New Perspectives in Folklore,* eds. Américo Paredes and Richard Bauman, p. 40.
21. Tedlock, "Introduction," to Sanchez, "A Prayer Over Dead Rabbits," trans. Dennis Tedlock and Andrew Peynetsa, *Alcheringa: Ethnopoetics* o.s. No. 4 (Autumn 1972): 60.
22. Toelken, p. 218.
23. Tedlock, "Translator's Introduction," p. 111.
24. Daniel J. Crowley, *I Could Talk Old-Story Good,* pp. 20-21.
25. Lawrence Ferlinghetti, "Constantly risking absurdity and death," *A Coney Island of the Mind,* p. 30.
26. Steiner, p. 296.
27. Ibid., pp. 297-98.
28. See Kenneth Goldstein, *A Guide for Field Workers in Folklore,* p. 98 for

suggestions on using film and video to record performances, and Jean Rouch, "The Camera and Man," *Studies in the Anthropology of Visual Communication* 1 (Fall 1974): 35-44.

29. Nida, *Toward a Science of Translating*, p. 147.
30. Steiner, pp. 298-300.
31. Ibid., p. 395.
32. George Quasha, "New Aspects of Translation," *The World of Translation*, p. 203.
33. Scheub, "Body and Image in Oral Narrative Performance."

7. An Illustration of a Performance-Centered Text

1. Roger Abrahams, *Deep Down in the Jungle . . . : Negro Narrative Folklore from the Streets of Philadelphia*, first rev. ed., p. 112; Bruce Jackson, *"Get Your Ass in the Water and Swim Like Me": Narrative from Black Oral Tradition*, p. 5.
2. Although *Alcheringa* has published a selection of Afro-American toasts, the texts transcribed by Onwuchekwa Jemie are not really performance-centered. No information is given about the specific performance event, nor are audience reactions, paralinguistic, or kinesic features recorded. See Onwuchekwa Jemie, "Signifying, Dozens, and Toasts: A Selection," *Alcheringa: Ethnopoetics*, n.s. 2, No. 1 (1976), pp. 27-41.
3. Julius Lester, *Black Folktales*, pp. 78-135.
4. See H. C. Brearly, "Ba-ad Nigger," *The South Atlantic Quarterly* 38 (1939): 75-81, reprinted in *Mother-Wit from the Laughing Barrel: Readings in the Interpretation of Afro-American Folklore*, ed. Alan Dundes, pp. 578, 585, for a discussion of the term "ba-ad nigger." Brearly points out that a speaker can use "bad" to mean "good" by prolonging the "*a*."
5. William Labov, Paul Cohen, Clarence Robins, and John David Evans, "Toasts," in *Mother-Wit from the Laughing Barrel*, p. 330.
6. A good summary of these debated issues appears in David Evans, "The Toast in Context," *Journal of American Folklore* 90 (1977): 129-48.
7. Abrahams, pp. 139, 100.
8. See Evans, pp. 130, 131, 135; William R. Ferris, Jr., "Black Prose Narratives from the Mississippi Delta," *Jassforschung*, 6/7 (1974/75): 75-81. Labov, et al., p. 347, discuss rhymed toasts which contain "prose transitions."
9. See Labov, Cohen, et al., pp. 330, 342.
10. Jackson, p. 12.
11. Evans, p. 131.
12. Jackson, p. 5
13. Abrahams, pp. 94, 92.
14. Labov, Cohen, et al., p. 341.
15. See Abrahams, pp. 100-08, for a description of the stylistic features of toasts.
16. A note about my relationship with James Hutchinson should help place his comments in perspective. Although we had a friendly student-teacher relationship, we were not close friends. Perhaps he would have given a different or fuller account to a close friend of the same sex and race.
17. I am indebted to A. Arnold, Marilyn Carreño and Melissa Walker for their help.

18. Benjamin G. Cooke, "Nonverbal Communication Among Afro-Americans: An Initial Classification," *Rappin' and Stylin' Out: Communication in Urban Black America,* ed. Thomas Kochman, pp. 43-44.
19. Robert Farris Thompson noted this connection between the poses in a personal communication, 1981. The quotation is from Robert Farris Thompson, "No. 37 Steatite Seated Image in Nobleman's Hat (fig. 3)," *The Four Moments of the Sun: Kongo Art in Two Worlds,* Catalogue by Robert Farris Thompson and Joseph Cornet, National Gallery of Art.
20. Cooke, p. 40.
21. Ibid., pp. 52-54.
22. Ibid., p. 55.
23. Jackson, pp. 32-35.
24. See David Dalby, "The African Element in American English," *Rappin' and Stylin' Out,* p. 177; see note 4, above.
25. Claude Brown, "The Language of Soul," *Rappin' and Stylin' Out,* p. 136.
26. See Jackson, p. 7, and Evans, p. 133. See also the introduction to Kenneth S. Goldstein and Robert D. Bethke, eds., *Monologues and Folk Recitation, Southern Folklore Quarterly* 40 (1974), Nos. 1 and 2.
27. Lester, pp. 114-16.
28. Ibid., pp. 122-23.
29. Ibid., p. 120.
30. See Jackson, p. 17.
31. Lester, pp. 117, 123.
32. Lester, p. 125.
33. Labov, Cohen, et al., p. 331.
34. Lester, p. 125.
35. See pp. 186, 190-94.
36. William J. Brandt, *The Rhetoric or Argumentation,* p. 165.
37. Lester, p. 134.
38. Ibid., pp. 116-17.
39. Harold Scheub, "Body and Image in Oral Narrative Performance," *New Literary History* 8 (Spring 1977): 355.
40. Ibid., p. 350.
41. Ibid., p. 351.
42. Toelken, "The 'Pretty Language' of Yellowman."

Abercrombie, David. *Elements of General Phonetics*. Chicago: Aldine Publishing Co., 1967.

Abrahams, Roger. *Deep Down in the Jungle . . . : Negro Narrative Folklore from the Streets of Philadelphia*. Rev. ed. Chicago: Aldine Publishing Co., 1970.

_____. "A Performance-Centered Approach to Gossip." *Man* 5 (1970): 290-301.

_____. "Enactments." Paper delivered at the meeting of the American Association for the Advancement of Science, 1977.

_____. "Folklore and Literature as Performance." *Journal of the Folklore Institute* 8 (1972): 75-94.

_____. "In and Out of Performance." MS. University of Texas at Austin, 1976.

_____. "Introductory Remarks to a Rhetorical Theory of Folklore." *Journal of American Folklore* 81 (April-June 1968): 143-58.

_____. "Joking: The Training of the Man of Words in Talking Broad." In *Rappin' and Stylin' Out: Communication in Urban Black America*, pp. 215-40. Edited by Thomas Kochman. Urbana: University of Illinois Press, 1972.

_____. "License to Repeat and Be Predictable." Paper presented at the Annual Meeting of the American Folklore Society, 1977.

Abrams, Meyer H. *The Mirror and the Lamp*. New York: Oxford University Press, 1953.

Arewa, E. Ojo, and Dundes, Alan. "Proverbs and the Ethnography of Speaking Folklore." *American Anthropologist* 66, part 2 (1964): 70-85. Special Publication, *The Ethnography of Communication*. Edited by John J. Gumperz and Dell Hymes.

Aristotle. *The Art of Rhetoric*. Translated by John Henry Freese. London: William Heinemann, LTD, Loeb, Classical Library, 1967.

Austin, Gilbert. *Chironomia; or a Treatise on Rhetorical Delivery*. Edited by Mary Margaret Robb and Lester Thonssen. London: W. Bulmer & Co., 1806, Reprint. Carbondale: Southern Illinois University Press, 1966.

Babcock, Barbara A. "The Story in the Story: Metanarration in Folk Narrative." In *Verbal Art as Performance*, pp. 61-80. By Richard Bauman. Series in Sociolinguistics. Edited by Roger W. Shuy. Rowley, Mass.: Newbury House, 1977.

Bacon, Wallace. "The Dangerous Shores a Decade Later." In *The Study of Interpretation: Theory and Comment*, pp. 221-28. Edited by Richard Haas and David Williams. Indianapolis: Bobbs-Merrill, 1975.

Ball, John. "Style in the Folktale." *Folk-lore* 65 (December 1954): 170-72.

Barker, Roger G., and Wright, Herbert F. *Midwest and Its Children: The Psychological Ecology of an American Town*. Evanston, Illinois: Row, Peterson and Co., 1954.

Barrax, Gerald W. "The Dozens: A Small Drama in One Act, One Scene." In *Understanding the New Black Poetry*, pp. 360-61. Edited by Stephen Henderson. New York: William Morrow and Co., 1973.

Bartenieff, Irmgard, and Davis, Martha Ann. "Effort-Shape Analysis of Movement: The Unity of Expression and Function." In *Body Movement: Perspectives in Research*. Edited by Martha Davis. New York: Arno Press, 1972.

Bascom, William R. "Folklore and Anthropology." In *The Study of Folklore*, pp. 25-33. Edited by Alan Dundes. Englewood Cliffs, New Jersey: Prentice-Hall, 1965.

———. "Verbal Art." *Journal of American Folklore* 68 (1955): 245-52.

Bateson, Gregory. "A Theory of Play and Fantasy." In *Steps to an Ecology of Mind*, pp. 177-93. New York: Ballantine Books, 1972.

———. "Problems in Cetacean and Other Mammalian Communication." In *Steps to an Ecology of Mind*, pp. 364-78. New York: Ballantine Books, 1972.

Bauman, Richard. "Differential Identity and the Social Base of Folklore." In *Toward New Perspectives in Folklore*, pp. 31-41. Edited by Américo Paredes and Richard Bauman. Austin: University of Texas Press, 1972.

———. "Linguistics, Anthropology, and Verbal Art: Toward a Unified Perspective, with a special discussion of Children's Folklore." In *Linguistics and Anthropology*. Georgetown University Round Table on Languages and Linguistics, 1977, pp. 13-36. Edited by Muriel Saville-Troike. Washington, D.C.: Georgetown University Press, 1977.

———. "Introduction." In *Toward New Perspectives in Folklore*, pp. v-ix. Edited by Américo Paredes and Richard Bauman. Austin: University of Texas Press, 1972.

———. "Settlement Patterns on the Frontiers of Folklore." In *Frontiers of Folklore*, pp. 121-31. Edited by William Bascom. Washington, D.C.: American Association for the Advancement of Science, 1977.

———. "Verbal Art as Performance." *American Anthropologist* 77 (1975): 290-311.

———. *Verbal Art as Performance*. Series in Sociolinguistics. Edited by Roger W. Shuy. Rowley, Mass.: Newbury House Publishers, 1977.

Bauman, Richard, and Abrahams, Roger D. with Kalcik, Susan. "American Folklore and American Studies." *American Quarterly* 28 (1976): 360-77.

Bauman, Richard, and Sherzer, Joel. "The Ethnography of Speaking." *Annual Review of Anthropology* 4 (1975): 95-119.

Beck, Horace P. "MacEdward Leach—1896-1967," *Keystone Folk Quarterly* (Fall 1967): 195.

Bell, Alexander Melville. *Visible Speech: the Science of Universal Alphabetics*. London: Simpkin, Marshall, 1867.

Bell, Michael J. "William Wells Newell and the Foundation of American Folklore Scholarship." *Special Issue: American Folklore Historiography*. In *Journal of the Folklore Institute* 10 (1973): 7-22.

Ben-Amos, Dan. "Analytical Categories and Ethnic Genres." *Genre* 2 (1969): 275-301.

———. "Folklore: The Definition Game Once Again." Unpublished paper read at the meeting of the American Folklore Sociey, Toronto, Ontario, 1967.

———. "Toward a Definition of Folklore in Context." *Toward New Perspectives in Folklore*, pp. 3-15. Edited by Américo Paredes and Richard Bauman. Austin: University of Texas Press, 1972.

Ben-Amos, Dan, and Goldstein, Kenneth S., eds. "Introduction." In *Folklore: Performance and Communication*. The Hague: Mouton, 1975.

Benedict, Ruth. *Zuni Mythology*, 2 Volumes. Columbia University Contributions to Anthropoloy, Vol. 21. New York: Columbia University Press, 1935.

Berleant, Arnold. *The Aesthetic Field: A Phenomenology of Aesthetic Experience*. Springfield, Illinois: Charles C. Thomas, 1970.

Birdwhistell, Ray L. *Kinesics and Context: Essays on Body Motion Communication*. New York: Ballantine Books, 1970; Philadelphia: University of Pennsylvania Press, 1970.

Boas, Franz. "The Central Eskimo." *Sixth Annual Report of the Bureau of American Ethnology*. Washington, D.C.: Government Printing Office, 1884-1885.

———. *Chinook Texts*. Smithsonian Institution, Bureau of Ethnology. Washington, D.C.: Government Printing Office, 1894.

———. "The Documentary Function of the Text." Letter to Professor Holmes, Bureau of American Ethnology, 1905. In *The Shaping of American Anthropology 1883-1911: A Franz Boas Reader*. Edited by George W. Stocking, Jr. New York: Basic Books, 1974.

Bogatyrev, Petr. "Folk Song from a Functional Point of View." In *Semiotics of Art: Prague School Contributions*, pp. 20-32. Edited by Ladislav Matejka and Irwin A. Titunik. Cambridge and London, The MIT Press, 1976.

———. "Forms and Functions of Folk Theater." In *Semiotics of Art: Prague School Contributions*, pp. 51-56. Edited by Ladislav Matejka and Irwin A. Titunik. Cambridge and London, The MIT Press, 1976.

———. "Semiotics in the Folk Theater." In *Semiotics of Art: Prague School Contributions*, pp. 33-50. Edited by Ladislav Matejka and Irwin A. Titunik. Cambridge and London, The MIT Press, 1976.

Bolton, Janet. "Response." In *The Study of Oral Interpretation*, pp. 85-91. Edited by Richard Haas and David Williams. Indianapolis: Bobbs-Merrill, 1975.

Bowdre, Paul H., Jr. "Eye Dialect as a Literary Device." In *A Various Language: Perspectives on American Dialects*, pp. 178-86. Edited by Juanita V. Williamson and Virginia M. Burke. New York: Holt, Rinehart and Winston, 1971.

Brandon-Sweeney, Beverly. "Kinesics and Its Interpretation." *Folklore Annual of the University Folklore Association*. 4/5 (1972/1973): 23-51.

Brandt, William J. *The Rhetoric of Argumentation*. Indianapolis: Bobbs-Merrill, 1970.

Brown, Claude. "The Language of Soul." In *Rappin' and Stylin' Out: Communication in Urban Black America*, pp. 134-39. Edited by Thomas Kochman. Urbana: University of Illinois Press, 1972.

Brearly, H. C. "Ba-ad Nigger." *The South Atlantic Quarterly* 38 (1939): 75-81. Reprint in *Mother-Wit from the Laughing Barrel: Readings in the Interpretation of Afro-American Folklore*, pp. 578-85. Edited by Alan Dundes. Englewood Cliffs, New Jersey: Prentice Hall, 1973.

Bright, William. "Language and Music: Areas for Cooperation." *Ethnomusicology* 7 (1963): 26-32.

Bright, William, ed. *Sociolinguistics*. The Hague: Mouton, 1966.

Browning, Larry D., and Hopper, Robert. "How Messages Get to Mean-- Influences in a Bureaucratic Organization." Paper presented at the Central States Speech Association Conference, 1977.

Brunvand, Jan Harold. *Folklore: A Study and Research Guide*. New York: St. Martin's Press, 1976.

Bunzel, Ruth. *Zuni Texts*. Publications of the American Ethnological Society, 15. New York: G.E. Stechert & Co., 1933.

Burke, Kenneth. *A Grammar of Motives.* Berkeley: University of California Press, 1945.

Burns, Elizabeth. *Theatricality: A Study of Convention in the Theatre and in Social Life.* London: Longman, 1972.

Burns, Thomas A. "Folkloristics: A Conception of Theory." *Western Folklore* 36 (1977): 109-34.

Catford, J. C. "Phonation Types: The Classification of Some Laryngeal Components of Speech Production." In *In Honor of Daniel Jones,* pp. 26-37. Edited by David Abercrombie. London: Longmans, 1964.

Chatman, Seymour. "A Study of James Mason's Interpretation of 'The Bishop Orders His Tomb'." *The Oral Study of Literature,* pp. 94-132. Edited by Thomas O. Sloan. New York: John Wiley & Sons, 1966.

Cohen, Edwin. "The Role of the Interpreter in Identifying the Concept of 'Folk'." *Western Speech* 37 (1974): 170-75.

Colby, Benjamin, and Peacock, James. "Narrative." In *Handbook of Social and Cultural Anthropology.* Edited by John J. Honigmann. Chicago: Rand McNally, 1973.

Cooke, Benjamin G. "Nonverbal Communication Among Afro-Americans: An Initial Classification." In *Rappin' and Stylin' Out: Communication in Urban Black America,* pp. 32-64. Edited by Thomas Kochman. Urbana: University of Illinois Press, 1972.

Crowley, Daniel J. *I Could Talk Old-Story Good: Creativity in Bahamian Folklore.* In *Folklore Studies* 17. Berkeley: University of California Press, 1966.

Crystal, David. *Prosodic Systems and Intonation in English.* Cambridge: Cambridge University Press, 1969.

Culler, Jonathan. *Structuralist Poetics: Structuralism, Linguistics, and the Study of Literature.* Ithaca, New York: Cornell University Press, 1975.

Cushing, Frank. *Zuni Folktales.* New York: G.P. Putnam's Sons, 1901.

Dalby, David. "The African Element in American English." In *Rappin' and Stylin' Out: Communication in Urban Black America,* pp. 170-86. Edited by Thomas Kochman. Urbana: University of Illinois Press, 1972.

Daniel, Jack L., and Smitherman, Geneva. "How I Got Over: Communication Dynamics in the Black Community." *Quarterly Journal of Speech* 62 (1976): 26-39.

Darnell, Regna. "Correlates of Cree Narrative Performance." *Explorations in the Ethnography of Speaking,* pp. 315-36. Edited by Richard Bauman and Joel Sherzer. London: Cambridge University Press, 1974.

Dauenhauer, Richard. "Notes on Swanton Numbers 80 and 81." *Journal of American Folklore* 94 (1981): 358-64.

Dégh, Linda. *Folktales and Society: Storytelling in a Hungarian Peasant Community.* Translated by Emily Schossberger. Bloomington: Indiana University Press, 1969.

Dégh, Linda and Vazsonyi, Andrew. "Legend and Belief." *Genre* 4 (September 1971): 281-304; reprinted in *Folklore Genres,* pp. 94-123. Edited by Dan Ben-Amos. Austin: University of Texas Press, 1976.

Delia, Jesse G. "Constructivism and the Study of Human Communication." *Quarterly Journal of Speech* 63 (February 1977): 66-83.

Dewey, John. *Art as Experience.* New York: Minton, Balch, 1934.

Doherty, Joseph. "Towards a Poetics of Performance." MS. University of Texas at Austin.

Dorsey, J.O.; Gatschet, A. S.; and Riggs, S. R. "Illustration of the Method of Recording Indian Languages." *First Annual Report of the Bureau of American Ethnology*. Washington, D.C.: Government Printing Office, 1879-1880.

Dorson, Richard M., ed. *Buying the Wind: Regional Folklore in the United States*. Chicago: University of Chicago Press, 1964.

_____ *Negro Folktales in Michigan*. Cambridge, Massachusetts: Harvard University Press, 1956.

_____ "Oral Styles of American Folk Narrators." In *Style in Language*, pp. 27-51. Edited by Thomas A. Sebeok. New York: John Wiley & Sons, 1960.

_____ "Print and American Folk Tales." *California Folklore Quarterly* 4 (1945): 207-15.

_____ "Standards for Collecting and Publishing American Folktales." *Journal of American Folklore* 70 (1957): 53-57.

Dundes, Alan. "From Etic to Emic Units in the Structural Study of Folktales." *Journal of American Folklore* 75 (1962): 95-105.

_____ "Texture, Text, and Context." *Southern Folklore Quarterly* 28 (1964): 251-65.

_____ "The American Concept of Folklore." *Journal of the Folklore Institute* 3 (1966): 226-49.

_____ "The Devolutionary Premise in Folklore Theory." *Journal of the Folklore Institute* 6 (1969): 5-19.

Eco, Umberto. *A Theory of Semiotics*. Bloomington: Indiana University Press, 1976.

Ekman, Paul, and Friesen, Wallace V. "The Repertoire of Nonverbal Behavior: Categories, Origins, Usage, and Coding." *Semiotica* 1 (1969): 49-98.

Ellison, Ralph. *Invisible Man*. New York: Vintage Books, 1972.

Evans, David. "The Toast in Context." *Journal of American Folklore* 90 (1977): 129-48.

Farrell, Thomas B. "Knowledge, Consensus and Rhetorical Theory." *The Quarterly Journal of Speech* 62 (February 1976): 1-14.

Ferlinghetti, Lawrence. "Constantly risking absurdity and death." *A Coney Island of the Mind*. New York: New Directions, 1958.

Ferris, William R., Jr. "Black Prose Narratives from the Mississippi Delta." *Jassforschung* 6/7 (74/75): 75-81.

Fine, Elizabeth C. "In Defense of Literary Dialect: A Response to Dennis R. Preston." *Journal of American Folklore* 96 (July-September 1983): 323-30.

_____ Review of *Traditional American Indian Literature: Text and Interpretations*, edited by Karl Kroeber. *Journal of American Folklore* 96 (1983): 225-27.

Fine, Elizabeth C., and Speer, Jean Haskell. "A New Look at Performance." *Communication Monographs* 44 (November 1977): 374-89.

Finnegan, Ruth. *Limba Stories and Storytelling*. Oxford: Oxford University Press, 1967.

_____ "What is Oral Literature Anyway?" *Oral Literature and the Formula*. Edited by Benjamin A. Stolz and Richard S. Shannon. Ann Arbor: Center for Coordination of Ancient and Modern Studies, University of Michigan, 1976.

Fleischhauer, Carl, and Jabbour, Alan, eds. *The Hammons Family: A Study of a*

West Virginia Family's Traditions. Washington, D.C.: Library of Congress, 1973.

Folb, Edith A. *Runnin' Down Some Lines: The Language and Culture of Black Teenagers.* Cambridge, Massachusetts: Harvard University Press, 1980.

Freedman, Norbert. "Toward a Mathematization of Kinetic Behavior: A Review of Paul Bouissac's *La Mesure Des Gestes*." *Approaches to Semiotics.* Paperback Series, 3. The Hague: Mouton, 1973. *Semiotica* 15 (1976): 83-96.

Galantière, Lewis. "Introduction." In *The World of Translation.* Papers delivered at the Conference on Literary Translation, New York, May 1970 under the auspices of P.E.N. American Center.

Geertz, Clifford. "Blurred Genres: The Refiguration of Social Thought." *The American Scholar* 49 (Spring 1980):165-79.

_____. "Deep Play: Notes on the Balinese Cockfight." In *The Interpretation of Cultures,* pp. 412-53. New York: Basic Books, 1973.

_____. "Thick Description: Toward an Interpretive Theory of Culture." In *The Interpretation of Cultures,* pp. 3-30. New York: Basic Books, 1973.

Georges, Robert A. "Toward an Understanding of Storytelling Events." *Journal of American Folklore* 82 (1969): 313-28.

Gibbs, George. "Instructions for Research Relative to the Ethnology and Philology of America." *Smithsonian Miscellaneous Collections* 7, No. 160, Washington, D.C.: Government Printing Office, 1863.

Goffman, Erving. *Encounters: Two Studies in the Sociology of Interaction.* Indianapolis and New York: The Bobbs-Merrill Co., 1961.

_____. *Frame Analysis.* New York: Harper Colophon, 1974.

_____. *Interaction Ritual: Essays on Face to Face Behavior.* New York: Anchor Books, 1967.

_____. *The Presentation of Self in Everyday Life.* Garden City, N.Y.: Doubleday Anchor Books, 1959.

Goldstein, Kenneth L. *A Guide for Field Workers in Folklore.* Hatboro, Pennsylvania: Folklore Associates, 1964.

Goldstein, Kenneth L., and Bethke, Robert D., eds. *Monologues and Folk Recitation, Southern Folklore Quarterly* 40 (March-June 1976).

Goodman, Nelson. *Languages of Art: An Approach to a Theory of Symbols.* Indianapolis and New York: The Bobbs-Merrill Co., 1968.

Gossen, Gary H. "Chamula Genres of Verbal Behavior." *Toward New Perspectives in Folklore,* pp. 145-67. Edited by Américo Paredes and Richard Bauman. Austin: The University of Texas Press, 1972.

_____. *Chamulas in the World of the Sun: Time and Space in a Maya Oral Tradition.* Cambridge, Mass.: Harvard University Press, 1974.

Graham, Donald L. (Dante). "April 5th." *Understanding the New Black Poetry,* p. 320. Edited by Stephen Henderson. New York: William Morrow Co., 1973.

Hall, Edward T. *The Hidden Dimension.* New York: Anchor Books, 1966.

Halpert, Herbert. "American Regional Folklore." In "Folklore Research in North America: Reports of the Committee on Research in Folklore, 1945-1946." *Journal of American Folklore* 60 (1947): 355-66.

Harrison, Randall P., and Knapp, Mark L. "Toward an Understanding of

Nonverbal Communication Systems." *The Journal of Communication* 22 (December 1972): 339-52.

Hein, Hilde. "Performance as an Aesthetic Category." *Journal of Aesthetics and Art Criticism* 28 (Spring 1970): 381-86.

Hendricks, William O. *Essays on Semiolinguistics and Verbal Art.* The Hague: Mouton, 1973.

———. "Linguistics and Folkloristics." *Linguistics and Adjacent Arts and Sciences.* Vol. 12, pp. 661-81. In *Current Trends in Linguistics.* Edited by Thomas A. Sebeok. The Hague: Mouton, 1974.

Henson, Hilary. *British Social Anthropologists and Language: A History of Separate Development.* Oxford: Clarendon Press, 1974.

Herndon, Marcia. "Analysis: The Herding of Sacred Cows." *Ethnomusicology* 18 (1974): 219-62.

Herskovits, Melville J. *Franz Boas: The Science of Man in the Making.* New York: Charles Scribner's Sons, 1953.

Herskovits, Melville, and Herskovits, Frances. *Dahomean Narrative: A Cross-Cultural Approach.* Evanston, Illinois: Northwestern University Press, 1958.

Hirsch, E.D., Jr. *The Aims of Interpretation.* Chicago and London: The University of Chicago Press, 1976.

Hockett, Charles F. "Translation Via Immediate Constituents." *International Journal of American Linguistics* 20 (1954): 313-15.

Hrdličková, V. "Japanese Professional Storytellers." *Genre* 2 (1969): 179-210.

Hudson, Lee. "Beat Generation Poetics and the Oral Tradition of Literature." Ph.D. dissertation. University of Texas at Austin, 1972.

Hunt, Everett Lee. "Plato and Aristotle on Rhetoric and Rhetoricians." *Historical Studies of Rhetoric and Rhetoricians,* pp. 19-70. Edited by Raymond F. Howes. Ithaca, New York: Cornell University Press, 1961.

Hutchinson, Ann. *Labanotation.* Norfolk, Conn.: New Directions, 1961.

Hymes, Dell. "An Ethnographic Perspective." *New Literary History* 4 (Autumn 1973): 187-201.

———. "Breakthrough Into Performance." In *Folklore: Communication and Performance,* pp. 11-74. Edited by Dan Ben-Amos and Kenneth Goldstein. The Hague: Mouton, 1975.

———. "Discovering Oral Performance and Measured Verse in American Indian Narrative." *New Literary History* 8 (1977): 431-58.

———. "Folklore's Nature and the Sun's Myth." *Journal of American Folklore* 84 (1975): 345-69.

———. "Models of the Interaction of Language and Social Life." In *Directions in Sociolinguistics,* pp. 35-71. Edited by J. J. Gumperz and Dell Hymes. New York: Holt, Rinehart & Winston, 1972.

———. "Reading Clackamas Texts." In *Traditional American Indian Literatures: Texts and Interpretations,* pp. 117-59. Edited by Karl Kroeber. Lincoln and London: University of Nebraska Press, 1981.

———. "The Contribution of Folklore to Sociolinguistic Research." In *Toward New Perspectives in Folklore,* pp. 42-50. Edited by Américo Paredes and Richard Bauman. Austin: University of Texas Press, 1972.

Ives, Sumner. "A Theory of Literary Dialect." In *A Various Language: Perspectives on American Dialects*, pp. 145-77. Edited by Juanita V. Williamson and Virginia M. Burke. New York: Holt, Rinehart and Winston, 1971.

Jackson, Bruce. *"Get Your Ass in the Water and Swim Like Me": Narrative from Black Oral Tradition.* Cambridge, Massachusetts: Harvard University Press, 1974.

Jacobs, Melville. *Clackamas Chinook Texts.* Indiana University Publications of the Research Center in Anthropology, Folklore and Linguistics, Nos. 8 and 11. Bloomington: Indiana University, 1958, 1959.

———. "Folklore." In *The Anthropology of Franz Boas*, pp. 119-38. Edited by Walter Goldschmidt. *Memoirs of the American Anthropological Association*, No. 89, 1959.

———. *The Content and Style of an Oral Literature.* Chicago: University of Chicago Press, 1959.

———. *The People Are Coming Soon.* Seattle: University of Washington Press, 1960.

Jakobson, Roman. "Closing Statement: Linguistics and Poetics." In *Style in Language*, pp. 350-77. Edited by T. A. Sebeok. New York: John Wiley and Sons, 1960.

———. "On Linguistic Aspects of Translation." In *On Translation*, pp. 232-39. Edited by Reuben A. Brower. Cambridge: Harvard University Press, 1959.

Jakobson, Roman, and Bogatyrev, P. "Die Folklore als besondere Form des Schaffens." In *Donum Natalicium Schrijnen: Verzameling van opstellen door oud-leerlingen en bevriende vakgenooten opgedragen aan Mgr. Prof. Dr. Jos. Schrijnen*, pp. 900-913. Nÿmegen-Utrecht: Dekker, 1929.

Jansen, William Hugh. "Classifying Performance in the Study of Verbal Folklore." In *Studies in Folklore*, pp. 110-18. Edited by W. Edson Richmond. Bloomington: Indiana University Press, 1957.

Jemie, Onwuchekwa. "Signifying, Dozens, and Toasts: A Selection." *Alcheringa: Ethnopoetics* n.s. 2, No. 1 (1976): 27-41.

Johnson, David W. "Increasing Your Communication Skills." In *Interpersonal Communication in Action*, pp. 13-30. Edited by Bobby R. Patton and Kim Giffin. New York: Harper & Row, 1977.

Jowett, Benjamin. *Preface to the Dialogues of Plato*, 2nd ed. London: Oxford University Press, 1891.

Kellogg, Robert. "Oral Literature." *New Literary History* 5 (1973): 55-66.

Kirshenblatt-Gimblett, Barbara. "A Parable in Context." In *Folklore: Performance and Communication*, pp. 105-130. Edited by Dan Ben-Amos and Kenneth Goldstein. The Hague: Mouton, 1975.

Köngäs-Maranda, Elli. "Theory and Practice of Riddle Analysis." In *Toward New Perspectives in Folklore*, pp. 51-61. Edited by Américo Paredes and Richard Bauman. Austin: University of Texas Press, 1972.

Knox, Ronald A. *On English Translation.* London: Oxford University Press, 1957.

Laban, Juana de. "Movement Notation: Its Significance to the Folklorist." *Journal of American Folklore* 67 (1954): 291-95.

Labov, William. "Rules for Ritual Insults." In *Rappin' and Stylin' Out: Communication in Urban Black America*, pp. 265-314. Edited by Thomas Kochman. Urbana: University of Illinois Press, 1972.

Labov, William; Cohen, Paul; Robins, Clarence; and Lewis, John. "Toasts." In *Mother-Wit from the Laughing Barrel: Readings in the Interpretation of Afro-American Folklore*, pp. 329-47. Edited by Alan Dundes. Englewood Cliffs, New Jersey: Prentice-Hall, 1973.

Lazaro, Patricio. "A Survey of Approaches in Philippine Oral Literature Scholarship." Ph.D. dissertation. Northwestern University, 1974.

Leach, MacEdward. "Problems of Collecting Oral Literature." *Publications of the Modern Language Association* 77 (1962): 335-40.

Leathers, Dale C. *Nonverbal Communication Systems*. Boston: Allyn and Bacon, 1976.

Lester, Julius. *Black Folktales*. New York: Richard V. Baron, 1969.

Lévi-Strauss, Claude. "The Structural Study of Myth." *Journal of American Folklore* 78 (1955): 428-44.

Loesch, Katherine. "Empirical Studies in Interpretation: The Text." *Western Speech* 33 (1969): 250-68.

Lomax, Alan. *Folk Song Style and Culture*. Washington, D.C.: American Association for the Advancement of Science, 1968.

Lord, Albert B. *The Singer of Tales*. New York: Atheneum, 1970. Reprinted from Harvard University Press, 1960.

Lotman, J. M. "The Discrete Text and the Iconic Text." *New Literary History* 6 (1975): 333-38.

Lotman, Ju. M.; Uspenskij, B.A.; V.V. Ivanov; V.N. Toporov; and A.M. Pjatigorskij. "Theses on the Semiotic Study of Cultures (As Applied to Slavic Texts)." In *The Tell-Tale Sign: A Survey of Semiotics*, pp. 57-83. Edited by Thomas A. Sebeok. Lisse, Netherlands: The Peter De Ridder Press, 1975.

Lowie, Robert H. *The History of Ethnological Theory*. New York: Farrar & Rinehart, 1937.

MacLeish, Archibald. "Ars Poetica." *Collected Poems, 1917-1952*. Boston: Houghton-Mifflin, 1952.

Malinowski, Bronislaw. *Coral Gardens and Their Magic II: The Language of Magic and Gardening*. 1935. Reprint. Bloomington: Indiana University Press, 1965.

_____. *Myth in Primitive Psychology*. New York: W.W. Norton, 1926.

Mallery, Garrick. "Sign Language Among North American Indians Compared with That Among Other Peoples and Deaf Mutes." *First Annual Report of the Bureau of American Ethnology*, pp. 263-549. Washington, D.C.: Government Printing Office, 1879-1880.

Mandelbaum, David G., ed. "Editor's Introduction." In *Selected Writings of Edward Sapir in Language, Culture and Personality*, pp. v-xii. Berkeley and Los Angeles: University of California Press, 1963.

Maranda, Elli Köngäs. "Theory and Practice of Riddle Analysis." In *Toward New Perspectives in Folklore*, pp. 51-61. Edited by Américo Paredes and Richard Bauman. Austin: University of Texas Press, 1972.

Martin, Howard Rodney. *The Prosodic and Paralinguistic Analysis of Dramatic Speech: A Practical System*. Ann Arbor: The Phonetics Laboratory, The University of Michigan, 1977.

Matejka, Ladislav. "Postscript: Prague School Semiotics." In *Semiotics of Art: Prague School Contributions*, pp. 265-90. Edited by Ladislav Matejka and Irwin A. Titunik. Cambridge and London: The MIT Press, 1976.

McDowell, John H. "Some Aspects of Verbal Art in Bolivian Quechua." *Folklore Annual of the University Folklore Association*, No. 6 (1974): 68-81.

McElroy, Hilda-Njoki. "Traditional Wit and Humour in Pan-African Drama." Ph.D. dissertation. Northwestern University, 1973.

Michelson, Truman. "The Autobiography of a Fox Indian Woman." *40th Annual Report of the Bureau of American Ethnology*. Washington, D.C.: Government Printing Office, 1918-1919.

Mills, George. "Art: An Introduction to Qualitative Anthropology." In *Art and Aesthetics in Primitive Societies*, pp. 73-98. Edited by Carol F. Jopling. New York: E.P. Dutton & Co., 1971.

Miller, George A. *The Psychology of Communication: Seven Essays*. New York and London: Basic Books, 1967.

Mitchell-Kernan, Claudia. "Signifying, Loud-Talking, and Marking." In *Rappin' and Stylin' Out: Communication in Black America*, pp. 315-35. Edited by Thomas Kochman. Urbana: University of Illinois Press, 1972.

Moles, Abraham. *Information Theory and Esthetic Perception*. Translated by Joel E. Cohen. Chicago: University of Illinois Press, 1966.

Mukařovský, Jan. "Poetic Reference." In *Semiotics of Art: Prague School Contributions*, pp. 155-63. Edited by Ladislav Matejka and Irwin A. Titunik. Cambridge and London: The MIT Press, 1976.

_____. "Standard Language and Poetic Language." In *A Prague School Reader on Esthetics, Literary Structure, and Style*, pp. 17-30. Translated by Paul L. Garvin. Washington, D.C.: Georgetown University Press, 1964.

Nida, Eugene A. "A Framework for the Analysis and Evaluation of Theories of Translation." In *Translation: Applications and Research*, pp. 47-91. Edited by Richard W. Brislin. New York: Gardner Press, 1976.

_____. "Principles of Translation as Exemplified by Bible Translating." In *Language Structure and Translation: Essays by Eugene A. Nida*, pp. 24-46. Edited by Anwar S. Dil. Stanford, California: Stanford University Press, 1975.

_____. *Toward a Science of Translating*. Leiden: E. J. Brill, 1964.

Nida, Eugene, and Taber, Charles R. *The Theory and Practice of Translation*. Leiden, Netherlands: E. J. Brill, 1974.

Noelke, Virginia Hull McKimmon. "The Origin and Early History of the Bureau of American Ethnology, 1879-1910." Ph.D. dissertation. University of Texas at Austin, 1974.

Ong, Walter J. *The Presence of the Word: Some Prolegomena for Cultural and Religious History*. New Haven, Connecticut: Yale University Press, 1967.

Peacock, James L. *Rites of Modernization: Symbolic and Social Aspects of Indonesian Proletarian Drama*. Chicago: University of Chicago Press, 1968.

Pike, Kenneth L. *Language in Relation to a Unified Theory of the Structure of Human Behavior, Part I*. Preliminary Edition. Glendale, California: Summer Institute of Linguistics, 1954.

———. *Phonetics: A Critical Analysis of Phonetic Theory and a Technic for the Practical Description of Sounds.* Ann Arbor: University of Michigan Press, 1943.

———. *The Intonation of American English.* University of Michigan Publications, Linguistics, Vol. I. Ann Arbor: University of Michigan Press, 1945.

Pittenger, Robert E.; Hockett, Charles F.; and Danehy, John J. *The First Five Minutes.* Ithaca, New York: Paul Martineau, 1960.

Powell, John Wesley. *Introduction to the Study of Indian Languages, with Words, Phrases, and Sentences to be Collected.* 2nd edition. Washington, D.C.: Government Printing Office, 1880.

———. "Limitations to the Use of Anthropologic Data." *First Annual Report of the Bureau of American Ethnology,* pp. 73-88. Washington, D.C.: Government Printing Office, 1879-1880.

———. "Report of the Director." *First Annual Report of the Bureau of American Ethnology.* Washington, D.C.: Government Printing Office, 1879-1880.

———. "Report of the Director." *Second Annual Report of the Bureau of American Ethnology.* Washington, D.C.: Government Printing Office, 1880-1881.

———. "Sketch of the Mythology of the North American Indians." *First Annual Report of the Bureau of American Ethnology.* Washington, D.C.: Government Printing Office, 1879-1880.

Poole, Roger. "Objective Sign and Subjective Meaning." In *The Body as a Medium of Expression,* pp. 74-106. Edited by Jonathan Benthall and Ted Polhemus. New York: E. P. Dutton & Co., 1975.

Preston, Dennis R. "Mowr Bayud Spellin': A Reply to Fine." *Journal of American Folklore* 96(1983):330-39.

———. "'Ritin' Fowklower Daun 'Rong: Folklorists' Failures in Phonology." *Journal of American Folklore* 95 (1982): 304-26.

Procházka, Vladimir. "Notes on Translating Technique." In *A Prague School Reader on Esthetics, Literary Structure and Style,* pp. 108-30. Edited and translated by Paul L. Garvin. Washington: Washington Linguistic Club, 1955.

Quasha, George. "New Aspects of Translation." In *The World of Translation,* pp. 203-22. Papers delivered at the Conference on Literary Translation held in New York City in May 1970 under the auspices of P.E.N. American Center.

Radin, Paul. "The Literature of Primitive Peoples." *Diogenes* 12 (1955): 1-28.

Report of Committee of American Anthropological Association. "Phonetic Transcription of Indian Languages." *Smithsonian Miscellaneous Collections* 66, No. 6 (1915): 1-15.

Reynolds, L.D., and Wilson, N.G. *Scribes and Scholars: A Guide to the Transmission of Greek and Latin Literature.* London: Oxford University Press, 1968.

Richards, I. A. "Toward a Theory of Translating." *Studies in Chinese Thought.* American Anthropological Association, Vol. 55, Memoir 75. Chicago: University of Chicago Press, 1953.

Ricoeur, Paul. "The Model of the Text: Meaningful Action Considered as a Text." *New Literary History* 5 (Autumn 1973): 91-117.

Roberts, Leonard. *Sang Branch Settlers: Folksongs and Tales of a Kentucky Mountain Family.* Austin: University of Texas Press for the American Folklore Society, 1974.

Roloff, Leland. "The Field of Interpretation: Instructive Wonder." *Interpretation Division Newsletter* (Spring 1973): 7-8.

———. *The Perception and Evocation of Literature.* Glenview: Scott, Foresman, 1973.

Rosenberg, Bruce. *The Art of the American Folk Preacher.* New York: Oxford University Press, 1970.

———. "Oral Sermons and Oral Narrative." In *Folklore: Performance and Communication,* pp. 75-104. Edited by Dan Ben-Amos and Kenneth S. Goldstein. The Hague: Mouton, 1975.

Rosenfield, Lawrence W. "An Autopsy of the Rhetorical Tradition." In *The Prospect of Rhetoric: Report of the National Developmental Project,* pp. 64-77. Edited by Lloyd F. Bitzer and Edwin Black. Englewood Cliffs, New Jersey: Prentice-Hall, 1971.

Rothenberg, Jerome, ed. *Shaking the Pumpkin: Traditional Poetry of the Indian North Americas.* New York: Doubleday, 1972.

———. "Total Translation: An Experiment in the Presentation of American Indian Poetry." *Stony Brook* 3/4 (1969). Reprinted in George Quasha, "New Aspects of Translation." *The World of Translation,* pp. 203-22. Papers delivered at the Conference on Literary Translation held in New York City in May 1970 under the auspices of P.E.N. American Center.

Rothenberg, Jerome, and Tedlock, Dennis, eds. "Statement of Intention." *Alcheringa: Ethnopoetics* 1 (1970).

Rouch, Jean. "The Camera and Man." *Studies in the Anthropology of Visual Communication* 1 (Fall 1974): 35-44.

Rush, James. *The Philosophy of the Human Voice.* Sixth ed. Philadelphia: J. B. Lippencott & Co., 1867.

Sacks, Harvey. "An Analysis of the Course of a Joke's Telling in Conversation." *Explorations in the Ethnography of Speaking,* pp. 337-53. Edited by Richard Bauman and Joel Sherzer. London: Cambridge University Press, 1974.

Sanchez, Sonia. "chant for young brothas & sistuhs." *Talkin and Testifyin: The Language of Black America,* p. 181. By Geneva Smitherman. Boston: Houghton-Mifflin, 1977.

Sándor, István. "Dramaturgy of Tale-Telling." *Acta Ethnographica: Academiae Scientarium Hungaricae* 16 (1967): 303-38.

Sapir, Edward, ed. *Wishram Texts, together with Wasco Tales and Myths.* Collected by Jeremiah Curtin. Publications of the American Ethnological Society, II. Leyden: E. J. Brill, 1909.

———. "Abnormal Types of Speech in Nootka." In *Selected Writings of Edward Sapir in Language, Culture and Personality,* pp. 179-96. Edited by David G. Mandelbaum. Berkeley and Los Angeles: University of California Press, 1963.

———. "Song Recitative in Paiute Mythology." In *Selected Writings of Edward Sapir in Language, Culture and Personality,* pp. 463-67. Edited by David G. Mandelbaum. Berkeley and Los Angeles: University of California Press, 1963.

Saussure, Ferdinand de. *Course in General Linguistics.* Edited by Charles Bally and Albert Sechehaye, in collaboration with Albert Riedlinger. Translated, with an introduction and notes by Wade Baskin. New York: The Philosophical Library, 1959. Reprint. New York: McGraw-Hill, 1966.

Scheflen, Albert E. *Communicational Structure: Analysis of a Psychotherapy Transaction.* Bloomington: Indiana University Press, 1973.

Scheub, Harold. "Body and Image in Oral Narrative Performance." *New Literary History* 8 (Spring 1977): 345-67.

_____. "Translation of African Oral Narrative-Performances to the Written Word." *Yearbook of Comparative and General Literature* 20 (1971): 28-36.

Sebeok, Thomas A. "Six Species of Signs: Some Propositions and Strictures." *Semiotica* 13 (1975): 233-60.

Sloan, Thomas O. "Oral Interpretation in the Ages Before Sheridan and Walker." *Western Speech* 35 (1971): 147-54.

Smith, David H. "Communication Research and the Idea of Process." *Speech Monographs* 39 (August 1972): 174-82.

Smitherman, Geneva. *Talkin and Testifyin: The Language of Black America.* Boston: Houghton-Mifflin, 1977.

Souter, Alexander. *Hints on Translation from Latin into English.* London: Society for Promoting Christian Knowledge, 1920.

Speer, Jean Haskell. "Folklore and Interpretation: Symbiosis." *Southern Speech Communication Journal* 40 (1975): 365-76.

_____. "Folkloristics and the Performance of Literature." Ph.D. dissertation. University of Texas at Austin, 1978.

Steele, Joshua. *Prosodia Rationalis, or An Essay Toward Establishing the Melody and Measure of Speech, to be Expressed and Perpetuated by Peculiar Symbols.* 2nd edition. London: J. Nichols, 1779.

Steiner, George. *After Babel: Aspects of Language and Translation.* New York and London: Oxford University Press, 1975.

Sutton-Smith, Brian. "The Expressive Profile." In *Toward New Perspectives in Folklore*, pp. 80-92. Edited by Américo Paredes and Richard Bauman. Austin: University of Texas Press, 1972.

Taylor, Archer. *The Black Ox.* In *Folklore Fellows Communications* No. 70. Helsinki, 1927.

Tedlock, Dennis. *Finding the Center: Narrative Poetry of the Zuni Indians.* Translated by Dennis Tedlock. New York: The Dial Press, 1972; reprint ed., Lincoln and London: Univeristy of Nebraska Press, 1978.

_____. "Introduction" to Walter Sanchez, "A Prayer Over Dead Rabbits." Translated by Dennis Tedlock and Andrew Peynetsa. *Alcheringa: Ethnopoetics* o.s. No. 4 (Autumn 1972): 60.

_____. "Learning to Listen: Oral History as Poetry." In *Envelopes of Sound.* pp. 106-25. Edited by Ronald J. Grele. Chicago: Precedent Publishing, 1975.

_____. "On the Translation of Style in Oral Narrative." *Journal of American Folklore* 84 (1971): 114-33.

_____. "Toward an Oral Poetics." *New Literary History* 8 (Spring 1977): 507-19.

_____. "Translator's Introduction," to Walter Sanchez "The Girl and the Protector." *Alcheringa: Ethnopoetics* n.s. 1, No. 1 (1975): 111.

Thompson, David W. "Teaching the History of Interpretation." *Speech Teacher* 22 (1973): 38-40.

Thompson, Robert Farris. "No. 37 Steatite Seated Image in Nobleman's Hat (fig. 3)." *The Four Moments of the Sun: Kongo Art in Two Worlds.* Catalogue by

Robert Farris Thompson and Joseph Cornet. Washington, D.C.: National
Gallery of Art, n.d.

Thompson, Stith. "Folktale." In *Funk and Wagnalls Standard Dictionary of
Folklore, Mythology, and Legend,* Vol. I. Edited by Maria Leach. New York:
1949.

―――― *The Folktale.* New York: Holt, Rinehart and Winston, 1946.

Toelken, J. Barre. "The 'Pretty Language' of Yellowman: Genre, Mode, and
Texture in Navaho Coyote Narratives." *Genre* 2 (1969): 211-35.

Toelken, Barre, and Scott, Tacheeni. "Poetic Retranslation and the 'Pretty
Languages' of Yellowman." In *Traditional American Indian Literatures: Texts
and Interpretations,* pp. 211-35. Edited by Karl Kroeber. Lincoln and London:
University of Nebraska Press, 1981.

Trager, George L. "Paralanguage: A First Approximation." In *Language in
Culture and Society,* pp. 274-88. Edited by Dell Hymes. New York: Harper and
Row, 1964.

Trager, George L., and Smith, Henry Lee, Jr. *An Outline of English Structure.
Studies in Linguistics: Occasional Papers* 3. Norman, Oklahoma: Battenburg
Press, 1951.

Turner, Victor. *The Ritual Process: Structure and Anti-Structure.* Chicago:
Aldine Publishing Company, 1969.

Turpin, Thomas J. "The Cheyenne World View as Reflected in the Oral
Traditions of the Culture Heroes, Sweet Medicine and Erect Horns." Ph.D.
dissertation. University of Southern California, 1974.

Utley, Francis Lee. "Conflict and Promise in Folklore." *Journal of American
Folklore* 70 (1952): 111-18.

Vachek, Josef. *The Lingusitic School of Prague: An Introduction To Its Theory
and Practice.* Bloomington and London: Indiana University Press, 1966.

Valéry, Paul. "The Course in Poetics: First Lesson." In *The Creative Process: A
Symposium,* pp. 92-105. Edited by Brewster Ghiselin. Berkeley: University of
California Press, 1954.

Voeglin, C. F. "A Modern Method for Field Work Treatment of Previously
Collected Texts." *Journal of American Folklore* 67 (1954): 15-20.

―――― "Multiple Stage Translation." *International Journal of American
Linguistics* 20 (1954): 271-80.

Wells, Rulon S. "Comments to 'Part Five: Metrics.'" In *Style in Language,* pp.
197-209. Edited by Thomas A. Sebeok. New York: John Wiley & Sons, 1960.

Whitaker, Beverly. "Evaluating Performed Literature." In *Studies in Interpretation, II,* pp. 267-81. Edited by Esther M. Doyle and Virginia Hastings Floyd.
Amsterdam: Rodopi NV, 1977.

―――― "Research Directions in the Performance of Literature." *Speech
Monographs* 40 (1973): 238-42.

Wilgus, D. K. "The Text is the Thing." *Journal of American Folklore* 86 (1973):
241-52.

Winner, Irene Portis, and Winner, Thomas G. "The Semiotics of Cultural Texts."
Semiotica 18 (1975): 101-56.

Index

Abercrombie, David, 141, 144, 145
Abrahams, Roger, 34, 35, 46, 47, 48, 59-60, 61-62, 65-66, 79, 166, 168, 169
Abrams, M. H., 69
Aesthetic error, 74
Aesthetic experience, 72-73
Aesthetic facts: Experiential Facts, 14; Interdisciplinary Facts, 14-15; Judgmental Facts, 14; Objective Facts, 14; Situational Facts, 14
Aesthetic field framework, 68-73
Aesthetic theory, 68-73
Aesthetic transaction, characteristics of: active-receptive, 78-80; immediate, 80-81; integral, 82-83; intrinsic, 83-85; intuitive, 81; preanalytic, 81-82; sensuous, 80; unique, 83
Afro-American toasts, 11, 166, 168, 196, 198
American Folklore Society, 7, 16, 17, 29
American Indian languages, 18, 99; translation aids, 19-20, 22-23, 24
American Indian texts, 3, 17, 25, 39-40, 51-52, 151, 154, 203. See also Zuni Indians
Analogies, drama, 34-35
Analogies, game, 34, 35
Arewa, E. Ojo, 33, 41, 43
Aristotle, 82
Art, definition of, 85
Astrov, Margot, 52
Audience: performer/audience distinction, 74, 76; text adjustment for, 105-107
Audience relationships, 9, 100
Aural channel: linguistic structure, 115-16; paralinguistic structure, 116-18
Austin, Gilbert, 24, 142
Austin, J. L., 59

Babcock, Barbara, 36, 48
Bacon, Wallace, 11-12
BAE. See Bureau of American Ethnology
Barber, Jonathan, 142
Barker, Roger G., 10, 120, 127, 140-41, 153
Bartenieff, Irmgard, 119
Bascom, William, 17, 38-39
Bateson, Gregory, 34-36, 59, 130
Bauman, Richard, 28, 32, 34, 35-36, 37, 47-48, 58-59, 61, 63, 66
Behavior levels: molar, 127-28, 162, 164; molecular, 127-28, 140, 162, 164
Behavior study, 127-30
Bell, Alexander Melville, 144
Ben-Amos, Dan, 6, 26, 46, 47, 61
Benedict, Ruth, 37-38
Berleant, Arnold, 8, 14, 76, 78-84; aesthetic transaction model, 71-74, 75 (fig.)

Birdwhistell, Ray, 10, 53, 101-2, 106, 118-19, 120-30, 142, 153; linguistic and kinesic transcriptions, 101 (fig.)
Boas, Franz, 3, 18, 21-23, 28, 151
Body-base, definition of, 122
Body movement. See Kinesics
Body movement categories, 130
Body qualities, 122-23, 173
Bogatyrev, Petr, 33-34
Bolton, Janet, 12
Brandon-Sweeney, Beverly, 53
Browning, Larry D., 67
Bühler, Karl, 32, 33
Bureau of American Ethnology (BAE), 19, 21, 22
Burke, Kenneth, 34-35, 46, 64

Cantometrics, 43-44
Chomsky, Noam, 32
Choreometrics, 43-44
Cohen, Paul, 169
Communication: aesthetic, 68; as translation, 93
Comparative literature, 34
Connected discourse, terminology, 91
Context, 66-68
Corrigible schemata, 10-11, 155-58, 163, 165
Cronkhite, Gary, 12
Crowley, Daniel, 42, 45
Cultural evolutionism, 21, 24
Cultural relativism, 23
Cushing, Frank, 107

Darnell, Regna, 132
Dauenhauer, Richard, 51, 52
Davis, Marth Ann, 119
Dégh, Linda, 4, 42, 45, 54, 74
Dewey, John, 71
Dialects: Appalachian, 137-38; Black, 137, 138-39, 177, 198; literary, 136-40
Digital projection systems: alphabetic projections, 141, 143-44; analphabetic projections, 141-42, 143-44; natural language projections, 135-41
Dorsey, J. O., 20
Dorson, Richard, 16, 30, 40-41, 95, 100
Dundes, Alan, 33, 41, 43, 44-45

Eco, Umberto, 85, 134
Ekman, Paul, 130
Emergence, 63-64
Ethnographic research, 42-44
Ethnography of speaking, 36-37, 48, 67-68, 157-58

241

Ethnolinguistic texts: development 23-28, 55; format, 18-20; translation, 39
European comparative method. *See* Finnish historical-geographic method
Evans, David, 168

Finnegan, Ruth, 42, 45, 65
Finnish historical-geographic school of folklore, 5, 28, 29-30, 31
Fleischhauer, Carl, 151-52
Focus, 85
Folklore, definition of, 17, 44, 46, 60, 64
Folklore study: analytical perspectives, 16; fusion of anthropological and literary perspectives, 37-45; history of, 30-36; interdisciplinary nature, 11-12, 37, 66-67, 99-100, 120; performance approach, 2, 45-54, 71
Folklore texts: accuracy, 3; adjustment for audience, 105-7; criticism of, 3-6, 29, 37-38, 39, 40, 45, 46, 48, 50, 52-53, 68; definitions, 45, 48, 50, 55, 69, 90, 94, 95-97; historical development, 7-8; ideal, 87-88, 89; importance of, 16; notational and descriptive systems, 10, 24, 42-44, 48-49, 53-54, 101 (fig.), 134-48, 182-84; overloading, 105-9, 180; polyphonic, 54, 74, 76; popularized, 30, 40-46, 100-101, 151; scientific, 40-41, 100-101; translation difficulties, 1, 9, 52; underloading, 108-9; varying texts, 38
Folkloristics. *See* Folklore study
Folklorists: anthropological, 7, 16, 17, 18, 28; literary, 7, 16, 17, 28
Frame, 35-36, 59, 61
Freedman, Norbert, 119
Friesen, Wallace V., 130

Galantière, Lewis, 97
Gatschet, A. S., 20
Geertz, Clifford, 34-35, 90
Georges, Robert, 46
Gibbs, George, 19
Goffman, Erving, 34-36, 47, 61
Goldstein, Kenneth, 6, 26, 41, 42, 47
Gossen, Gary, 48, 67-68
Gregory, Dick, 64

Hall, Edward T., 131-33
Halpert, Herbert, 30
Harris, Joel Chandler, 136-37
Hein, Hilde, 69
Hendricks, W. O., 31, 91
Hermeneutic steps of translation, 11, 165; embodiment, 163-64; penetration, 162-63; restitution, 163-64; trust, 161-62
Hirsch, E. D., 10-11, 155-56
Holmes, William H., 22

Hopper, Robert, 67
Hrdlicková, V., 53, 131
Hutchinson, James, 167, 169-72, 181, 184, 196-202
Hymes, Dell, 2, 4-5, 11, 15, 36-37, 47, 51-52, 61, 94, 100, 157

Iconic actions, 131, 162
Ideophones, 135, 199
Information theory, 104-7, 111
International Phonetic Alphabet (IPA), 136, 137, 143
Interpretation, oral, 1-2, 11-13, 15, 24, 109, 203
Intersemiotic translation, 8-9; definition, 89, 96-97
Ives, Sumner, 136-37

Jabbour, Alan, 151-52
Jackson, Bruce, 166, 169
Jacobs, Melville, 39-40, 51
Jakobson, Roman, 8, 32, 33, 83, 85, 96
Jansen, William Hugh, 41

Kellogg, Robert, 76
Kine, definition of, 121
Kinemorph, definition of, 121
Kinemorphic construction, definition of, 121-22
Kinesic notations, 53-54
Kinesic units, 121-22
Kinesics, 118-22, 125, 200-202; coding, 130-31; effort-shape analysis, 119; models of 119-21; motion markers, 124; recording difficulties, 125-26; stance shifts, 162-63; structural linguistic model, 120-25. *See also* Parakinesics
Kirshenblatt-Gimblett, Barbara, 46-47

Laban, Rudolph, 119
Labanotation, 119
Labov, William, 169
Leach, MacEdward, 2, 41, 42
Legend texts, 54, 74
Lester, Julius, 11, 77, 167, 196-200
Lévi-Strauss, Claude, 5
Loesch, Katherine, 134-35
Lomax, Alan, 41, 43-44, 119
Lord, Albert, 18, 63, 77
Lotman, J. M., 134

McDowell, John H., 117
Malinowski, Bronislaw, 23, 26-28
Mallery, Garrick, 23-25, 140
Maranda, Elli Köngäs, 34
Marshman, J. T., 12
Mathesius, Vilém, 31
Mencken, H. L., 136-37
Metacommunication, 35, 36, 61

Michelson, Truman, 151
Mills, George, 85
Moles, Abraham, 85, 104
Mukařovský, Jan, 32-33, 47, 83
Musical notations in textmaking, 7, 22, 26, 143

Newell, William W., 17
Nida, Eugene, 8, 98, 102-6, 109, 113, 152

Olfactory channel, 133, 179-80
Ong, Walter, 92

Parakinesics, 122-23, 125, 173; action modifiers, 123; interaction modifiers, 123-24; motion qualifiers, 123
Paralinguistic features, 115-17, 163, 180
Paredes, Américo, 47
Parry, Milman, 18, 34, 63, 77
Parry-Lord hypothesis, 65-66
Performance: aesthetic transaction, 78-87; aesthetics, 13-14; characteristics of, 73-74; cultural specificity, 65-66; definitions, 47, 60, 61-62, 94; information theory, 104-7; organization, 66; performer/audience distinction, 74, 76; retranslation, 51-53; as social interaction, 13; as source medium, 113-33; translating, objections to, 90-94
Performance event, 62-65, 169-72; emergence, 63-64
Performance ground rules, 12-13, 62-63
Performance keys, 61
Performance record, 94-95, 158, 160, 184-95. See also Hermeneutic steps of translation
Performance report, 94-95, 158, 167-84; ends and act sequence, 159; key and instrumentalities, 160, 172-80; key to projections, 160, 180-84; norms and genre, 160-61; participants, 159; setting and scene, 159
Performance tradition, 76-78, 167-69
Performance translation: analytical equivalence, 153; dynamic equivalence, 151; formal equivalence, 150, 152-53; perceptual equivalence, 154
Performers, 13, 74, 76
Phillips, J. B., 103
Photography, 53-54, 145
Pike, Kenneth, 85, 115-16, 141-42, 145
Plato, 82
Poetry, definition of, 64
Poole, Roger, 126
Powell, John Wesley, 18, 19-21, 28
Prague School of linguistics, 18, 31-34
Preston, Dennis R., 137-39
Print: as receptor medium, 133-37; channel capacity, 133-34; definition of, 134
Printed signs: digital projection systems, 135-44; iconic projections, 144-45

Projection, definition of, 134-35
Projection devices, limitations of, 145-47
Projection key, 180-84

Quasha, George, 164

Radin, Paul, 38
Redundancy: cultural, 104-5; linguistic, 104
Ricoeur, Paul, 90
Riggs, S. R., 20
Roberts, Leonard, 152
Robinson, Rowland, 30
Roloff, Leland, 12, 96
Rosenberg, Bruce, 79
Rothenberg, Jerome, 4, 49-50, 95
Rouch, Jean, 110
Rush, James, 143
Russian Moscow-Tartu semioticians, 90-91

Sacks, Harvey, 54
Sándor, István, 13, 53, 138
Sapir, Edward, 23, 25-26, 143, 151
Saussure, Ferdinand de, 31-32
Scheflen, Albert E., 125
Scheub, Harold, 50, 53, 96, 164, 201, 202
Scott, Tacheeni, 53
Sebeok, Thomas, A., 130-31
Sensory channels of performance, 113-33
Scherzer, Joel, 47, 48
Service, Robert W., 196
Sloan, Thomas, 12
Smitherman, Geneva, 139
Social thought, refiguration of, 84-86
Speech: ethnography of, 36-37, 48, 67-68, 157-58; musical qualities of, 7, 22; typography, 49
Speech Communication Association, 12
Speer, Jean Haskell, 12
Stagolee, 11; iconic gestures, 131, 175-77; instrumentalities, analysis of, 172-80; kinesic features, 200-202; performance event, 84, 169-72; performance record, 184-95; performance report, 167-84; performance tradition, 167-69; pitch patterns, 199; projections, key to, 180-84; stance variations, 173-75; text comparisons, 195-202
Steele, Joshua, 143
Steiner, George, 11, 93, 97, 161-63, 165
Stocking, George W., 22
Structuralism, 5
Swanton, John, 22, 52

Tactile channel, 133, 179-80
Taylor, Archer, 5, 29-30
Tedlock, Dennis, 2, 3, 4, 15, 48-49, 50, 94, 95, 138, 145, 154, 158
Text types, 2, 101-2

Textmaker as audience, 109-10
Texts. *See* American Indian texts; Folklore
  texts; Legend texts
Thompson, David, 12
Thompson, Stith, 5, 29-30
Toelken, J. Barre, 4, 13, 15, 51, 52-53, 102,
  138, 140, 154, 203
Trager, George L., 116-17
Translation: adequate, 102-4; classes of,
  96-97; defense of, 93-94; definition of, 95-
  97; interlingual, 96; intralingual, 96;
  methodology, 98, total, 95. *See also*
  Hermeneutic steps of translation; Inter-
  semiotic translation; Performance transla-
  tion
Translation theory, 97-98
Trumbull, J. Hammond, 19
Tylor, Edward, 20, 24

Utley, Francis Lee, 40

Valéry, Paul, 96
Vazsonyi, Andrew, 54, 74
Verbal art: definition of, 58; object status,
  77-78
Visual channel: artifactual signals, 131,
  179-80; kinesic signals, 118-31; proxemic
  signals, 131-33, 179-80
Vocal devices, 7, 163, 177
Vocalizations, definition of, 116
Voeglin, C. F., 39, 51

Whitaker, Beverly, 12
Whitney, W. D., 19
Wilgus, D. K., 55
Winner, Irene Portis, 91
Winner, Thomas G., 91
Wright, Herbert F., 10, 120, 127, 140-41, 153

Zuni Indians, 4, 37, 48-49, 60-61, 107, 158